My Psychoanalytic Path:
Traversing the Thicket of Institutional Leadership

MY PSYCHOANALYTIC PATH

Traversing the Thicket of Institutional Leadership

Selected Papers of Harriet I. Basseches

International Psychoanalytic Books (IPBooks)
New York • http://www.IPBooks.net

My Psychoanalytic Path: Traversing the Thicket of Institutional Leadership: Selected Papers of Harriet I. Basseches

Published by IPBooks, Queens, NY
Online at: www.IPBooks.net

Cover painting by K. B. Basseches

ISBN: 978-1-956864-98-4

Contents

Foreword by Arlene Kramer Richards ix

Introduction by Harriet I. Basseches 1

Publications from *The American Psychoanalyst*

1. NAAP/ABAP Fail in Bid for COPA Approval as U.S. 9
2. A Conversation with Bruce H. Sklarew 13
3. A Conversation with Stanley Greenspan 23
4. CORPA Decision: End of the Road for ABAP 37
5. IPS, Now Three Years Old, Spurs Move toward Regional IPA Federation 41
6. IPS and APsaA: A Spirit of Cooperation 49
7. The Role of Psychoanalysis in Graduate Education Today 59
8. An Insecure Presence in Psychology Graduate Education 65
9. Transgenerational Haunting: Interview with Maurice Apprey ... 71
10. Chair of Psychoanalysis, Uncommon or Not? 77
11. Efforts Focus on Educational Criteria for Psychoanalysis in New York 83
12. NAPsaC—North American Psychoanalytic Confederation 87

Early Publications

13. The Relation of Color-Form Incongruity and Maladjustment to Reaction Time 93
14. Field Dependence in Young Anorectic and Obese Women 121

Presentations and Selected Publications

15. Hearing What Cannot Be Seen: A Psychoanalytic Research Group's Inquiry Into Female Sexuality 133

16. Into the Second Century: One Theory or Many? The Fit between Practice and Theory; Introduction to L. Rangell's Presentation.. 155

17. The Dynamic Surface of Psychic Realities in The Psychoanalytic Situation: Implications For Technique 161

18. The Riddle of Femininity: The Interplay of Primary Femininity and the Castration Complex in Analytic Listening 173

19. A Foreign Language: Voice for the Forbidden Thought........... 197

20. How Far Can the Frame Be Stretched Without Breaking: What Helps the Patient, and is it Psychoanalysis? 215

21. Battling the Life and Death Forces of Sadomasochism............ 227

22. The Challenge of Femininity: Conflicts about the Feminine and the Masculine in Men and Women................................ 235

23. Panel: The Challenge of Developing New IPA Psychoanalytic Groups Harriet Basseches, Co-Chair for North America 249

24. Infantile Sexuality and Trauma: Influence on Adult Sexuality.. 255

25. Presentation on Panel: When do the cure, our organizations and psychoanalysis become anchors?.. 265

Book Reviews

26. Before I Was I: Psychoanalysis and the Imagination by Enid Balint 277

27. Freud and Psychoanalysis 283

28. A Psychoanalytic Life.. 287

29. Thanks for HIB Distinguished Service Award..........................293

Closing Remarks by Harriet I. Basseches 295

Addendums

1. At Century's End: A Unitary Theory of Psychoanalysis
   by Leo Rangell 301
2. Developing, holding and containing new psychoanalytic
   groups by Cláudio Laks Eizirik 325

Foreword by Arlene Kramer Richards

Dr. Basseches presents us with an unconventional book and an unconventional attitude for a psychoanalyst. Instead of putting us into the history of a patient and discussing theoretical implications as has long been the way into a psychoanalytic discourse, she has begun with individual psychoanalysts, talking with them as human beings. Connecting with them illustrates her starting with connecting with individuals and continuing with connecting with them to form groups and even to connecting groups to each other.

In this volume, she records the history of a transformation in American psychoanalysis that she helped initiate. Her talent and passion for making connections, bringing people together and working within an organization has been a great contribution to the field. That contribution extends to being part of an ongoing study group, organizing a branch of an institute for studying and teaching psychoanalysis and keeping that branch connected to the original institute in a way that benefits both parts of what is now the Contemporary Freudian Society. From participating in forming an organization of several societies in the United States to forming and maintaining one that includes all analytic societies in the US that meet standards of the International Psychoanalytical Association, she shows how a gradual process can change organizations just as a gradual process of therapeutic work can change an individual.

Her thoughtful contributions to understanding the formation of new IPA groups are highlighted in the report by Dr Claudio Eizerik in which he highlights the contributions she made as a result of her experience shepherding a new group of the IPA from its initial gathering to its final status as an independent society in the IPA. He particularly cites her identification of rivalry as a major issue in the developing group and her description of the charismatic leader as a force for either cooperation within the group or a force for dissension. The need for that leader to develop and nurture younger colleagues to guide the group in the future is an important issue if the new group is to last.

But the work centers on what happens in the clinical situation. And here we come to the clinical work. Her paper with Nancy Goodman, Chapter 17 of this volume, is an important contribution to the theory of analytic technique. In this paper the clinical experience is conceptualized as dynamic interchange rather than a process of the analyst working on the patient. The idea that the analytic pair continually brings new thoughts and feelings in response to what they hear from each other and what they hear from themselves. Seeing the process this way makes it much more interesting and engaging for both people in the analytic room than seeing it as an analogue of the doctor patient relationship with the doctor healing the patient according to a prescribed procedure.

Chapter 19 presents another clinical issue: how to work with a multilingual or polyglot patient when you are a unilingual analyst? Her conclusion that the unilingual analyst can use clues from the counter-transference points to the importance of empathy and the multiple clues to meaning available aside from the linguistic. It gives hope and confidence to the analyst as well as the patient.

Another area of interest to psychoanalysts is addressed in Chapter 22. Here Basseches attempts a discussion of Femininity and Masculinity that emphasizes how much both men and women experience ambivalence about both active strivings and passive wishes, about both aggressive and passive feelings and about bodily appearance. Men and women are regarded as more alike than different in their repudiation of femininity.

Coming even closer to the clinical situation again she examines what it means to be a contemporary Freudian in Chapter 20. For me, the point of her paper and the crux of the issue of protecting the "frame" of the analytic work is contained in this one sentence of the chapter:

"My view of abstinence and neutrality feel solidly within contemporary Freudian thinking and rely on Loewald's thought (1989) that what counts is the underlying intentions of the analyst and her attitude of valuing that frame for the work."

This unusual and, indeed, original attitude can, I believe, protect the treatment from a premature ending. The case report in Chapter 21 shows the value of protecting the treatment so that more conversation leads to more understanding for both analyst and analysand.

In Chapter 20 Basseches shows how that ongoing discussion of the analysand's childhood, adolescent and adult memories lead both analyst and analysand to see the intertwining of ideas about separation, sexuality and compromise formation add to and make sense of the analysand's unhappiness. what she calls construction of masturbation fantasy seems to me an example of compromise formation. This implies the possibility of the analysand understanding other of his actions and choices as compromise formations as well.

Chapter 25 takes us to another facet of Basseches' work: reviews of psychoanalytic books. Here she generously reads each book for the best it has to offer, extracting a pearl from the rough shell even while describing that shell in some detail. Her selection of books by Balint, Meissner and Schafer is interesting in that all are complex compendia of the life work of contributors to psychoanalysts.

The Balint and Meissner books are edited versions of Balint's work and, in the case of Meissner, the work of Freud and some of his disciples. Schafer summarizes and synthesizes his own work. What does it mean to sum up a life's work? Basseches book is itself a summary of a life's work. Her choices of what to include in her own work display her achievements in individual, group and international organizations in psychoanalysis in dramatic form. Reader enjoy.

Introduction by Harriet I. Basseches

I want to begin by giving you some back story of my earliest experience in the psychoanalytic sphere of wanting psychoanalytic training so much that I was willing to travel to another city from Washington, DC to New York City to achieve that goal. I tell those details in part by way of introduction and in part to set the stage for the intensity of my interest and involvement in psychoanalytic institutions and functioning. Since my first efforts to get training as a psychoanalyst, I learned many lessons about institutional psychoanalysis. The first lesson was discovering how challenging it would be just to begin training. At the time I emerged from graduate school with my PhD in Clinical Psychology in 1979 and realized I needed more depth to my experience in order to do therapy, I went to apply at a local institute of the American Psychoanalytic Association (APsaA*) only to learn that regrettably I was not welcome.

I began my own official psychoanalytic journey in 1984. I say, "official" because of the APsaA Institute's rejection of me, unless I forswore an intention to do clinical work—something I and quite a few fellow psychologists in my community would not do despite an earnest interest in pursuing psychoanalytic training. In 1984, however, a group of us in Washington, DC who had learned of the New York Freudian Society

---

* At the time this article was published in TAP, APsaA was used as the acronym; at the time of publication of this book, it is now APsA.

(NYFS), an independent psychoanalytic Institute in New York City, one of a very few institutes housed on the coasts of the U.S. considered "good" programs outside of APsaA. NYFS allowed psychologists and social workers along with psychiatrists and some academics to train.

A group of psychologists and social workers approached them and invited them to consider offering us training. Happily, they agreed to go forward with what eventually became an additional chapter of the NYFS in DC. Thus began an adventure with our wonderful teachers and mentors from New York for a group originally of 14 people to become candidates for psychoanalytic training. During those years, our teachers travelled to Washington on alternating Saturdays and we went up to New York for supervision, once we had passed "Readiness for Control" and began seeing analytic patients. Our analyses were conducted by the few brave training analysts who bucked the system that forbade conducting such in their local APsaA affiliated organizations. As one can imagine, having been denied the opportunity and now having the training was extremely exhilarating. We were a very enthusiastic bunch. We, of course, gladly accepted the educational program that NYFS provided for us, but otherwise, we ran our on ship including the beginning functioning of committees, such as a scientific committee to plan presentations enriching our learning. Actually, I do not think the NYFS envisioned a long-term relationship with our group once we were launched, but in fact, we became increasingly integrated until it became clear that we would be a continuing branch of the NYFS and the organization eventually changed its name to the Contemporary Freudian Society (CFS).

Shortly before graduating, I was asked I believe because I lived in Washington, DC, where a national accrediting organization was located, to represent my institute and other "outside" but considered 'good' institutes, to work beside a representative from APsaA to keep a much further "outside" group which wanted to be named the organization to certify as the standard bearer for psychoanalysis in the United States from taking that mantel. We succeeded in arguing against the application, and at least for the time, kept the more outsiders from gaining dominance. Thus, I learned there existed degrees of outsiderness.

The next lesson in status issues occurred somewhat shortly afterward. The NYFS was in the process of a successful completion of its application to join the IPA, following that lawsuit to which I refer below. As a requirement for admission, all NYFS training analysts had to be reevaluated for their position in their institute, and some feared they would be rejected. While that mostly did not happen, it created an atmosphere of hostile groupings between those members who wanted to join the IPA and those who were happier to remain as they previously were—a stand-alone, independent institute. While the issues which precipitated the forming of these hostile attitudes between the two internal groups slowly became irrelevant as the NYFS settled in as part of the IPA, it took many years for the hostility to dissipate within the NYFS. It was during this period that I became increasingly active in the NYFS.

Being one of the oldest members of our candidate group, I was prepared to devote myself 100% to the endeavor in a way that other younger members could not yet do, and I finished training by 1990. At that point I began to be very active in the New York portion of our Society, invited and accepting membership on the Progressions Committee (Education Committee), which is the central pulse of the educational part of an analytic institute. While on that meaningful committee, I began to become interested in the organizational structure of the Institute, applying for and winning a spot on the Board as Vice President. I was welcomed enthusiastically by what I thought was the spirit of the NYFS group. I was then after a couple of years invited to apply to run for President. I won and I thought my love affair with the NYFS was continuing. It turned out that only a bit more than one half of the group joined me in my romance. A bit less than half resented me and thought that I was a foreigner and had no right to lead our group. Those were challenging times, especially as I had not understood that at that time there was a split in the group at least superficially focused on NYFS having begun a process of joining the International Psychoanalytical Association (IPA). Some members of the NYFS resented that they were required to be reevaluated in their long-held statuses, especially as training analysts, even though assured that this was proforma. In addition, there was a feeling of unease over how much we would be accepted and welcomed into the IPA, especially since we were a group made up mostly of psychologists and social workers with a smattering of psychiatrists but basically a part of that group that had been unwelcome at APsaA and IPA until the successful lawsuit requiring admittance to APsaA and IPA concluded at about the time the Washington group began our training. Moreover, the NYFS had great pride in its independence and success as a stand-alone institute. All of that led to a division for a time among members for and against this new status of participating in the IPA. This undercurrent, with which I was only dimly aware, was an important divide that I as a President coming from our then new subsidiary failed to address. I mention all this background as a kind of preliminary contextual note to my introduction, because I believe it helps demonstrate my learning curve regarding psychoanalytic group dynamics and functioning. I hope to describe more of what I learned, as I also share through my papers which follow about meaningful events in the psychoanalytic timetable, during my years of most activity.

I close my discussion of my thoughts on this section with a couple of observations. In the case of psychoanalysis, I believe the attitude of who was "in" and who was "out" actually began with Freud himself. In his effort to preserve and protect his unique contribution of psychoanalysis, I believe he had difficulty tolerating a range of views among his followers so that some while originally embraced by him, eventually were excluded and minimized. Similarly, those who studied with him varied in how closely they followed him, and for some their attitudes seemed more rivalrous and oppositional. Thus, following this lead, there was a core set of controversial positions that seemed to occur throughout the history of psychoanalysis: the inside and the outside. That divisiveness was replicated when shortly before, during and after World War II, psychoanalysts of European origin came to the United States and also to England from the European Continent, where Freud originally resided. Further, even within the core groups of psychoanalytic thinking which formed, the capacity to integrate a broad range of ideas for inclusion has not seemed to be the chosen path; rather schools of thought, skeptical of other schools, seemed to be the way the history has developed.

It seems likely that this spirit of competitiveness, rivalry and difficulty valuing other points of view from one's own is not exclusive to psychoanalysis, but it certainly has had a powerful effect on its history. I believe it has had both positive and negative impacts: the positive, in that the field is rich with a broad range of interesting and exciting ideas available; regarding the negative, I think psychoanalysis is perceived in the culture as a boutique, elite, set of ideas and even though influential, the ideas while often adopted, are often viewed by all but psychoanalysts as outdated, outmoded, and rarely relevant—a sad loss to society and to psychoanalysis.

I would like to conclude these introductory remarks with a description of how the papers and presentations have been organized in the book. One category of papers focuses on my reporting, views, and experiences to do with psychoanalytic institutional matters. That section, the TAP articles, give a part of the historical record from a period of significant activity and changes in the institutional world of psychoanalysis in North America in particular. Another includes papers or presentations connected with my clinical views and experiences. In the clinical group, I was sole author for some, and others were written with other colleagues. Finally, there is a category primarily centered on book reviews and interviews. Within a given category, I have tried to present the material chronologically from the earliest to later papers.

I acknowledge that this compendium neither includes all of my solo papers or all of my papers with other colleagues, nor includes reference to the book with Paula Ellman and Nancy Goodman and myself, published by Karnac entitled, ***Battling the Life and Death Forces of Sadomasochism***.

PUBLICATIONS FROM

THE AMERICAN PSYCHOANALYST

CHAPTER 1

NAAP/ABAP Fail in Bid for COPA Approval as U.S.

Accrediting Body for Psychoanalysis

Harriet I. Basseches, Ph.D., Oscar Legault, M.D. & Jonathan H. Slavin, Ph.D.

TAP 25:4 p. 2

Few who read the headline above will readily grasp its meaning despite its considerable importance.

COPA is the Council on Postsecondary Accreditation, a nongovernmental organization that sanctions accrediting bodies for institutions and programs of higher education, including most colleges, universities, and medical schools in the United States.

NAAP is the National Association for the Advancement of Psychoanalysis, an association claiming a membership of 40 independent psychoanalytic institutes. many of them rather obscure. NAAP formed ABAP, the American Board for Accreditation in Psychoanalysis, with the intent, as the name might imply. of accrediting (and regulating standards for) programs in psychoanalysis throughout the United States. As under COPA's rules there can be but one accrediting body per profession, designation of such a body is a serious matter with far reaching effects. Acceptance by COPA of the NAAP/ABAP application would position ABAP as the sole accrediting body for psychoanalytic training programs in this country.

Learning of ABAP's pending application, five United States psychoanalytic organizations sent letters to COPA expressing their opposition: the American Psychoanalytic Association, the New York Freudian Society, the American Psychological Association, the Institute for Psychoanalytic Training and Research (IPTAR), and the Academy of Psychoanalysis. On July 1, 1991, the first three of these groups accepted invitations to testify before the COPA Committee on Recognition as it considered initial recognition of ABAP. At hearings held, Oscar Legault and Harriet I. Basseches testified on behalf of the American Psychoanalytic and the New York Freudian Society, respectively. Jonathan Slavin, President of the Division of Psychoanalysis (Division 39), represented the American Psychological Association. A sixth psychoanalytic organization, the Council of Psychoanalytic Psychotherapists, was also in opposition and sent their president, Miriam Pierce, as an observer. A past president of this organization, Harvey Kaplan (also a member of the New York Freudian Society), was the first to sound the alert, informing Freudian Society president Abby Adams-Silvan of the ABAP application. Adams-Silvan then notified Presidents Joseph Sandler of the International Psychoanalytical Association and Bernard Pacella of The American.

The opposition attacked the application on the grounds that NAAP lacks universal recognition within the psychoanalytic community and that its membership standards fall well below those of mainstream psychoanalytic programs. According to a letter from Marianne R. Phelps, COPA Coordinator of Recognition, announcing the committee's decision, the application was declined on the basis of a failure to demonstrate compliance with the following COPA provisions:

> *"A4. Accredits programs which are generally accepted as preparing for entry-level into a profession Or occupation.*
>
> *B1. Provides evidence that accreditation protects the interests of students, benefits the public, and improves the quality of teaching, learning, research, and professional practice."*

"B2. Provides evidence that its policies, evaluative criteria, procedures, and evaluative decisions are accepted by the appropriate communities of interest such as educators, educational institutions, other accrediting bodies, practitioners, employers, and public agencies."

COPA discouraged past exploration by the American Psychoanalytic Association for such designation on the basis that the American both accredited training institutions and certified their graduates. Approximately ten years ago NAAP made its first attempt to become the accrediting body. Since that time, NAAP/ABAP has expended great effort toward achieving that goal. NAAP/ABAP's reception at the COPA meeting in July gave the appearance that attention had been paid to the cultivation of good will.

According to the letter from Phelps, NAAP/ABAP may reapply for initial recognition by "submitting additional information to demonstrate compliance with [the above-mentioned] provisions... and another public hearing [would be scheduled]. A document reported to have been circulated by the NAAP/ABAP leadership to its members after the current application was deferred, rather than sounding the death knell for their quest for recognition, is said to read more like a celebratory victory statement. The thought that ABAP was turned down on the basis of only three provisions seems to encourage the leadership that they are close to success; moreover, they are preparing to reapply before the next COPA deadline of October 11, 1991. Clearly, NAAP/ABAP has not taken no for an answer, and the organization's efforts at achieving accreditation rights must continue to be a concern. Even more important, however, is the need to face up finally to the thorny issues posed for the profession by the question of accreditation.

CHAPTER 2

A Conversation with Bruce H. Sklarew

TAP 27:4, pp. 12–13.

Basseches: You were one of the founders of the Forum for the Psychoanalytic Study of Film Tell me, How did the Forum originate?

Sklarew: Let me begin before the Forum. The first organized program in which psychoanalysts discussed films was originated by Steve Steury in the early eighties when he was director of the Extension Division of the Baltimore-Washington Institute. He coordinated four series of films in collaboration with the American Film Institute at the Kennedy Center. When Steve moved to Milwaukee, 1 organized a discussion series on Bergman's view of women in the context of female development, as the first of eight series with the Smithsonian Institution and AFI. *Then we planned a more ambitious project, a retrospective of the work of Bernardo Bertolucci with his participation. The conference included four analysts, as well as four prominent film scholars, two of whom had written books on Bertolucci. It was to be a joint venture between the Baltimore-Washington Institute and AFI in New York, but as the budget approached ten thousand dollars, both AFI and the Institute pulled out I then asked Bertolucci if he would consider doing it in Washington. As an Italian Communist, his response was, "I only know one person in Washington, Ronald Reagan. I don't think 1 want to do it in Washington." So, we scurried around to find a venue in New York. It was like producing an off-Broadway show. Without institutional sponsorship, four analysts—Paula Atkeson, Marianne Goldberger, Gene

Gordon, and myself—decided to give ourselves a name: "The Society for the Psychoanalytic Study of Film." Since we had a name and a grand beginning, Gene Gordon and I decided to form an organization, as though that's what the world needs. Later, we changed "Society" to "Forum." Today we have a national membership of over four hundred, and some overseas.

Basseches: Tell me about the range of the Forum's projects and interests.

Sklarew: They range from the large and ambitious, like two weekend conferences with Bertolucci, to smaller local projects. We organized our fourth program last spring with the Film Society of Lincoln Center on the works of Jean Vigo, who directed the acclaimed [*Atalante* and *Zero for Conduct*]. Other projects include series with AFI and the Smithsonian, discussions at Columbia and other universities, collaborations on Jewish films with the Jewish Community Center of D.C and the George Washington University Hillel, four programs with the Washington School of Psychiatry, and many at local community centers. We publish a newsletter of announcements and film discussions, called *Projections,* which we hope to develop into a journal. We also make available to members a bibliography on psychoanalysis and film, as well as lists of films discussed and programs. The Forum has chapters in Washington, New York, and San Francisco.

Basseches: So, you've been very active. Who belongs to the organization, and who is on your Board?

Sklarew: Gene Gordon and I are co-chair; half of the Board are psychoanalysts from the Baltimore-Washington and Washington Institutes. Bertolucci is *a* nominal member. The rest are psychologists and social worker, an attorney, filmmakers, and film and literary scholars knowledgeable about psychoanalysis. The membership consists predominantly of people in the mental health field, as well as film scholars and others interested in film.

Basseches: Through the Forum's activities, I understand that you have become friends with Bertolucci, and that he has invited you on the set of his films. What did you learn?

Sklarew: I was invited by Bertolucci to the set of *The Sheltering Sky* in Morocco. I felt like 1 was in the midst of a magnificent primal, scene experience, The set was a relatively small room, and 1 was cramped in a dark small room and needing to get out of the way not only of the camera and the lights, but also out of the line-of-sight of the actors—Debra Winger and John Malkovich. It was like hiding and watching the world being created. Last November I spent two weeks in Katmandu, Nepal, and then a week **in** Seattle on the set of the not yet released *Little Buddha*. Part of the movie was shot around the supposed Bodhi tree, where Buddha experienced his enlightenment. In reality it is a tree about twenty feet **in** circumference, with a branch span of over a hundred feet. The tree was growing at the edge of a cliff, but since the director wanted space on all sides, they erected scaffolding that was about seventy-five feet high and put in about twenty-five feet of filler solid enough to hold thirty or forty people. So, they literally remade the earth. I noticed an unusual daily rhythmic tension on the set. The morning started very slowly, with the director and crew seeming to meander around, mainly adjusting the lighting. The tension· accelerated over the next hour or two, as they got closer to doing the first shot, and then repeating it over and over again with small variances of camera angle, lighting, and positioning. The tension would build and build until the shot was finished, followed by a huge sense of relaxation. Of course, there might be two minutes of actual film used in the whole day of shooting.

Basseches: *You were impressed.*

Sklarew: Yes. Bertolucci does his own research, is very erudite, mostly self-educated, and fluent in French and English. He sets up his own scenes. He's very much in control, yet very casual, accessible, and creative. It is well known that he has had extensive experience with psychoanalysis, and he read Freud. He speaks of cinema as made from raw materials woven on a dream loom and has said that "psychoanalysis is another lens of my camera." In seeming contrast to his enthusiasm for psychoanalysis, however, he once said to me, "You biopsy my films," a most overdetermined idea.

Basseches: You remind me of an article I read about the filming of Casablanca. It suggested that the filmmakers were deciding and writing what was going to happen right on the set. The actors were expected to play their roles when they did not know the outcome, yet it worked.

Sklarew: Yes. Ingrid Bergman wanted to know with whom she was leaving Casablanca. The director, Michael Curtiz, said, 'We don't know and you don't need to know." So, film can be created in a helter-skelter way and still come out well.

Basseches: I know that you have collaborated with film scholars who use psychoanalytic ideas. Tell me how that works.

Sklarew: Such film scholars as Jeff Kline, who wrote a magnificent book, *Bertolucci's Dream Loom,* that l reviewed in the Quarterly, Krin Gabbard, the brother of Glen, and Ira Konigsberg at the University of Michigan have a good sense of applied analysis and have discussed films for the Forum and The American. We usually include film scholars so each discipline can inform the other. Because the ideas and language are used in disparate ways, the Forum tries to bridge the interdisciplinary gap. Film scholars usually do not have an historical sense of the development of psychoanalysis. For example, at one meeting of the Society for Cinema Studies, a scholar referred to the 1895 Project as if it were the last word in psychoanalysis. In another instance, l was approached by a scholar who had been reading oedipal interpretations in the literature on *King Kong*. But he had heard something about preoedipal issues that he didn't quite comprehend, yet thought might apply. He really wanted to check it out with an analyst.

Basseches: *You have mentioned The American. You have a project going there as well. ls the Forum cosponsor?*

Sklarew: The forum has no official function at The American, although it has presented three films in collaboration with the International. The American has a long tradition of showing a film and discussing it on Thursday nights at the meetings. In 1987 I proposed a more elaborate film program. We now have a two-or three-part workshop of viewings and discussions. For the past four years we have also had a discussion group on the same theme as the workshop. Themes have included the works of Bertolucci and Bergman, Images of Mothers and Daughters in the Maternal Melodrama. Film and Dreams, Voyeurism and Film, Surrealism and Film, Cinematic Projection/ Psychotic Projection, Sadism and Masochism. Jewish Identity, Political Extremism, Gay/Lesbian Representations, Psychoanalysts in Film, and the Phallic Woman.

Basseches: Do you find that you've been getting a good response?

Sklarew: We've had a strong response, nearly thirty in the discussion group in San Francisco on analysts and therapists in film, and often fifty at the workshops.

Basseches: I heard on PBS that the film industry is going to be doubling its output in the coming year. Rather than people being less interested in going to the movies because of videos and TV, movies have been doing a booming business.

Sklarew: There are several reasons for that. First, watching a video at home is a very different, much less intense experience. It's easily interrupted, or you can interrupt yourself, lessening the regression. The TV screen is small, rather than being life-size or larger. The resolution is never as sharp, and on a TV screen the original film is incomplete because of the film's aspect ratio. Moreover, film viewing has a greater immediate visual and auditory impact; it resonates more directly with unconscious processes. It places us in close contact with the primary process and affects, as in dreaming, and stimulates a range of fantasies. We imagine that early idealized love-objects still exist for us in the form of movie stars. Reality testing is in abeyance. The desire for cinema is like the curiosity for a forbidden primal scene experience as the viewer sits in a darkened theater riveted on exciting and often puzzling sights and sounds. Robert Eberwein, in *Film and The Dream Screen,* described a temporary dissolution of the ego that results in a merger of viewer and object. Michelline Frank and Ira Konigsberg have discussed viewing film as an intermediate zone between internal and external experience that functions as a transitional phenomenon. Arlow writes that art forms-including film-give us a vicarious opportunity to act out our sexual and aggressive impulses with exculpation from superego censorship. Further, film can inspire us to try on different roles, identify and find ego ideals in the characters, and "do the right thing." Hollywood has been described as "the ultimate dream factory. It allows us to have the dreams we've never had, the dream we yet await."

Basseches: What further ideas do you have about the relationship between dreams and film?

Sklarew: Fellini said that "film is a dream for the waking mind." Films can present bizarre and vivid images, puzzling juxtapositions, and gaps in time and continuity, all of which are characteristic of our experience with dreams, particularly those that do not have a lot of secondary elaboration. Dream work, the use of displacement, condensation, visual representation, and sometimes symbolism, parallels what one might call "film work," even though the latter is a collective enterprise including script writers, the director, and sometimes a novelist. The regressive experience of sitting in a darkened theater, stilled and tightly placed in a passive-receptive position, is like the motor inhibition of dreams. Having viewed a complex film, one often leaves the theater with a sense of puzzlement about what has been seen, much like awakening from a dream.

Basseches: I know there are many ways one can think about the relation of psychoanalysis and film. What does the psychoanalyst bring to our understanding of films, and, alternatively, what does film have to offer of value to the psychoanalyst? Would you address that reciprocity?

Sklarew: Historically, this popular visual medium originated at the same time Freud explored the transformation of thought into visual representations in *The Interpretation of Dreams*. Film continued as the new art form of the twentieth century, just as psychoanalysis became the science of the mind. It is speculative to suggest that studying film will teach us about psychoanalysis, but there are parallels between "film work" and dream work. We use our psychoanalytic skills to illuminate the many levels of motivation and conflict in the characters and their interactions as if it were all condensed clinical material. We approach film as an assemblage or montage of manifest dreams projected onto a dream screen. Of course, we do not have the transferences or associations as we do from patients, but we are alert to juxtapositions, symbolizations, and other demonstrations of the workings of the unconscious of the director, the screen writer, and sometimes the novelist. Bob Winer speaks of the voyeurism common to both watching film and listening to patients, a voyeurism that is sublimated in the interest of understanding. In both film and clinical work, we attend to thoughts and feelings stirred up in us, in order to learn more. Our clarifications and interpretations of film to lay audiences can convey psychoanalytic ideas in an acceptable, palatable way.

Basseches: The representation of psychoanalysis and psychotherapy in film is not very positive.

Sklarew: Irv Schneider wrote that moviemakers thought they invented a profession they called "psychiatry." It characterized film therapists starting with the 1906 sanatorium superintendent, Dr. Dippy. There are a few Dr. Wonderfuls and an increasing number of Dr. Evils. This is also clear in the excellent book written by the Gabbards, *Psychiatry in the Cinema*. Therapists are often presented showing unethical and bizarre behavior, personal problems, or using strange and naive methods making them easy to associate as we do from patients, but we are alert to juxtapositions, symbolizations, and other demonstrations of the workings of the unconscious of the director, the screen writer, and others even the actors. We are represented in these ways for various defensive reasons. Transference to therapists as authorities, parents, mind readers, noxious controller—modern forms of witch doctors, demons, Greek or Roman gods-leads people lo want to make us seem less powerful. Like the voyeur, the filmgoer reverses the patient's point of view, observing the life of the therapist from the shadows and thus feeling some defensive power over the therapist. In addition, the film viewer can project his or her conflicts onto the therapist, who becomes a repository for issues that can then be avoided.

21

Basseches: We do have to stop for now. I was delighted to learn more about the Forum and about film. Thank you.

CHAPTER 3

A Conversation with Stanley Greenspan

TAP 28:3, pp. 26–27.

Basseches: *You have always been closely associated with infant research. Can you tell us how you came to that field?*

Greenspan: I was trained in both adult and child psychiatry. As I was finishing my child psychiatric training, I started psychoanalytic training and did both the adult and child programs. Now I'm a supervising child analyst at the Washington Psychoanalytic Institute. Around the time I was in analytic training, I also started doing research at NIMH. That is where we initiated the research on infants and young children's emotional development, as well as clinical problems and intervention strategies. That research program went on for around fifteen years at NIMH and now continues in a number of other settings, including the Reginald Lourie Infant Center in Rockville, Maryland, and the University of Maryland at College Park. During this time, I was also involved in clinical practice, including child and adult psychoanalysis, as well as work with infant and very young children and their families. For most of my career I have been involved in both research and clinical practice, learning about development from both perspectives.

Basseches: Do you recall what spurred your interest in this area?

Greenspan: Well, it grew out of curiosity about how adults become the way they are. So, I did some child training. But even older children had earlier roots, so I went back still further to infants. But I suspect that the real reason, or another reason, was that I was getting ready to be a parent. I was about to have my first child when we started the baby research. Earlier, when I was an undergraduate at Harvard, I became interested in-depth psychology from reading Erikson and Freud. My parents, having gone through the depression, had always emphasized my doing something like medicine, which would be "secure." My brother was already in medical school. In my sophomore year in college, I was interested in science and was thinking about becoming a doctor. l became fascinated with depth psychology and at that point the idea of becoming a psychiatrist started taking shape. Then I went on to medical school at Yale.

Basseches: Did you have a mentor or someone who particularly influenced your thinking?

Greenspan: Well, Reginald Lourie, a psychoanalyst and the director of child psychiatry at Children's Hospital during my child psychiatry residency, was a very important influence, in terms both of his interest in infants and young children and of his overall broad-based clinical perspective. He was an important teacher and mentor to many. He retired from Children's Hospital right around the time I was beginning the NIMH Clinical Infant Development research program, and Reg was able to join me in developing it. We worked together for many years, studying infants and young children in multi-risk families, developing preventive intervention strategies, and starting the Zero to Three National Center for Clinical Infant Programs and the Reginald Lourie Center I mentioned earlier.

Basseches Of the many books and articles you have published—I counted over a hundred articles and chapters, 20 monographs and books either authored or edited—are there some you would mention that would best show the direction of your thinking,

Greenspan: An early book, one that serves as a theoretical foundation for much of the later work. is Intelligence *and Adaptation: An Integration of Psychoanalytic and Pugetian Developmental Psychology* (1979). The monographs *Psychopathology and Adaptation* in *Infancy and Early Childhood* (1981) and *Infants in Multi-Risk Families* (1987) describe some of the findings from the NlMH research. More recent books that further refine and apply this general theoretical structure to clinical problems include *Infancy and Early Childhood: The Practice of Clinical Assessment and Intervention with Emotional and Developmental Challenges* (1992) and *The Development of the Ego* (1989). The latter explores the implications of this work for psychoanalytic theory and technique. Books for parents and educators include a very recent one, *Playground Politics: The Emotional Life of the* School-*Aged Child* (1993), as well as two that I wrote with my wife, Nancy T. *Greenspan—First Feelings: Milestones in the Emotional Development of Your Infant and Child from Birth to Age Four* (1985) and *The Emotional Partnership: How Parents and Children Can Meet the Emotional Challenges of Infancy and Childhood* (1989). Many of the ideas we will be talking about are discussed in a book due out from International Universities Press in a few months entitled *Developmentally Based Psychotherapy.* It discusses new psychotherapeutic strategies that build on an understanding of early development.

While the major part of my writing has been directed to scientific and professional groups, including pediatricians and educators, about a quarter of my effort has been toward communicating directly with the general public. The goal is to create a greater awareness of in-depth emotional development throughout all the developmental stages, from infancy up through adulthood, to facilitate healthier child rearing, and to encourage preventively oriented interventions. In that regard, I might mention that our work on the milestones of early emotional development was incorporated into the American Academy of Pediatrics' guidelines for the well-baby exam. It was also featured in a PBS *Nova* documentary entitled "Life's First Feelings" which has been shown yearly on public television. A videotape based on the milestones was made by the Institute for Mental Health Initiatives, a nonprofit foundation called "Exploring First Feelings". It is being shown to new mothers in over two hundred hospitals. Another videotape, made for both educators and parents, is called "Floor Time." Produced by Scholastic Inc. of New York, it presents both the emotional tones and various strategies for promoting healthy emotional and intellectual growth in young children. In addition, a number of books based on this work have been written for educators and parents.

Basseches: I know you have received many awards. Could you highlight a few?

Greenspan: I am especially proud of the American Psychiatric Association's Gittleson Prize for Contributions to Child Psychiatry Research, and of the Edward A. Strecker Award for Contributions to American Psychiatry. They indicate a recognition of the importance of early emotional development and preventive approaches.

Basseches: There is so much more to discuss in terms of your theoretical ideas and research. Perhaps we can begin by discussing your belief that psychoanalysis needs an improved developmental model for understanding normal and pathological patterns, as well as the therapeutic process.

Greenspan: Our current developmental model has provided unique insights. The work of pioneers like Mahler, Anna Freud, Spitz, Erikson, and Hartmann, Kris, and Loewenstein has focused on early experience contributing to intrapsychic phenomena. However, the focus has for the most part been on the content of intrapsychic phenomena. By content I mean the nature of wishes, conflicts, prohibitions, and various aspects of the ego mechanisms.

Yet there is another very important aspect of intrapsychic phenomena that has been relatively neglected in our current developmental perspectives. It's hinted at by Anna Freud's work on the nature of ego mechanisms of defense, Mahler's work on object constancy, and some of Spitz's observations, as well as some of Hartmann, Kris, and Loewenstein's work on psychic structure formation. But overall, we haven't had a detailed road map of how intrapsychic structure builds up. For example, we haven't had a complete understanding of how the ego develops and how its different mechanisms develop and come to play their particular functional roles. To use an analogy, we have had a relatively good understanding of the drama that is enacted, but an insufficient understanding of the structure of the stage that supports that drama.

There are two aspects of intrapsychic structure formation that clinical work with infants and young children, as well as psychoanalytic work with children and adults, has begun to reveal. One of these has to do with the sequence of intrapsychic organizations that characterize early structure formation, including the organization of experience that precedes the ability to represent it. The second builds on Freud's goal for psychoanalysis regarding an understanding of the biological aspects of ego development, especially the biological aspects of defenses. Emerging is an understanding of how individual differences, in terms of biological aspects of constitutional and maturational phenomena, contribute to the structure of the ego. We are beginning, then, to understand the individual biological differences that contribute to the differences in ego structure and organizational levels of experience that characterize early ego development.

Basseches: Can you give some examples of these organizational levels and biological differences?

Greenspan: In *The Development of the Ego* I describe in some detail a total of six such levels, as well as the types of problems that are related to each: (1) self-regulation, where perceptual differences in sensory-affective reactivity and processing contribute to the development of personality or character structure; (2) forming and maintaining relationships as a basis for the capacity for object relatedness; (3) self/object boundary-defining pre-representational interactions; (4) self- and object pre-representational "personhood," characterizing interactions; (5) representational elaboration as a basis for internal self- and object representational elaborations; and (6) representational differentiation as a basis for internal self- and object differentiations and integration.

The biologically based constitutional and maturational differences we describe are based on differences we have observed in infants and young children, as well as older children and adults, and appear to contribute significantly to character formation and pathology. In each sensory pathway, sensory and affective experience can be characterized as hypo- or hyper-reactive. In addition, each sensory channel can have differences in the way interpersonal and affective information is processed (e.g., auditory/verbal, visual/spatial). Further, motor tone and motor planning abilities can vary significantly. What Hartmann described as the autonomous ego functions can actually vary quite a bit from person to person and contribute to both character and pathology.

Basseches: Can you give an example?

Greenspan, When certain biological patterns are coupled with certain environmental patterns, they can intensify each other. We see what Freud had anticipated, a biological basis for character structure and selection of defenses. For example, individuals who are overreactive to touch or sound, and have stronger auditory processing abilities and relatively weaker visual/spatial powers, tend toward the hysterical, depressive, and anxiety disorders. Those who have difficulty with movement in space tend toward phobic disorders.

It should be emphasized that when environmental conditions enhance flexibility rather than pathology, we tend to see healthy character formation, but with a tendency toward one or another of these characteristics. For example, instead of panic and/or anxiety or depression, we see a reactive, sensitive person who is very alert to others' moods and tendencies to be reactive themselves.

Basseches: Do you see an antithesis between this structural perspective and dynamic perspectives that focus on unconscious wishes and conflict?

Greenspan: Not at all. Each is an essential aspect of the multiple perspective psychoanalysis has traditionally employed in understanding the mind. It's easy to focus on only one perspective, say the dynamic, and to lose sight of the fact that every dynamic drama must take place in the context of a particular structure or set of structures. In addition, when focusing on structural perspectives, it's easy to lose sight of the fact that structures provide the foundation—the housing, so to speak—for different dynamic dramas, each with its own content or meanings.

Basseches: From a practical clinical point of view, why is it important to have a structural perspective?

Greenspan: It's especially important clinically to understand the structure of the ego, in addition to the particular dynamic phenomenon the ego is struggling with at any moment. Many individuals who come for psychoanalytic or psychodynamic treatment, or who could benefit from such treatment, have important structural limitations. It is rare that individuals who come into treatment already have highly differentiated ego structures whereby, for example, they could observe their own wishes and abstracted feeling states, make connections between different wishes and feelings (as well as different sides of a conflict), and understand these in historical, current, and future contexts.

The "ideal" neurotic patient allegedly has all these capacities working for him, and needs only the therapeutic process, including a transference relationship and the skillful guidance of a seasoned therapist, to avail himself of opportunities for new insight and growth. But in fact, relatively few patients come into the treatment situation with highly differentiated ego structures. The majority come in with significant compromises in one or another aspect of their basic ego structure. That is why having a road map of the structural components of ego development, to go alongside our road map of intrapsychic content (e.g., wishes, fears, conflicts), could increase our understanding of the mind and improve the efficacy of our therapeutic strategies.

Basseches: What does the developmental-structural perspective alert us to clinically that dynamic considerations don't?

Greenspan: The dynamic perspective has been elucidated over many years by skillful analytic inquiry. For the most part, however, this work provides a rich description of the various dramas played out in our intrapsychic life. By contrast, understanding the structural development of the mind provides us a way of comprehending how an individual learns to regulate the intensity of sensations and, later, the intensity of internal wishes and affects. It also provides us a way of understanding how individuals process—that is, comprehend and organize—sensations, wishes, and affects, and how they organize both motor and communication patterns.

Further, the structural perspective explores how individuals learn such fundamental capacities as how to become part of a relationship and share a sense of humanity with others. It demarcates the processes involved in early pre-representational self- and object interactions and differentiations. Beginning with part-internal object interactions and partial differentiations, it describes how we progress to pre-representational (presymbolic) whole self- and object patterns and further pre-representational differentiations. It demarcates how these pre-representational patterns serve as a foundation for the construction of a representational system, that is, the ability to abstract wishes and affects in a representational form. Most important, it helps us to understand biologically based constitutional and maturational differences.

The structural perspective seeks to understand how early representational capacities coalesce into internal self- and object organizations, and how constitutional and maturational deficiencies contribute to these early structural capacities—how, for example, overreactivity to sound and touch will lead to one type of organization, while underreactivity will lead to another. It also helps us identify specific interactive patterns that support or undermine particular structural capacities. In addition, it helps us understand how representational, internalized self- and object organizations become further differentiated as a foundation for the development of basic ego functions, including reality testing, impulse control, stable mood, stable internal representations of self and object, and stable differentiations between those representations. It also outlines how a differentiated ego structure leads to further growth and development, in terms of shifts from dyadic to triadic structures, and then to structures dealing with group phenomena, as well as more advanced, internalized phenomena.

Basseches: Could you give an example?

Greenspan: Consider a conflict over aggression, having to do with a wish to hurt the object and, in turn, a fear of being annihilated by the object. There are enormous differences in one's approach, depending on whether this conflict is operating at one level of structural organization or another. Consider that it is operating at a representational level. We may see it reflected in the play of a child, who has one doll hit another doll, followed by a hurricane, where the first doll gets submerged under crumbling buildings. There may be affects of fear and anxiety. While playing this out, however, the child is using words, maintains a descriptive or reflective attitude, and, when getting anxious about the hurricane, can put into words aspects of the anxiety and say, perhaps, "Mommy, I need a hug."

The same conflict played out at a pre-representational level, where experience can't be represented, might have the child yelling and screaming at the real object, not the pretend toys, or biting, kicking, or hitting the real object. Following this, in anticipation of severe punishment, the child might experience diffuse anxiety in a more bodily and behavioral sense (increased diffuse aggressive activity, changes in heart rate and muscle tone, etc.).

A child at the pre-representational level can't represent the expected retaliation. It's more like a person in a fight who throws a punch and, simply from the other person's behavioral pattern, anticipates a punch back. Our pre-representational, conflicted individual may therefore pinch, bite, or throw a tantrum and then up the stakes, increasing his own aggression because of the anticipation of counter-aggression. Or he may withdraw into a state of unrelatedness. In either case, he doesn't have the capacity to represent (i.e., create) a multisensory, affective picture of the pattern. The pattern is simply acted out, including expectations of the other's behavior.

What we see here is a drama that is not represented, but that rather is played out in the actual reality of a relationship. The content of the drama is not representational elements symbolized in pretending or elaborated in words (as in free association), but instead is behaviorally enacted, directly and viscerally. The drama is perceived as real, not as a set of feelings or wishes, as "He is going to hurt me" rather than "I feel as though I will be hurt." One may further speculate that a drama acted out behaviorally and viscerally might be associated with more primitive and overwhelming fears.

In this sense, the structure of the ego affects the content and vice versa. But it would be a mistake to think of these fears as having representational forms. Rather, they are experienced in a visceral and behavioral sense ("My muscles were exploding as I was hitting him").

Using traditional diagnostic thinking, one would see the more representational individual as having a more mature personality structure, capable of more traditional therapeutic exploration, whether it's a child using pretend play or an adult using words and descriptions or reporting associations or dreams. The individual who expresses the conflict in terms of direct behavioral phenomena we would view as a more primitive character disorder. Such individuals might come in having been involved in barroom brawls or severe, acting-out marital problems. We might feel less optimistic about their ability to participate in a dynamic therapeutic exploration.

But, regardless of our prognostic thinking about such persons, the structure of the personality and the ego is obviously critical in understanding the nature of their conflicts and anticipating the type of therapeutic work to come. Helping individuals shift from the level of acting out conflicts to the level of representing them might be seen, in fact, as the first order of business. Without this step, little growth could occur in their overall personality.

Basseches: How would these concepts play out in the treatment of patients?

Greenspan: Simply clarifying and interpreting these patterns would not be sufficient, and in fact might be counterproductive. First, one must always meet patients at the developmental level of their ego structure. Some of the strategies I propose are no different from what many therapists have been doing for years. But these approaches are too often viewed as intuitive rather than systematic or central to therapeutic growth. The developmental perspective can help systematize them and open up new areas for inclusion, such as constitutional and maturational differences, and the various developmental levels, that are not always grasped intuitively. Some, of course, will argue that these developmentally guided clinical strategies are preparatory to analysis, a preanalytic or analytic psychology phase of the work. To those who take this point of view, I would suggest that many more patients have these early difficulties than is often recognized, and that some of the limitations of analytic treatment relate to too narrow a view of the developmental levels in need of reworking.

Basseches: You seem to be saying that psychoanalysis should not define itself simply as a treatment for neurotic patients already capable of representing, differentiating, and observing their own experience. Instead, in order to deal with the issues you raise about early ego structure, it must define itself more broadly.

Greenspan: Psychoanalysis, as an approach to understanding the mind, has no choice. To remain vigorous and grow, it must embrace new findings. As a clinical treatment, it must continually bring in new discoveries to strengthen its clinical strategies. It must be careful, however, to build on its foundation systematically. As a discipline, psychoanalysis should be defined most broadly by its general principles and refrain from becoming too rigidly tied to one or another set of procedures.

Psychoanalysis has the opportunity to integrate findings about the mind, biological as well as psychodynamic and psychosocial. The developmental perspective can be especially useful in understanding how the different factors that influence development work together throughout the course of life. In this sense, the developmental perspective can guide the growth of psychoanalysis.

Basseches: Thank you for sharing your views so generously, and for giving our readers this opportunity to think about the important issues you raise.

CHAPTER 4

CORPA Decision: End of the Road for ABAP

TAP 29:3, p. 7.

The American Board for Accreditation in Psychoanalysis (ABAP) has at long last failed in its bid to become sole accrediting body for psychoanalysis in the U.S. On August 18, the Appeals Panel of the Commission on Recognition of Postsecondary Accreditation (CORPA) upheld the decision of its Committee on Recognition (COR) to deny ABAP recognition as an Accrediting Body for Postsecondary Educational Institutions or Programs.

For many years, The American Psychoanalytic Association (APSaA), the Confederation of Independent Psychoanalytic Societies of the United States (IPS), and other psychoanalytic organizations have opposed the ABAP application. In a letter, CORPA informed the organization that "consideration of ABAP's application for recognition is now complete. The action of the Appeals Panel is final and ABAP's application for recognition has been denied." That means no more reversals, last-minute cancellation of meetings, or appeals. The decision, however, does not rule out future bids by ABAP should it, according to the CORPA letter, "correct the deficiencies… that precluded a recognition decision."

The American and IPS have an ongoing history of cooperation in opposing the ABAP bid. Those testifying against ABAP, a nominally independent offshoot of the National Association for the Advancement of Psychoanalysis (NAAP), have included Donald Burnham, Oscar

Legault, and Allan Rosenblatt on behalf of The American, and Harriet Basseches representing both IPS and the New York Freudian Society, one of its constituent organizations. Since 1990 the NAAP/ABAP effort has been successfully opposed, with CORPA repeatedly deferring the ABAP application at a preliminary stage. In closed-door maneuvers, however, NAAP/ABAP succeeded in reversing that decision and moving the application along to the next stage. A hearing was then set for January 1994, with an array of third-party testifiers (The American, IPS, and others) scheduled to appear. Then, at the eleventh hour, NAAP/ABAP declined to proceed. The hearing was finally held in August 1994, the last point at which third parties were able to testify.

The outcome of the August hearing was a "failure to grant" recognition to ABAP. The applicant then launched an appeal at the next CORPA meeting, in October 1994. As reported in the NAAP newsletter, this appeal was heard, and the decision to remand the application back to CORPA for consideration presumably occurred at the CORPA meeting last February. At its own February meeting, CORPA again reviewed the file. The decision was confidential until all recognition procedures had been followed. At that point, a letter announcing CORPA's rejection of the ABAP bid was sent to all interested parties.

THIRD PARTIES ACKNOWLEDGED

In presenting its decision, CORPA acknowledged third-party testimony from several organizations, including The American and IPS, and from educators and practitioners affiliated with New York Hospital–Cornell Medical Center, the College of Physicians and Surgeons of Columbia University, and Yale University School of Medicine.

On a separate but related front, NAAP/ABAP temporarily withdrew its application to the Department of Education earlier this year. That situation is being monitored. Obviously, the question of who shall accredit continues to be a thorny issue. This may be the time for seriously considering the formation of a more appropriate accrediting body, one that would better represent the psychoanalytic community, and an application for CORPA and/or DOE recognition.

===

CONSORTIUM MEMBERS PRESENT UNITED FRONT

Members of the Psychoanalytic Consortium—Division 39 of the American Psychological Association. the National Membership Committee on Psychoanalysis, and the American Academy of Psychoanalysis—were each represented by separate counsel at the CORPA hearings but submitted joint written statements. This United front, though not specifically mentioned in the CORPA decision, was undoubtedly a significant factor in the successful opposition to the NAAP/ABAP bid for recognition as sole accrediting body for U.S. psychoanalysis.

CHAPTER 5

IPS, Now Three Years Old, Spurs Move toward Regional IPA Federation
TAP 29:2, pp. 26-27.

The Confederation of Independent Psychoanalytic Societies in the United States, or the IPS, as it has quickly come to be known (but later called the Confederation of Independent Psychoanalytic Societies or CIPS), comprises all U.S. psychoanalytic societies that, though unaffiliated with The American, are component societies of the IPA.

TAP has been faithful in documenting the histories of psychoanalytic societies and institutes within The American. With the IPS such a close neighbor, one might say sibling, TAP thought readers would have similar interest in its development and its history. The initial impetus for its formation arose immediately following the Rome Congress in 1989. At that time a convergence of events in the United States, South America, and Europe had led to a greater receptivity to nonmedical psychoanalytic organizations. At the Rome Congress, three societies from the United States unaffiliated with The American had been accepted into the IPA as provisional societies, the Institute for Psychoanalytic Training and Research (IPTAR), the New York Freudian Society (NYFS), and the Psychoanalytic Center of California (PCC).

PROVISIONAL STATUS FOR INDEPENDENTS

In 1993, in the IPA newsletter (2/2), Robert Wallerstein looked back at that event: "Of any business meeting that I've attended in the IPA and I have been attending them for twenty or thirty year now—the most moving was the time when that vote was announced, and the new members came into the room to take part for the rest of the day in the proceedings." Here was recognition for a constituency that previously had gone unrecognized: a nucleus of U.S. organizations maintaining the standards of the IPA, distinct from both The American and the American Psychological Association's Division 39.

It was Norbert Freedman, then president of IPTAR, who took the initiative in conceiving a separate IPA entity in the United States. A phone call from Charles Hanly, chair of the IPA Committee on New Groups, informed Freedman that the Los Angeles Institute and Society for Psychoanalytic Studies (LAISPS) had also been accepted as a provisional society. This provided the impetus for concrete action· To lay the groundwork, Freedman began talking with senior analysts from the other new groups- Sheldon Bach, Abby Adams-Silvan, and Mark Silvan from NYFS. Ernest Lawrence from LAISPS, and Albert Mason from PCC.

The next opportunity to advance the project was the Buenos Aires Congress in 1991, where Freedman arranged an informal meeting for representatives from the four groups. There they learned more about each other and agreed to exchange catalogues, bulletins, and other information. From that point on, the four groups began to communicate on a regular basis.

Perhaps the greatest spur to the official formation of the independent group, however, came out of the Presidents' Meeting held in London on July 24, 1992. At Buenos Aires there had been a call for greater democracy in the governance of the IPA; this was to be the topic of the London meeting.

From all over the world came presidents of the component societies, led by Joseph Sandler, then IPA President, to set in motion a successful drive toward the IPAs democratization. The meeting set a framework for establishing a House of Delegates that would share governance with the Executive Board and Council, and made plans for a working party, comprising representatives from the three main regions—Europe, Latin America, and North America—to draft new IPA bylaws. While in the past The American would without question have provided the representation from North America, that role had now for the first time to be clarified with both the Canadian Psychoanalytic Society and the four new groups in the US.

At a dinner meeting preceding the historic gathering in London, Adams-Silvan, Freedman, Mason, and Jean Sanville—then presidents of the four independent societies—had set themselves the task of communicating to the assembled presidents a new reality—the presence of the new IPA groups in the United States. This was to signal the first full participation of the independent U.S. groups in the shaping of IPA policy. Now, with the call for a House of Delegates, the times seemed propitious for creating the long-envisaged new IPA entity in the United States.

During the summer of 1992, immediately after the London meeting, the decision was made to establish a formal confederation, which at first was called the Coalition of Independent Psychoanalytic Societies in North America. The four over the ensuing months coalesced despite the immense continental distances involved. Through conference calls, faxes, and letters, as well as occasional meetings in person, they managed to discuss a wide range of issues, including such matters as training standards, accreditation, and scientific exchanges.

A FLEDGLING COALITION'S EARLY STRIDES

The first big task the coalition undertook was to explore with The American and the Canadian Society the formation of a North American federation of IPA groups on the order of FEPAL, the regional grouping for Latin America, or the European Psychoanalytic Federation. The first exploratory talks were held in New York on October 24, 1992. Chaired by Bernard Pacella, then president of The American, the meeting was a frank and open working session, at times confrontational but ending up in an amiable resolve regarding the coordination of regional representation to the IPA Many months of delay and negotiations ensued before a consensus was reached, but by the winter of 1993 the Canadian and !PS governing boards had approved the agreement. Finally, in April of that year, The American agreed that the three North American organizations should present a coherent grouping at the Amsterdam Congress fast approaching. A mutually satisfactory arrangement for a combined North American representation to the IPA was then worked out.

Meanwhile, underscoring a potential for further cooperation, the IPS and The American were coordinating closely in another area, that of protecting American psychoanalysis from the efforts of the National Association for the Advancement of Psychoanalysis (NAAP) to claim for its organization, the American Board for Accreditation in Psychoanalysis (ABAP), the status of sole accrediting body for psychoanalytic institutes in the United States. Sheldon Bach and Harriet Basseches, as cochairs of the IPS Committee on Accreditation (and later Basseches alone as chair), joined forces (and legal counsel) with Allan Rosenblatt, their opposite number in The American, to oppose NAAP/ABAPs application. Hearings were held in Washington, D.C.: over a period beginning in 1990 and are still in process. Similar opposition to the NAAP/ ABAP application to the US Department of Education is also being coordinated.

In other areas, the IPS and its societies were vigorously entering into the life and functioning of the IPA. For example, many IPS analysts were involved in the programming of the Amsterdam Congress and pre-Congress, as well as participating in panels and presenting papers. Ethel Person, editor of the IPA newsletter, appointed Adams-Silvan as a contributing editor responsible for news and notes from the IPS was later to be extended to include special full-length articles. For the upcoming Congress in San Francisco, the IPS not only is represented on the Arrangements Committee but is cohosting the event with The American. In May 1993, Freedman and Sanville wrote formally to Sandler as president and to Horacio Etchegoyen, who would succeed him, informing them officially that the coalition had been renamed the Confederation of Independent Psychoanalytic Societies. further, that Freedman and Sanville had been selected by the presidents of the four societies to cochair the IPS Steering Committee for the coming year, and that the group had established formal relations with The American and with the Canadian Society This communication was formally acknowledged by Sandler in a letter welcoming the new group and containing recommendations for its future development. Later, Etchegoyen too sent his good wishes.

AMSTERDAM AND BEYOND

Then, in July 1993, came the Amsterdam Congress. At the business meeting on July 28, full component status was awarded by acclamation to the three independent societies elected earliest to provisional status—IPTAR, NYFS, and PCC. Later that day, in celebration of this event and in appreciation of those who had helped make it happen, the IPS hosted a reception. Invited guests included members of the IPA Executive Committee (Wallerstein, Sandler, Etchegoyen, and Valerie Tufnell}, new vice presidents Otto

Kernberg and Harold Blum, Ethel Person in her newsletter capacity, and the site visitors who had led the three groups along the path to full recognition. Among the visitors present were Hanly, chair of the Committee on New Groups, and David Sachs, who followed Owen Renik as chair for North America. Officially representing The American were president Bernard Pacella and secretary Donald Meyers.

Norbert Freedman, raising a toast, spoke warmly of all those involved: 'This is a homecoming for members of the Confederation of Independent Psychoanalytic Societies, who have been guests in a house which they considered to be home for many decades. This situation was corrected, and since the memorable Rome and Buenos Aires meetings, we have been guests no longer. Today we are completely home. We are appreciative of a new working relationship that has been established with our colleagues from the American Psychoanalytic Association … [W]e have come to work collaboratively and cooperatively to deal with the many problems which beset psychoanalysis in our own land…. We have [also] become aware of the importance of our colleagues from north of the border…. [with whom] we have developed a close relationship….' Following closely upon the reception was an IPS celebratory dinner, wonderfully arranged by Harriet Wrye, in an historic canal house.

After the Amsterdam Congress, from the fall of 1993 through the following spring, representatives of the three North American groups-IPS, Canada, and The American-proceeded with their dialogue in a working group, a kind of steering committee. The previous spring, at a meeting called by Pacella, Helen Fischer had coined the acronym NAIPAG (North American IPA Groups), and a liaison committee had been appointed to formulate an agenda for a North American entity. In the fall of 1993, this committee. consisting of six representatives-Helen Meyers and Owen Renik for The American, Carlos Featherston and Brian Robertson for the Canadian Society, and

Steven Ellman and Mark Silvan for IPS-met in Montreal. Setting as their first task the composition of the North American delegation to the new House of Delegates, they agreed on a formula based on the relative numbers belonging to the three groups (and therefore open to revision in the event of significant shifts). From a total of nine delegates, five would be from The American, two from the IPS, and two from Canada. In addition, since IPA bylaws require that one of the nine be the regional representative to the Executive Council, every two years a new council representative is to be selected from the nine-member North American delegation, this position to be rotated on the basis of parity among the three component groups. Helen Meyers of The American is the first such representative to the Council, a position she will hold until the summer of 1996.

The first formal meeting of the North American delegation was held in London preceding the first semiannual meeting of the House of Delegates. A spirit of cooperation allowed the delegation to prepare a constructive agenda that was to set the tone for the House of Delegates the next day.

The IPS steering committee, which continues to meet in person or by conference call on a monthly basis, consists currently of Steven Ellman and Norbert Freedman from IPTAR, Jean Sanville from LAISPS, Barbara Stimmel and Fred Pine from NYFS, and James Gooch and Albert Mason from PCC. Pine is serving out the term of his friend and colleague Fred Wolkenfeld, who died suddenly on March 10. Sanville and Freedman continue as cochairs, with Florence Williams as treasurer.

A major current project of the IPS is the Post-Congress to be held in Los Angeles immediately following the San Francisco Congress. The Post-Congress will focus on the unique contribution of film to American culture and will examine in depth the relationship between film and psychoanalysis. Last November, in preparation for the Los Angeles event, the two East Coast IPS societies (IPTAR and NYFS) held a fund-raising gala to provide scholarships for attendance at the Post-Congress.

In the light of these many early achievements, it will be interesting to follow the further development of the IPS, this energetic young sibling of The American, in years to come.

CHAPTER 6

IPS and APsaA: A Spirit of Cooperation

TAP 34:1, pp. 27-29.

The IPS—that is, the Confederation of Independent Psychoanalytic Societies in the United States—is eight years old this year. The IPS includes four component societies and one study group of the IPA, none of which is affiliated with the American Psychoanalytic Association. Today, the IPS works more and more closely with the American in a variety of formal and informal ways, but this cooperation was not always the case. Without attempting to explicate the complex intent of those in APsaA leadership during the early years of the growth of psychoanalysis in this country, I believe that by and large they rebuffed most efforts at application for training and membership by non-medical mental health professionals as well as others who could at that time find welcome in other parts of the world where psychoanalysis was developing.

The IPS grew from those origins of discrimination and exclusion by the medical community that controlled psychoanalysis and psychoanalytic training in the United States. Despite that discrimination and exclusion, psychoanalysis influenced thinking in academic settings, particularly among academics, who were also lay mental health professionals. These non-medical people sustained their interest, creating flourishing institutes outside the aegis of the American, in particular in New York and Southern California. Four societies/institutes would later form the IPS: the Institute for Psychoanalytic Training and Research (IPTAR) and the New York Freudian Society (NYFS) in New York, and the Los Angeles Institute and

Society for Psychoanalytic Studies (LAISPS) and the Psychoanalytic Center of California (PCC) in Los Angeles. In the mid-1980s, the New York Freudian Society added a Washington, D.C., program, drawn initially from psychologists and social workers who had been unable to obtain training via institutes of the American in the Washington area and soon changed the name to the Contemporary Freudian Society (CFS).

At about that time, another development had far-reaching implications for the demographics of psychoanalysis in this country. Several psychologists supported by the American Psychological Association filed a restraint of trade lawsuit against the American and the IPA. Settlement of that Lawsuit opened the door to membership in the IPA. The lawsuit also had an impact on the American itself, which moved its approach—nudged in response to the lawsuit—from the previous trickle of acceptances of lay professionals for psychoanalytic training to the current open policy toward qualified non-medical applicants. Some even have claimed that the lawsuit was instrumental in re-energizing the American.

INDEPENDENTS JOIN IPA

On the basis of the lawsuit settlement, the four groups mentioned above: IPTAR NYFS, LAISPS, and PCC—applied directly to the IPA for membership, and by 1991 they had all achieved provisional status. Within the IPA, they came to be known as "the Independents."

In 1992, another step toward the formation of the IPS occurred at a meeting of the presidents of component societies of the IPA with the president of the IPA Joseph Sandler. A successful drive toward the IPA's democratization led to the framework for establishing a new House of Delegate; to share governance with the Executive Board and Council and to draft new IPA by-laws. The need for a work group representing the three regions of Europe, South America, and North America to plan for these new developments highlighted the presence of the new groups from North America. No longer the sole representative, the American acknowledged its new partners in the Canadian Psychoanalytic and the four new groups in the United States.

This signal of the first full participation of the new U.S. groups in IPA policy-making generated the decision on the part of the four groups to inaugurate a formal confederation, called at first the Coalition of Independent Psychoanalytic Societies in North America. The awareness of their shared goal of wanting to join the larger psychoanalytic world of the IPA dedicated to high standards of training and the preservation of psychoanalysis, at the same time remaining a voice for diversity and independence, united the four groups to a common cause. The leadership from the brand-new coalition joined with those of the Canadian and the American to hammer out an equitable arrangement for North American representation in the IPA. A new regional organization was formed: the North American International Psychoanalytical Association Groups or NAIPAG, similar to those of FEPAL in South America and the European Psychoanalytic Federation.

This successful cooperation followed coordination in another critical area: protecting American psychoanalysis from the efforts of the National Association for the Advancement of Psychoanalysis (NAAP) to claim for its ability to Accredit in Psychoanalysis (ABAP), the status of sole accrediting body for psychoanalytic institutes in the United States. Led by the NYFS in 1990 and continuing through 1995, the IPS and the American joined in opposition and worked together, ultimately helping to defeat that application of the NAAP/ABAP. (Ramifications relevant to the subject of accreditation have, of course, continued to evolve but may best be left for another context, since they take the narrative too far afield of the specific development of the IPS.) Throughout the 1990s the IPS groups—first provisional, then component societies of the IPA—were fully integrated into the IPA fabric, participating in its life and functioning at many levels of organization. As individuals, IPS members have been represented on many committees and activities associated with the governance of the IPA. They have not only participated in the planning for pre-congress and congress events but have presented papers and programs as well. As a fitting exemplar of the changing times, the IPS shared with the American the responsibility for hosting the last IPA Congress held in the United States in 1995.

IPS-APSAA COOPERATION

Meanwhile, NAIPAG has continued to meet, not only to deal with common political interests but also to consider the strengthening of joint scientific undertakings. Coordination between IPS and institutes of the American have blossomed in several locations. In Los Angeles [see "As LAPIS Celebrates 50th, LA Seeks Concord." TAP 30/4], a federation of LA societies including LAISPS (IPS), LAPSI (APsaA), PCC (IPS), and SCPS/I (APsaA) was formed to cooperate on projects. Beginning with a shared project centered on the Freud exhibit at the Library of Congress, the Baltimore Society for Psychoanalysis (APsaA), the NYFS Washington Program (IPS), and the Washington Psychoanalytic Society (APsaA) have planned programs with both candidates and members, shared public information data, and participated with still larger local groups, of psychoanalytically oriented organizations (in a unit called the consortium) to present research in the Washington, DC area as well. In New York, five societies or institutes— Columbia University Center for Psychoanalytic Training and Research (APsaA), IPTAR (IPS), the NYFS (IPS). the New York Psychoanalytic Institute (APsaA), and NYU Psychoanalytic Institute (APsaA)—have made similar strides of presenting jointly sponsored meetings and conferences.

While Marvin Margolis was president of the American, the leaders in the American and the IPS began to meet for regular twice-yearly discussions. This liaison committee has found it a meaningful forum to discuss matters of importance to psychoanalysis as well as to discuss IPA issues of significance to the United States. Talks initially centered on issues of accreditation and the Psychoanalytic Consortium, an organization that does not include the IPS despite clear overlapping concerns (see "A Guide for the Perplexed Reader," page 15). As time has passed, however, the focus has increasingly turned to the ways that the two organizations, the IPS and the American, could work meaningfully together on a variety of projects. Many such collaborations have resulted from these dialogues. One example is representatives from the IPS becoming members of committees of the American relevant to psychoanalysis and the community, such as the Public Information Committee and the Committee on Governmental Relations and Insurance. Other examples are participation by members of both organizations in workshops and shared knowledge from the work on the establishment of associated foundations. (Of course, some members of IPS who have also become members of the American have been active on other committees as well.)

TAP has been in the forefront of this exchange, having formally invited the IPS to place an IPS liaison on its roster during the editorship of William Jeffrey, and informally under Arnold Richards' stewardship. This salutary approach is also illustrated by the frequency of articles published by IPS members, as well as the new glossary that mentions the IPS prominently. It is clear that the APsaA of today is a very different organization than it was in those early days of rejection that led to the building of the IPS. Now a welcoming manner permeates exchange between these two organizations with so much in common. In 1995, I wrote in TAP [see "IPS, Now Three Years Old, Spurs Move Toward Regional IPA Federation," 29/2].

It is such a pleasure, five years later, to see how much the IPS and the American have been able to thrive and enjoy the benefits of working side by side. It seems that the relationship has strengthened both organizations—a trend that we hope will deepen in the years to come!

INTERNAL DEVELOPMENT

With the IPS solidly functioning alongside it, peer organizations are well integrated into the lPA, the IPS board and its constituent society boards considered it time to focus on the IPS's own internal structure and development along several avenues. One direction was in increasing communication and mutual scientific inquiry, to better get to know each other and our diversity of psychoanalytic thinking. The IPS has begun publishing a newsletter for its members. It has also held a variety of major receptions and meetings. Inaugurated at the reception at the 1993 congress in Amsterdam, the IPS has sponsored a reception at each of the congresses since, in 1995, 1997, and 1999. There has also been a major west coast scientific conference on film in psychoanalysis and an east coast symposium on Matte Blanco, both events open to the psychoanalytic and mental health communities. In addition to these, the IPS offered clinical meetings to its members and candidates.

One was hosted in Palm Springs in 1998, another in the Hudson River Valley in New York in 1999. Each time, meeting over several days in small groups balanced among members from all the constituent societies, participants found these clinical events deeply satisfying. Clinical material heard within the intimacy of the small group setting gave IPS members the experience of learning from each other and appreciating the diversity of perspectives. The non-competitive atmosphere engendered a common bond with ample respect for differences.

Another direction relates to the structure and governance of the IPS. The principle of an equal partnership among organization participants is the foundation of the IPS. This led to setting up an Executive Board made up of two representatives from each constituent organization (currently totaling eight), selected in whatever way each organization chose, to be on the board for staggered terms. The Executive Board itself elected co-chairs from among those representatives, keeping representation balanced among the constituent organizations.

All committees are made up of balanced members from each constituent society. The House of Delegates representatives and NAIPAG representatives have been elected from the Executive Board, again attentive to balance among the constituent organizations.

While this system worked more than satisfactorily for the first years of the IPS, it has become increasingly clear that a more democratic process would expand the participation and vital involvement of more of the members. Thus, the current board is orchestrating a new plan to elect officers nationally. this will require new by-laws since, under the principle of confederation, all decisions made by the committees of the IPS and by the Executive Board must be approved by the individual boards of the constituent societies before becoming available to the full individual members for voting. The details are being worked out, but there will be a new structural governance soon.

NEW INTEREST IN PSYCHOANALYSIS

One other significant direction of the IPS bears mention. Paralleling the growth of the IPS and the re-invigoration of the American, interest in psychoanalysis has increased markedly among mental health professionals. This intensification speaks to the sustaining power of psychoanalytic ideas even at a time when the public is often discouraged from turning to psychoanalysis. It is possible that the increased interest was encouraged by the news of the settlement of the lawsuit, the admittance of new societies into the IPA, and the changes in the American.

However these events may be explained, new groups have been forming in the United States. One such group, the Northwestern Psychoanalytic Society (NPS), has become a study group of the IPA and has joined the IPS. The study group status allows the NPS and the IPS time to work out this new relationship. The IPS hopes to integrate the NPS in the spirit thus far sustained in the IPS: a value for diversity and independence, while working together for a shared psychoanalytic future.

Many people both within and without the IPS have been important to its beginnings and growth. This article can only touch on some. The earliest planners include Norbert Freedman (IPTAR), Abby Adams-Silvan (NYFS), Ernie Lawrence (LAISPS), and Albert Mason (PCC).

The first steering committee was co-chaired by Norbert Freedman and Jean Sanville (LAISPS). They later became the first co-chairs of the IPS. Steven Ellman (IPTAR) and Abby Adams-Silvan worked with the Canadian and the American to establish NAIPAG and an equitable plan of North American representation. Later co-chairs have included Albert Mason, Steven Ellman, James Gooch (PCC), Harriet Basseches (NYFS), Terrence McBride {LAISPS), and Ann Rudovsky (NYFS}. Others who have been members of the IPS Executive Board include Fred Wolkenfeld (NYFS), Fred Pine (NYFS), and Barbara Stimmel (NYFS), who also has been chair of NAIPAG. The current Executive Board has James Gooch and Doris Silverman (IPTAR) as co-chairs and also includes Ann Rudovsky, Jeffrey Golland (NYFS), Harriet Wrye (LAISPS}, Beth Kalish Weiss (LAISPS), Steven Ellman, and Jeanette Gadt (PCC). The current representatives to the IPA House of Delegates are Ann Rudovsky and Steven Ellman; Ellman is also serving on the IPA Executive Council.

Thus, a major task lies before us as psychoanalysts, as significant time and energy must be devoted to a number of major research questions. Success though, will require a shift in the traditional approach of psychoanalysts.

For psychoanalysis to thrive as a part of modem psychiatry, we must undergo this shift of culture and apply the methodologies that most senior colleagues have developed over the last several decades. As an active researcher myself, I know first-hand that trust is not always a comfortable or easy process. But it is an essential process if we are to take our appropriate role within modem psychiatry.

CLINICAL PRACTICE

In recent years many articles, within both the scientific literature and the popular media, have predicted the death of psychoanalysis as a clinical enterprise. My own view is that the future of the clinical practice of psychoanalysis in this country is very difficult to predict. While we are well aware of the economic forces at work that drive choices of treatment and of the advances in other aspects of psychiatric knowledge and practice, involving both psychopharmacologic interventions as well as other psychotherapeutic interventions, we clearly don't have enough data to predict accurately the future.

There are several factors, though, that I believe will be important in predicting the future of psychoanalysis as a clinical enterprise both within and outside psychiatry. One issue has to do with not only political trends and economic forces, but career pathways and the choices that graduating psychiatric residents are making. Over the last two decades there has been a steady decline in the number of psychiatric practitioners entering training in psychoanalysis. This is not surprising to me since, as 1 mentioned earlier, many residents no longer have early educational imprinting experiences with psychoanalysts, and many do not even receive any teaching by psychoanalysts throughout residency. To be blunt, we shouldn't expect someone will choose a career pathway that they know little about or have no role models after whom to pattern their careers.

Whether this trend will shift depends in large part on psychoanalysts' willingness to reengage in psychiatric residency teaching programs, as I discussed earlier, My best judgment is that in the clinical arena there are major contributions psychoanalysis has to make to psychiatric practice regardless of the economic environment. To me, the major determinant regarding the clinical relationship between psychiatry and psychoanalysis in the future has more to do with how many psychiatrists choose psychoanalysis as a career path rather than any other issue. Unfortunately. unless some of the major shifts that I have discussed in the educational and research arenas take place, l think we will be forced to conclude that fewer and fewer psychiatrists in the United States will choose to become psychoanalysts. In spite of all other factors, this in itself would lead to a distancing of psychoanalysis from psychiatry.

To summarize, l have no doubt there are tremendous opportunities for interaction between psychiatry and psychoanalysis in the areas of education, research, and clinical practice. Many uncertainties lie before us, however, and the maintenance of a close clinical collaboration between psychoanalysis and mainstream psychiatry relies, I believe, on major shifts in education and research in psychoanalysis.

Without such shifts, l fear an ongoing divergence between psychoanalysis and psychiatry which would impoverish both disciplines. While much work needs to be done to ensure that this does not become the path we take, I am optimistic that we have the resources, knowledge, and skills to succeed. What remains to be seen is whether we also have the will.

*Later designated by the acronym, CIPS

CHAPTER 7

The Role of Psychoanalysis in Graduate Education Today

TAP 35:4, pp. 19 & 24.

Recently, TAP received an announcement by a psychiatric group offering to introduce a psychodynamic approach to interested residents. Introduce? Although the core of medical psychiatry was once not merely psychodynamic in orientation but solidly psychoanalytic, it is now axiomatic that psychoanalysis has lost its exalted status in psychiatric education. It has been replaced by biology and pharmacology, reinforced by managed care's emphasis on economics and efficiency and parallel insistence on short-term, research-based treatments.

This idea of "introducing" psychodynamics to residents led members of TAP's editorial board to wonder about the current place of psychoanalytic and psychodynamic ideas in psychiatry, psychology, and social work graduate education.

Psychoanalysis has been largely shut out of psychiatric academia, stemming the flow of potential analysts coming from psychiatry. But what about psychology and social work? The impositions of managed care and the emphases on biology have played their frustrating role in those fields as well, but there are additional factors.

PSYCHODYNAMIC IDEAS

Devalued In psychology doctoral programs accredited by the American Psychological Association, despite some important and outstanding examples to the contrary, there has been an increasing push toward a return to traditional areas of psychology. These include a strong programmatic content focused more on academic interests and experimental research and less on psychotherapy and a psychodynamic or psychoanalytic point of view. Short-term-cognitive-behavioral approaches originating in psychology have preempted psychoanalytically oriented therapy in more and more university settings. Social work schools—again with notable and important exceptions—have moved their programs away from psychotherapy and toward societal, management, and policy issues.

Thus, the thrust in all three professional sectors has been to devalue psychoanalytic ideas and psychotherapy, particularly long-term dynamic therapy and psychoanalysis. While these trends have been playing out, the psychoanalytic movement has been divided, even within the APsaA itself. As we also know, there has been a history of rancor and inhospitableness between the APsaA and other groups.

Perhaps distracted by internal and intergroup differences, but also perhaps because of an inability to clearly assess and organize ways to deal with the shifting tides, psychoanalysts seemed for a long time relatively passive in the face of these seemingly inevitable and discouraging trends. In the last decade, however, there has been a renewed detente among psychoanalysts of every persuasion and professional grouping. Aware of the erosion of psychoanalysis in the public arena, there has been a palpable change in the degree of activity and integration both within the APsaA and in the larger psychoanalytic world. For the American Psychoanalytic Association, a new era of vitality has emerged through efforts to include other professional groups and respect for a broadening spectrum of psychoanalytic views. The

APsaA has also made innovative efforts to investigate and communicate ways to turn the trend back toward appreciation of the richness that psychoanalysis has to offer.

Originally, the APsaA's Joint Committee on University and Medical Education had full responsibility for all matters pertaining to graduate education. In 1996, the association doubled its efforts by establishing a second committee, the Joint Committee on Graduate Education, mandated to develop projects designed to create a greater psychoanalytic presence in graduate psychology and social work programs. Having two committees permits a detailed focus on the philosophy, curriculum requirements, and specific needs of each discipline.

This special section of TAP attempts to take stock of the current role of psychoanalytic thought in the graduate education of the three largest mental health groups. Hinda Simon, a member of TAP's editorial board, focuses on the situation in social work schools. She highlights the dissonances between the goals of most social work curricula and a psychoanalytic perspective. I am also a member of the editorial board and discuss psychology doctoral programs, with input from interviews of psychology colleagues associated with graduate education and survey information from the Committee on Graduate Education. Lisa Mellman, who among her many "hats" is associate director of the Psychiatry Residency Program at Columbia University, brings us exciting news about the possibilities for increasing psychoanalytic input into psychiatric residency training.

THOUGHTS FOR THE FUTURE

In many respects, the news from the three reports is not unexpected. Yet there are surprising and promising new initiatives. For example, renewed possibilities for analysts in residency programs suggests that perhaps the pendulum is swinging back toward valuing our central activities. Now it will be up to those analysts who are appropriately aligned to support the efforts. Psychologists at one university have taken on the challenge of making psychoanalysis meaningful within new constraints; at another, they have created new opportunities that fit well with psychoanalytic expertise. From social work we learn that two years of training leave little room for clinical interests, pointing up the need for further post-graduate clinical development of a psychoanalytic nature.

Eric Marcus, chair of the Joint Committee on University and Medical Education, said that every student in the seminar he teaches at Columbia who comes to understand psychoanalytic principles will potentially affect hundreds of others. Stephanie Smith, chair of the Joint Committee on Graduate Education, emphasized the importance of encouraging collaboration between analysts and academic faculty, including attempts to draw graduate faculty into closer contact with the APsaA. Her committee invites graduate faculty to participate in scientific programs and welcomes graduate faculty as full and active members of the committee. The committee has also designed a project to explore multiple methods for arranging elective credit within graduate programs for students taking institute extension courses, studying with psychoanalysts, and the like.

In December, at the New York meetings, Smith and Marcus will co-chair a new and ongoing interdisciplinary discussion group, "On Teaching Psychoanalytic Views of Mind: Forum for Analysts and Academic Professional Faculty Teaching and Supervising in Graduate Psychiatry, Psychology, and Social Work Programs." Also at the meetings, the Joint Committee on Graduate Education will co-sponsor a presidential symposium with Dick Fox on psychoanalysis and graduate social work education. Symposium co-chairs are Helen Rosen, committee co-chair for social work, and committee member Ann Abbott, past president of the National Association for Social Work.

The challenge is to get the word out through faculty already in place and to encourage younger psychoanalysts to turn their energy toward becoming the psychoanalytic educators of tomorrow. Then psychoanalysis can again be taught through graduate curricula, and faculty and students can again learn psychoanalytic ideas.

CHAPTER 8

An Insecure Presence in Psychology Graduate Education

TAP 35:4, pp. 21 & 24.

I did an informal search of the websites of the American Psychological Association (APA) concerning its approved psychology doctoral and Psy.D. programs to get a sense of the extent that psychoanalytic or psychodynamic courses were included in its curricula. Limited as the investigation was, the territory looked discouragingly barren. I did discover, however, that in certain locales the psychology programs offered more psychoanalytic input, particularly New York City, Washington, D.C., and Michigan. Edward Shafranske, co-chair for psychology of the APsaA's Committee on Graduate Education, writes that

> the committee has sponsored two research projects to assess the current status of psychoanalysis in graduate psychology programs. The first study examined archival catalog data from a random sample of clinical psychology doctoral programs accredited by the American Psychological Association. The findings confirmed that psychoanalysis is underrepresented. Few programs include concentrations in psychoanalytic psychology and very few count psychoanalysts among their faculty.

Shafranske's second project, which was to be administered in late 2001, is a survey to examine clinical psychology graduate students' knowledge of and exposure to psychoanalysis and their attendant attitudes and beliefs.

As the first group of surveys makes clear, for several decades few psychology doctoral programs have espoused or included psychoanalytic ideas, and few analysts have participated in the programs. Instead, the teaching of even the shadow of psychoanalytic ideas is, by and large, in a different venue. No longer the domain of Ph.D. granting psychology doctoral programs, such teaching, irrespective of quality, is primarily the realm of the professional schools of psychology that award Psy.D. degrees.

This creates a divide between imparting knowledge of a general psychological nature, including research skills, from knowledge and experience of a clinical nature, which may include developmental ideas, psychopathology, and psychological testing. Not surprisingly, Division 39, the Division of Psychoanalysis of the APA, has been concerned about these matters for some ten years, according to Ruth Ochroch, a psychologist/ psychoanalyst involved in academia for fifty years. Division 39 members have also undertaken surveys, beginning with the efforts of Spyros Orfanos, a past president of Division 39, to study doctoral training.

The results of this and other surveys have led the Division 39 leadership to conclude that the division needs to find ways to advocate for and influence undergraduate and graduate curricula, to make psychoanalysis more accessible to the public, and to expand the thinking of psychoanalytic psychologists toward offering the community their skills outside the consultation room.

CAUSE FOR OPTIMISM IN CALIFORNIA, MICHIGAN

The next step in this inquiry was to interview psychologist/psychoanalysts who are faculty members in programs that are more developed psychoanalytically. I spoke to Hedda Bolgar, who has supervised students graduating from the California School of Professional Psychology in Los Angeles. She found that CSPP-LA, similarly to other psychology programs purport to teach psychoanalytic ideas or at least give passing reference to them. When students of these programs are questioned, however, it becomes clear that many have been provided little understanding of these concepts. Only if an instructor happens to be an analyst, or perhaps a knowledgeable, psychoanalytically oriented therapist, do students actually learn anything of use on the topic.

Bolgar sees such teaching as "accidental islands." On the other hand, she points out that those students given any exposure to psychoanalytic concepts often wish to learn more. At the California School, the student may have an analytic supervisor who alerts the student to the literature and to a psychoanalytically receptive internship where the student can receive further exposure to analytic concepts.

The Psychology Department at the University of Michigan, according to James Hansell, was until approximately fifteen years ago a stronghold of psychoanalytic thinking. At that lime the department became a smaller, more eclectic, more research-oriented program. The analytic faculty members were replaced and psychoanalytic theory reduced to a modest component, as the clinical program began to focus on life historical issues and behavioral and family systems. Nevertheless, even with these dramatic changes of emphasis, there are some positive aspects, particularly at an internship site that continues to be psychoanalytic and effective. Hansell explained that one-third of all the clinical students rotate through the university's psychological clinic and are exposed to psychoanalytic ideas through psychoanalysts' supervision and training.

Kim Leary, the associate director of the clinic, added to the optimistic picture, explaining that the clinic has been conducting psychoanalytic research on the therapeutic alliance, under the leadership of its director of the last decade, analyst Robert Hatcher. The clinic is publishing articles in journals of the APA—normally read by research-oriented psychologists— and is creating a body of work from projects where one article builds on the findings in another.

As the clinic broadens its psychoanalytic perspective to include interpersonal and relational ideas, students are gaining in enthusiasm. These students differ from their predecessors at the clinic in that they intend to pursue research rather than clinical careers, but their exposure to psychoanalytic ideas invites continued interest. One more note from Hansell, he and a colleague have received funding to write a textbook for undergraduates. Instead of a purely behavioral/symptom orientation, his textbook will include what he calls "stealth psychoanalysis."

CAUSE FOR CONCERN IN NEW YORK

We know that New York has long been a mecca for psychoanalysis. Many of the psychological doctoral programs in the New York City area opened in the 1960s. Most of those were strongly psychoanalytic. Today many of these programs have followed the national trend toward emphasis on (non-psychoanalysis friendly) research. Others seem uncertain of their direction. However, some strong, psychoanalytically receptive programs are still thriving, such as those at Adelphi, City University, and Long Island University-Brooklyn Center. Those that are thriving seem propelled by having psychoanalysts as faculty, such as Marvin Hurvich at LIU.

These programs have come to maturity, however, and over the next few years, as leadership faculty retire (for example, George Goldman at Adelphi and Steven Ellman at City), the psychoanalytic orientation in New York doctoral programs may be challenged. In some respects, this picture may follow a similar trajectory to that of psychiatric centers from the 1950s through the 1970s During this period the arc of public policy support shifted away from psychoanalysis even as the budding psychological interest was blossoming.

A MODEL PROGRAM IN WASHINGTON

Although many of the professional schools with responsibility for clinical training are unsympathetic or superficial in their treatment of psychoanalysis, at least one Psy.D. program is different. In Washington D.C., at George Washington University, James Miller heads what might be characterized as a model psychoanalytically informed program. The members of the core faculty are psychoanalysts, and supervisors are psychoanalysts and psychoanalytically oriented therapists.

The program developed from a previously successful psychodynamic track of the university's doctoral psychology program. The president of the university, Stephen J. Trachtenberg, encouraged its creation, perhaps for economic reasons. Moving from its first class in 1996 to full APA accreditation in 2001, the program graduates approximately forty students per year, the largest numbers of any program in GWU's School of Arts and Sciences.

GWU's Psy.D. program replaces a dissertation with a case-based project, from which each student masters in-depth understanding and writes a publishable paper. These students, exposed to a broad range of psychoanalytic ideas, have practical experience in their psychotherapy and testing work—

and for some, through their own treatments. Some go on to psychoanalytic training. The Psy.D. program at GWU seems to meet all the criteria that would support a psychoanalytically informed psychology program: curricula, faculty, student learning, and the support of the funding institution.

Psychology graduate training includes a genuine psychoanalytic component in only a very few programs in a few locations. The new program in Washington provides a basis for optimism and a model for emulation.

CHAPTER 9

Transgenerational Haunting: Interview with Maurice Apprey

TAP 36:4, pp. 15 & 32.

[Ed. note: This is one of a series of profiles by TAP Editorial Board Members of intriguing psychoanalysts we think you would want to know about.]

Maurice Apprey is a tenured, full professor at the University of Virginia School of Medicine. A prolific writer and book review essayist for a number of journals, he has caught the attention of our membership for his thinking and writing on ethnicity and culture and theories of technique. A remarkable teacher, in one year he's able to teach students from the first year of college all the way to fifth year fellows of child psychiatry. He teaches a course called "Psychoanalysis; Repetition and the Human Sciences" to college freshmen, "The Practice of Medicine," where he focuses on teaching interviewing skills to first year medical students, an "Introduction to Psychoanalytic Theory" course to fourth year medical students, "Psychodynamic Theories behind Psychotherapy" to third year psychiatry residents, and a human development course to fifth year fellows in psychiatry.

Now he has added the teaching of a human development course to the New York Freudian Society (Washington DC), added to his already full load. As if that were not enough, he carries a regular load of psychoanalytic patients and still functions as Associate Dean in the medical school. He also undertakes projects on community change for local groups, as well as international groups, for example, in the Baltics. From the standpoint of human interest, therefore, his career carries a curious mixture of altruism, commitment to social change, integrity in the teaching of metapsychology, and interdisciplinary projects in the human sciences. He hails from Ghana, West Africa, trained in London, and is an American citizen.

Basseches: Thanks for meeting with me. Your work has been attracting attention. You have been espousing a phenomenon called "transgenerational haunting." What are you referring to?

Apprey: Nicolas Abraham and Maria Torok, two French psychoanalysts, first used the term in their work on the phantom as a metapsychological construct. I am interested in how toxic psychological projects of prior generations are subtly injected, deferred and/or transmitted into subsequent generations in multifarious ways.

Basseches: How did you come to think of trauma in this particular way?

Apprey: The inspiration for this line of inquiry presented itself to me as an adolescent of fifteen when l was studying the poetry of W H. Auden and was struck by the line in his poem, "On This Island," where he writes: "Ships diverge on urgent voluntary errands." have come to see through clinical work and also in the communal memory of Traumatized groups of humans carry errands to reduce themselves to ashes or derivatives thereof at the behest of their ancestral transgressors. One of the most powerful depictions of this comes from Robert Stoller's account of his work with the mother of a transsexual boy where the mother reported a recurrent dream: "I had died but my mother was so busy sending me to the store on errands that she did not know I was already dead. "These errands become mentalized and are subsequently carried out in a different form so that the motor remains the same but the license plate changes. Clinically l have observed echoes of the phenomenon of transgenerational haunting in anorexia nervosa, gender identity disorder, some criminal psychopathic conditions, and in the larger societal arena, [among] groups that have undergone massive trauma such as African Americans, Holocaust victims and so on. I encourage those who read my work to do so along with the writings of llany Kogan of Israel, Haydee Faimberg of France and Vamik Volkan.

Basseches: What basic assumptions underlie your description of this phenomenon?

Apprey: Three passages from Heinz Hartmann serve as a pivot for my thinking about this phenomenon. The first speaks to how humans are subject to the influence of tradition and how they take over from others a great many of their methods for solving problems. In so doing, they live in past generations as well as in their own contemporary one. The second speaks to the notion of change of function where defensive operations that were once anchored in instincts may subsequently be carried out in the service of the ego with new apparatuses taking over prior and primitive functions. The third is Hartmann's view that the results of phenomenological psychology are a necessary foundation upon which explanatory psychology build results that could also be used in psychoanalytic research. !n my clinical or psychoanalytic research work, therefore, description precedes interpretation. Often there is tension between the two, I am reluctant to resolve [it]. Why? Because a good description and good interpretation, both seek a prior latency in taking us to primordial places.

Basseches: You mentioned that there are several other influential sources to your thinking.

Apprey: Many. 1 should mention Georges Pulitzer, a Hungarian who emigrated to France in the 1920s. He was a Hegelian Socialist in those days when it was a good thing to be a Socialist. He taught philosophy to workers in France. But the Nazis gave him an ultimatum, he should either discontinue educating the public or be executed. He chose to die, but not before he wrote one of the finest critiques of psychoanalysis. He privileged the latent content and dismissed manifest content as nothing but "a conventional story" and correlatively, the analytic surface as a non-sequitur. He regretted that so much of the structural theory pointed to formalism and abstraction and in so doing, lost the story of the analysand at the level of the first person. Two lessons follow my interest in his critique: Firstly, keep the tension between the topographical and the structural theories, and secondly, we are sometimes so busy interpreting that we lose sight of that which is staring us in the face.

Basseches: I see your thoughts go from philosophy to psychology, and from individuals to groups.

Apprey: That is true. In my view one must have a resume of skills that allows one to go from representations of knowledge to the transfer of knowledge. But in whatever I do, rigor [involves] fidelity to the phenomenon under observation. In the past, infant observation and work with at-risk mothers gave me the opportunity to sharpen my observational skills. So, whatever I do, I must start at the level of naive description. Accordingly, I can faithfully listen to a child while we play on the floor; listen to an adolescent chide me for not knowing the name of a rock star; sit behind the couch as I listen to an adult patient; and mediate ethnonational conflicts in Eastern Europe. Whatever I do, I can hear the sedimentations of historical grievances, observe how they are reactivated, as well as [listen for] what the individual or traumatized group expect[s] of me by paying particular attention to how they supplement that which has now been reactivated.

Basseches: The person who is notably absent in your list of influences, but I do not believe you ignore, is Freud. Perhaps it is too obvious to mention, but certainly the echo of Freud's ideas permeate and resonate with these other sources.

Apprey: Yes indeed. Allow me to put together a bald and representative way that I think. Freud showed us that a drive has a source, operates under pressure, has an aim and an object. What trans-generational haunting has shown me is that this notion of Freud's can be radicalized into a developmental history of instinctual goals by marrying concepts from drive theory and object relations theory. The result is that we can no longer say that the source of an instinct is the subject's body alone; rather, the source of an instinct can also be from an anterior other or even multiple agents. We can no longer say that an instinct operates exclusively with urgency; rather, an instinct can both be urgent and deferred through a deceptively dormant intercession between generations. We can no longer say that an instinct's aim, active and passive, is to seek satisfaction of libidinal or aggressive ends; rather, those instinctual aims can be collapsed into one another and compromised, as when a subject accepts an infanticidal project from an other only to contest it and/or transform it. We can no longer perceive an object that performs or participates in a subject's libidinal or aggressive aim as the object of desire or of hostile dependence and so on; rather we must think of objects as though they were simultaneously potentially independent, potentially intermediary, as well as potentially a member in a series of linkages, for example, across generations. So, Freud remains the anchor. It is difficult to train at the Anna Freud Centre and lose that basic foundation.

Basseches: I am truly grateful for this opportunity to talk with you about your work on transgenerational haunting. There is so much more we could share with our readers who I am sure will look forward to future publications of yours. Thank you!

CHAPTER 10

Chair of Psychoanalysis, Uncommon or Not?

TAP 37:4, pp. 9–10, 38.

Glen Gabbard has been appointed to be Chair of Psychoanalysis in the Department of Psychiatry at Baylor College of Medicine. The news triggered a question as to the frequency of such an appointment at a time when it is often claimed that psychoanalysis has been marginalized in our culture. The view of an eclipsed role for psychoanalysis and psychoanalysts contrasts with the situation in the 1950's when many psychiatry department chairs in medical schools were psychoanalysts. This article focuses on two areas: the notable details surrounding Dr. Gabbard's accomplishment; and TAP's attempt to determine how many others might hold similar positions. Named chairs of psychoanalysis give recognition not only to a particular distinguished psychoanalyst but equally to the field itself.

First, let's turn to Gabbard's appointment. He has been at Baylor since 2001. His appointment as the first Brown Foundation Chair of Psychoanalysis has recently been approved. He was recruited two years ago by Stuart Yudofsky, Chair of the Department of Psychiatry at Baylor. At that time, Gabbard was the Callaway Professor of Psychoanalysis and Education at the Karl Menninger School of Psychiatry, so he was already in a position of influence in an academic setting. He was promised a similar status at Baylor, where there has been a long history of sympathetic connection with psychoanalysis and close ties to the Houston- Galveston Psychoanalytic Institute. What prompted this important naming of a chair and how it was funded were questions that Gabbard considered more appropriately answered by Stuart Yudofsky. I interviewed them both for this article.

Yudofsky said it was his intention to make it possible financially for Gabbard to devote himself to his many and diverse psychoanalytic responsibilities, for example, his work as program chair for the APsaA meetings. He is also currently joint editor-in-chief (and the first non-British editor) of the International Journal of Psychoanalysis with Paul Williams. His duties at Baylor include directing the Psychiatry Clinic, where all the residents and psychology interns learn dynamic therapy, and being director of Psychotherapy Training. In those capacities, he has responsibility for revamping the residency curriculum to increase psychoanalytic therapy courses, in addition to teaching psychodynamic psychiatry and therapy to the residents. Gabbard remarked that many residents go on to psychoanalytic training at the Houston-Galveston Institute. He believes this choice is due to the presence of analyst/role models among their residency teachers.

A VISION FOR THE 21ST CENTURY

In my interview with Yudofsky, he explained that the creation of this appointment goes back to a planning initiative undertaken at Baylor College of Medicine in anticipation of the new century called, "Vision 2000." Yudofsky, a neuropsychiatrist, made a proposal to the Research Committee, composed mostly of biologically oriented scientists, to set up a Brain and Behavior Center that would be funded by the Brown Foundation for $25 million. This center was to consist of the full range of theoretical and academic pursuits, i.e., molecules and genetics, areas in which Baylor has always been strong, but also various perspectives of psychology, areas less strong at Baylor. In Yudofsky's view, Baylor has always been committed to a bio-psycho-social model, including a psychodynamic/psychoanalytic perspective. Setting up such a chair is challenging, because not only the person but the named chair has to be approved and funded. To arrange for a named chair, the Faculty Council, made up of all faculty—the entire basic science departments (strongly representing biological scientists) as well as the clinical faculty—must approve. This appears to have been quite a coup.

The Brown Foundation supports the arts, museums, performance arts, and education. This was the largest gift ever given to a medical school. Yudofsky explained why he had proposed a chair in psychoanalysis, rather than the broader category, psychotherapy. He values the psychoanalytic perspective, which he came to appreciate through his own psychoanalytic mentors, such as Hilde Bruch, Larry Kolb, Sherv Frazier, to name a few, and other influences, Bob Michels, Roger MacKinnon, Ethel Person, Michael Stone, Otto Kernberg, Harold Searles. He strongly believes that psychoanalysis must be supported in medical schools. He mentioned Jim Lomax, associate chair, who is also close with the Houston-Galveston Institute.

EIGHT PSYCHOANALYSIS CHAIRS

Following the news of Gabbard's appointment, TAP searched for other known chairs of psychoanalysis. The search yielded eight others so honored. These include Thomas Barrett, Schmule Erlich, Peter Fonagy, Ed Foulks, Steven Marans, Jon Meyer, Bill Meissner, and Leo Rangell. Detailed account of the positions of three of these distinguished colleagues follows. Peter Fonagy has held the position of Chair of Psychoanalysis at the University College of London since 1992. It was initially a visiting professorship, with

Roy Schafer the first holder, in 1975. The one-year model did not sufficiently meet the donor's aim of establishing psychoanalysis within the university, however, so a permanent chair was instated. Joseph Sandler was appointed the first permanent chair in 1985.

Finally, there is Leo Rangell, who has held the title of Chair of Psychoanalysis since 1971. He had been Clinical Professor of Psychiatry at the University of California, Los Angeles, for over 20 years. In 1976, when he was appointed to the faculty of a second University of California campus, in San Francisco—at that time the only double appointment in two branches of the University system—he was named Clinical Professor of Psychiatry (Psychoanalysis). Visiting professorships are another related category of honoring psychoanalysts in academia. The Heinz Kohut Visiting Professorship at the University of Chicago, named after a psychoanalyst, rather than the field of psychoanalysis, was reported to TAP by Jonathan Lear, one of the professors associated with the sponsoring group. Leading thinkers are invited for a year to enhance a strong psychoanalytic cadre of professors already teaching at the University of Chicago under the rubric of the Committee on Social Thought, chaired by Robert Pippin. Appointments have included Stanley Cavell from Harvard, Robert Hinschelwood from London, Robert Paul from Emory, and Bennett Simon from Harvard. Future honorees are John Riker from Colorado College (philosophy) and Mark Solms from the Anna Freud Centre, London.

The number of chairs of psychoanalysis is not large. Some of these positions have been held through many of the lean years of value for psychoanalytic thinking. But also new appointments have been increasing since the 1990's into the new century. Taken together, these represent outstanding people in our field. Their recognition clearly reflects on their own exceptional work. More than that, each of them without question strengthens the presence of psychoanalysis in academia and well beyond.

The discussion has focused on psychoanalysts who are in positions that directly identify psychoanalysis. Not to be overlooked, however, are the many analysts who function in academia in positions of honor and influence without the title of "Chair in Psychoanalysis."

CHAPTER 11

Efforts Focus on Educational Criteria for Psychoanalysis in New York

TAP 39, p. 18.

On January I, 2005, the New York State Board of Regents voted to approve regulations for the implementation of Article 63 of the Education Law which is scheduled to go into effect on February 3, 2005. The law establishes licenses for psychoanalysts who are not licensed in an "exempt" profession (medicine. psychology, social work, nursing). Licensed professionals in exempt professions will not need to obtain the new license to practice.

The passage of Article 163 in the summer of 2003 prompted growing concern among psychoanalysts and other mental health professionals because the educational requirements for a license in psychoanalysis are egregiously low; a master's degree in any field, completion of a program of training in psychoanalytic institute, 1500 hours of supervised clinical practice-and successful completion of a state administered exam. Most disturbing to many analysts was the omission of any frequency standards for psychoanalysis, permitting training and control analysis to be conducted once a week or less.

The licensing criteria in the law were clearly modeled on the educational standards of the National Association for the Advancement of Psychoanalysis, the group that lobbied for of the law, some of whose member institutes conduct and analysis at a frequency of one session per week.

FREQUENCY STANDARDS

Following passage of the law, APsaA and CIPS (Confederation of Independent Psychoanalytic Societies) initiated a joint effort to the State Education Department, the agency responsible for implementing the law, to promulgate regulations that would strengthen the licensing criteria specifying that training and control analyses must be conducted at a minimum of three to five five sessions per week in accordance with standards of the Psychoanalytic Consortium. (The Consortium, which comprises APsaA, Division 39 of the American Psychological Association, the American Academy of Psychoanalysis and Dynamic Psychotherapy and the National Membership Committee on Psychoanalysis in Clinical practice, created the Accreditation Council on Psychoanalytic Education in Social Work, works on political and ethical issues and created the Accreditation Council on Psychoanalytic Education.)

A large coalition was formed to lobby the state through efforts and petitions in support of a common set of recommendations. The coalition included APsaA, CIPS the American Academy of Psychoanalysis and Dynamic Psychotherapy, Division 39 of the American Psychological Association, as well as many other psychoanalytic institutes and societies in the State of New York.

Unfortunately, although the state was prompted to raise the initial standard of proposed regulations, the regulations, which were voted into effect by the Board of Regents on January 11, do little to improve educational criteria for licensure in psychoanalysis. Most significantly. the regulations remain silent with regard to frequency.

Psychoanalytic groups have been quick to respond to this situation. Within a week of the Regents vote, APsaA secured the resources of David Carroll, anAlbany lawyer and lobbyist. On January 20, Carroll addressed the APsaA Executive Council and reported that our situation in New York was difficult but not hopeless. In general, he favored an initial strategy of lobbying for favorable administrative guidelines. CIPS and other psychoanalytic groups in New York are similarly exploring both legal and lobbying options At a recent North American Psychoanalytic Confederation (NAPsaC) meeting Fredric T. Perlman, as BOPS public policy Chair, and president suggested that it might be possible for CIPS and other groups to join as co-clients of Carroll if there was agreement on his lobbying agenda. We are waiting to see the lobbying agenda before moving forward.

NAPsaC—North American Psychoanalytic Confederation

TAP 42:1, pp. 32-33.

Some of you may wonder, what is NAPsaC—a backpack? Actually, it is an acronym, representing the regional group of the International Psychoanalytical Association (IPA) Societies in North America. It is the only organization to unite all the IPA Societies in North America, giving them the opportunity to work and think together on matters of common concern.

NAPsaC, the North American Psychoanalytic Confederation, is composed of the American Psychoanalytic Association (APsaA), which is the only regional association in the IPA; the Canadian Psychoanalytic Society (CPS); the Confederation of Independent Psychoanalytic Societies of the United States (CIPS), which includes the Institute for Psychoanalytic Training and Research (IPTAR), the Los Angeles Institute and Society for Psychoanalytic Studies (LAISPS), the Psychoanalytic Center of California (PCC), the Northwestern Psychoanalytic Society (NPS), and the San Francisco Institute for Psychoanalytic Studies (IPS); and three otherwise unaffiliated societies of the IPA, including the Japan Psychoanalytic Society (JPS), the New York Freudian Society (NYFS), and the Psychoanalytic Institute of Northern California (PINC). Together, these groups make up the entirety of IPA Societies in North America. The Japan Society is included because, as yet, it is the only psychoanalytic voice in Asia and so we welcome them in our North American alliance.

You may have noticed that NAPsaC is a "regional group" of the IPA, and yet APsaA is the only "regional association." To clarify the distinction, APsaA is the only association within the IPA that completely undertakes its own educational oversight and accreditation, and represents all of its societies under one umbrella. NAPsaC's regionality refers to its geographical locale: It comprises the North American region. It has counterparts in Europe and Latin America known as the European Psychoanalytic Federation (EPF) and the Federation of Psychoanalytic Societies of Latin America (FEPAL). While none of the regional groups has any official IPA status, they are valued and encouraged by the IPA, as they afford each locale an opportunity for psychoanalysts from all the societies to work together and to dialogue with the IPA Board in ways that focus on the specific concerns of each region.

NAPsaC is a young organization that is eager to solidify and foster a North American psychoanalytic identity and to demonstrate its relevance to its constituency. With those intentions, NAPsaC has developed three projects with you in mind.

FIND AN ANALYST WEB SITE

NAPsaC Find An Analyst Web site (www.FindAnAnalyst.org) will enable prospective patients in the United States and Canada to find an IPA psychoanalyst near them. The Web site is a public service that allows us to promote psychoanalysis, the IPA, and our own practices in North America. The search functions on the site are linked to an IPA database.

Please note that inclusion in the database is not automatic. The IPA will not release your contact information without permission. You must register with the IPA to be included in the database. Registration is easy—just log onto the site www.FindAnAnalyst.org and click on "Get Listed."

FIPA—FELLOW OF THE IPA CREDENTIAL

This title was developed and promoted by NAPsaC's Committee on Credentialing. All members of the IPA living in the United States and Canada may obtain FIPA certificates. Log onto the IPA Web site www.ipa.org.uk, use your confidential user ID and password to enter the "Private Area," and click on "Order Certificates."

NAPsaC strongly encourages all IPA analysts living in North America to use the FIPA designation on business cards, billing statements, professional stationery, professional directories, and society bulletins. FIPA will soon become identified with IPA psychoanalysis in North America, the way "M.D.," "Ph.D.," and "C.S.W." are identified as professional credentials. For more information contact Fredric Perlman, the creator and organizer of the FIPA and Find an Analyst projects, at ftperlman@earthlink.net.

STUDY GROUPS AND WORKING PARTIES

The third project, a two-year pilot program, creates two educationally rich and unique opportunities, organized by Abbot Bronstein and his committee. The first is the formation of continent-wide study groups, whose members will meet yearly to focus on clinical material in depth. The second involves the formation of two working parties. One will study the implicit theories of the analyst; the other, comparative clinical methods. The working parties' model has been in successful operation in the EPF for some time. Two leaders of the European effort, David Tuckett and Jorge Canestri are consulting with NAPsaC to help set these up. FEPAL has plans to offer a similar opportunity in Latin America. If you are interested in pursuing the working parties project, contact chairman Abbot Bronstein (cladg@aol.

com); for the study groups, contact committee members Rich Reichbart (reichbart@earthlink.net) or Peter Ruderman (PRuderman@aol.com).

We on the NAPsaC Board understand the challenges we face as a new organization in a professional world already densely populated with psychoanalytic organizations. In the few short years of our existence, we have been providing a meaningful forum for our region. We will continue to do so in the belief that the more we find common cause among us, the more we will serve psychoanalysis.

The Board of NAPsaC is dedicated to creating better coordination between our constituent groups and the board of the IPA. The better we can identify the services and support we need in order to survive and thrive as a profession in North America, the better prepared we will be to help ourselves and our patients, and the more vigorously and effectively we will represent the IPA and the greater psychoanalytic world. Not a bad set of goals. We welcome your participation in our new projects.

EARLY PUBLICATIONS

CHAPTER 13

The Relation of Color-Form Incongruity and Maladjustment to Reaction Time[1]

Elsa Siipola and Harriet Basseches, Smith College.

In 1950 the senior author proposed a theory to identify the psychological processes underlying conceptual reactions to different types of ink blots (Siipola, pp 380 ff). This theory pertained to two separate stimulus dimensions of ink blots chromatic-achromatic color (which was the primary variable isolated in the research that gave rise to the theory) and form-color incongruity (which emerged as an unexpected factor influencing reactions to chromatic blots). In the theory developed at that time, differences between blots in these two stimulus dimensions were both viewed as differences in the degree of complexity of the problem-solving task presented to the S, and increasing complexity of the task was assumed to directly related to response latency under appropriate experimental conditions, The order of complexity assigned to various types of stimulus-forms was as follows:

Achromatic forms (incongruent as well as congruent) present the simplest task, because of their perceptual neutrality color. The only problem to be

---

1 This research originated as a cooperative enterprise involving two colleges, Amherst and Smith. The authors are indebted to Edwin I Megargee, who conducted a pilot study and gave invaluable assistance in the production of stimulus materials, Prof Theodore Koester, who designed the apparatus, and Prof Robert Birney, who contributed important critical advice. The authors are also indebted to Harold Israel of Smith College for assistance in all aspects of the research.

solved by S is that of matching the form to an appropriate concept (Siipola, 1950. p. 371).

Congruent chromatic forms present a slightly more complex task since, in addition to matching the form, S must simultaneously take account of and match the hue of the stimulus to an appropriate concept. This task turns out to be relatively simple, however, since the two cues of form and hue reinforce each other in this case.

Incongruent chromatic forms involved in a task clearly much more complex than either of the above. Here the cues for form and hue, both of which must be appropriately represented in a single concept, simultaneously arouse incompatible response-tendencies it is this hue-form incongruity in blots which is the complicating condition most likely to produce conceptual conflict resulting in primitivation of the conceptual process and the usual behavioral symptoms of conflict, including relatively long response latencies.

The primary aim of the present research is to subject the congruity-incongruity aspect of the above theory to a direct experimental test, which is to measure the effects of the variable of color-form incongruity upon the latency of response. Both achromatic and chromatic blots must be included in the design since, according to the theory, color-form incongruity should have a differential effect upon latency for these two different types of blots. In the case of achromatic blots, the effect should be negligible, S should respond just about as quickly to an achromatic blot when the black or gray color is clearly inappropriate to the form (e.g. black lion) as he does when black or gray is highly appropriate to the form (e g, black seal). On the other hand, in the case of chromatic blots, color-form congruity (e.g. purple lion) should be an effective variable under appropriate experimental conditions and should increase the latency of S's reactions as compared with the latency for matched congruent blots (e.g. tan lion). Moreover, since such incongruent chromatic blots are more likely than other types to induce symptoms of conflict, the responses to these blots should be more likely to reflect directly whether S's mode of handling conflictful situations is adjustive or maladjustive.

A secondary aim of this study is, then, that of relating individual differences in reaction time for congruent and incongruent blots to the personality variable of maladjustment in a college population. If our theory is valid, in comparison to adjusted Ss maladjusted Ss should give reliably longer reaction times for incongruent chromatic blots, whereas they are unlikely to show dependably greater latencies for congruent chromatic blots or for achromatic blots of either type. If the individual reaction times for the various types of blots are thus predictably connected with the variable of maladjustment, the theory will show real promise toward unraveling some of the tangled complexities in the lines of relationship between perceptual responses and dynamics.

The aspect of the theory which related the achromatic-chromatic variable to response latency involved a controversial issue of such great interest to investigators in this area that the result was an almost complete neglect of experimentation on the other essential aspect of the theory dealing with congruity-incongruity. This focus of interest is clearly demonstrated in Baughman's recent review (1958), which provides an excellent account of more than 20 related studies during the last decade. The empirical evidence from these studies provides no support for the Siipola (1950) finding of a significant relationship between the chromatic-achromatic variable in blots and response latency. An impressive amount of contrary evidence has accumulated to prove that the relationship we found does not hold under the usual conditions of experimentation (Baughman, 1958, pp. 124 ff). Actually, this lack of general support does not necessarily invalidate our finding since no one has replicated our unusual conditions which deliberately utilized simplified, ambiguous blots and strong time pressure. Moreover, recognition of the possibility that this high degree of time pressure night be of critical importance led us to repeat the experiment in 1952 (Siipola & Taylor) under the more usual free conditions. This change induced the Ss to respond to the same blots with average latency of 14 sec as compared with 4 sec in the original research. And when the time pressure was thus relaxed, the striking effects of chroma on reaction time disappeared, and even we had to report results contrary to the original finding (p. 44). Rather than a basis for real controversy, then, there seems only to be confusion deriving from the occurrence of different results under different conditions. Since it is evident that the relationship between color and latency is maximized by conditions of strong tune pressure, these conditions will be applied in the present experiment.

Although the congruity-incongruity aspect of the color problem has been neglected by experimenters, there are two studies in which the authors claim that they have disproved, either wholly or m part, this aspect of the theory (Sipola, 1950). The claim made by Berg and Polyot (1956, p. 15) that their data justifies rejection of our incongruity hypothesis seems exaggerated, their research was not even designed to isolate color-form Incongruity as an experimental variable.

Lazarus and Oldfield reported in 1955 an experiment which was specifically designed to isolate and vary color-form incongruity in blots. Our analysis of the predictions and results presented by Lazarus and Oldfield leads us, however, to conclusions different from those reached by these investigators (pp. 369 ff). From the specific predictions made by Lazarus and Oldfield (p 359), it is apparent that their predictions were drawn from a theoretical starting point somewhat different from ours, Although two of their predictions are agreement with our theory, one of them is the direct opposite Of that prescribed by our theory, namely the prediction that reaction time will be "longer for achromatic blots than for their mates with congruous color." Hence their finding of reliably shorter reaction times with achromatic blots than with congruent chromatic blots must be interpreted as refuting their own theory and confirming ours. Our theory predicts that the mere presence of hue in blots (even when this hue is congruent with the form) is likely to present a somewhat more complex perceptual task than that involved in responding to matched achromatic blots.

From the results presented by Lazarus and Oldfield we find considerable support for our theory of form-color incongruity in so far as it applies to unstructured, ambiguous blots. Even the authors themselves conclude at one point that "response times are significantly shorter for the congruous color-form combinations than for the incongruous ones. This is clear only m the ambiguous cards" (p 365). That not all of the evidence is conclusive, especially in the case of structured blots, is not surprising since this research was conducted under free, leisurely conditions producing long response latencies (13 sec for ambiguous blots as reported on p 370). Free conditions, as shown by Siipola and Taylor (1952), so effectively minimize the effect of color on response latency that it is remarkable that any differences were found under these conditions.

From all of the Rorschach-related research on color since Siipola's (1950) formulation of the theory, the conclusion seems evident that her predictions relating response latency to color variables should be limited to apply dependably only under conditions of time pressure. The critical question raised by the results of Lazarus and Oldfield is whether these predictions should further limited to apply only to ambiguous blots or whether, given the essential conditions of time pressure, they apply also to highly structured blots. The present research is designed to answer this question.

The first prediction to be tested here's that incongruent chromatic stimulus-forms will produce longer reaction times than matched congruent forms, whereas incongruent achromatic forms will fall to produce reliably longer latencies than matched congruent forms hypothesis was tested under the following conditions the Stimulus-forms were highly structured, strong time pressure was imposed upon S, and reaction time (measured separately for each stimulus item) was defined as the time required by S to produce his very first response when instructed to react as quickly as possible.

METHOD

Congruent and Incongruent Series

In designing this experiment, it was necessary to face the inherent difficulties involved in defining the experimental variable in a manner that would be both psychologically meaningful and would supply the basis for distinguishing between congruent and incongruent stimuli an objective, operational manner. Essentially, congruence refers simply to the appropriate or correct combination of the form of a familiar object with its natural or intrinsic color. There is, however, the complicating fact that many familiar objects occur naturally in many different colors (birds, dresses) and hence have no colors which are for incongruent. This complication was handled here by limiting the forms used to only those which identified familiar objects having a single distinctive color. A form-color combination was thus operationally defined as congruent only if the form identified an object which nature can be found typically in only one distinctive or intrinsic color and if in the experiment the form was presented in that natural color. Objects which have such distinctive colors into two different classes. Class I objects whose distinctive (congruent) color is achromatic (black seal), Class II objects whose distinctive (congruent) color s's chromatic (tan lion). Ten stimulus forms representing Class I objects and representing Class II objects were selected (see Table 1). When presented in various shades of gray appropriate to the objects (Class 1) or in their natural hues, (Class II) these stimulus forms provided two norm series representing the two basic types of congruence, achromatic and chromatic.

Table 1

Assignment of Hue in the Chromatic Series

Class I stimulus forms		Class II stimulus forms		
Object	Series	Object	Series	
	Incongruent hue (red seal)		Congruent hue (tan lion)	Incongruent hue (purple lion)
fork	purple	evergreen tree	green	orange (tan)
pliers	green	giraffe	orange (tan)	red
frying pan	purple	lips	red	yellow
seal	red	banana	yellow	red
snake	red	violin	orange (tan)	green
sword	yellow	grapes	purple	orange (flesh)
elephant	orange (flesh)	hand	orange (flesh)	green
squirrel	green	cactus	green	red
gun	orange (flesh)	fire hydrant	red	purple
tree trunk	red	lion	orange (tan)	purple

Note: Two of the series (black seal and black lion) do not appear in this table since all items in these series were achromatic

The effectiveness of various congruent stimulus forms was tested in a plot study using 80 Ss. To be acceptable an item had to satisfy the following criteria: it had to be initially perceived as the intended object by at least 75 per cent of the Ss, and the reaction time for the initial response had to fall within the range of 9 to 13 sec. From those items which met these criteria 20 stimulus forms were finally selected to make up norm series of the two basic types which would be approximately equal difficulty. The stimulus forms finally selected were very highly structured since for each norm series they were perceived correctly 90 per cent of the trials.

The selection of such highly structured blots yielded a critical advantage. Unless E knew in advance that a given form would dependably produce a particular identifiable concept, he could not judge whether a given color-form combination should be classed as congruent or incongruent, and hence he could not arrange an experiment to test the effects of the congruity-incongruity variable. The more highly structured the stimulus forms, the more precisely can E manipulate the experimental variable in advance.

Once the two congruent norm series (black seal, tan lion) had been established, the production of incongruent series employing the same stimulus forms was relatively simple A form-color combination was operationally defined as incongruent if the given form was presented in a color other than its natural congruent color. Thus, by simply reproducing in incongruent colors the 20 basic forms of the norm series, it was possible to obtain form color combinations representing the following three psychologically different types of incongruent series, each of which could be compared to a congruent norm series matched in form and shading.

Chromatic, Type 1, red seal series. Forms which identify objects natural color vs achromatic are inappropriately endowed with hue.

Chromatic, Type 2, purple lion series. Forms which identify objects with a particular intrinsic hue are colored in an incorrect hue.

Achromatic Type, black lion series. Forms which identify objects possessing a particular intrinsic hue are inappropriately represented m neutral shades of gray.

Experimental Design

Since the effects of the congruity-incongruity variable could be expected to appear only as minute differences between very rapid reaction times (about 1 sec.), extreme precautions were necessary to avoid having these subtle differences masked by much larger effects of factors as unequated stimulus series or unequated groups of Ss. A rather complex experimental design (see Table 2) was therefore developed to combine in a single the control procedure of holding the Ss constant for certain comparisons of congruent and incongruent series and the procedure of holding the stimulus forms constant for other comparisons of congruent and incongruent series. The design required three groups of Ss, and it provided for two different types of statistical comparison between congruent and incongruent series.

Table 2

The Experimental Design

Groups	Stimulus forms presented	
	Class I **Achromatic objects**	**Class II** **Chromatic objects**
Group A (*N* = 45) Achromatic stimuli	10 congruent items black seal series (Class I norm series)	10 incongruent items black lion series
Group C-1 (*N* = 45) Chromatic stimuli	10 incongruent items red seal series	10 congruent items tan lion series (Class II norm series)
Group C-2 (*N* = 45) Chromatic stimuli		10 incongruent items purple lion series

Note: This design provides for two different types of statistical comparison between congruent and incongruent series (a) Comparison of related samples presented one class of stimulus forms in congruent and the other class in incongruent color (horizontal comparisons for Group A and for group C-1) (b) Comparison of independent groups presented the same class of stimulus forms in either congruent or incongruent colors (vertical comparisons of two groups for Class I forms and three groups for Class II forms). For all groups the congruent and incongruent items were intersperse in a single continuous series, for group C-2 special congruent chromatic items had to be added to fill out the series.

1 Related samples, different stimuli forms. (Table 2, horizontal comparisons for groups A and C-1) Here a given group of Ss was presented one class of 10 stimulus forms in congruent color and a different class of 10 equated forms in incongruent color. Two groups of 45 Ss were utilized here. Group A presented achromatic forms exclusively, while group was presented chromatic forms exclusively (to avoid possible interaction effects between chromatic and achromatic stimuli). In the case of both groups the 10 congruent and the 10 incongruent items were interspersed and presented within single continuous series (to avoid establishing a set for either type of items). Thus except for the color of the 20 basic stimulus forms, all of the conditions including the order of presentation were exactly for these two groups.

2 Independent samples, same stimulus forms. (Table 2, vertical comparisons). Here independent groups of ss were presented the same class of 10 stimulus forms in either congruent or incongruent colors. For the Class I forms derived from achromatic norms (black seal) there is only one type of incongruent series possible, the chromatic (red seal). For the Class II forms derived from chromatic norms (tan lion) two types of incongruent series are possible achromatic and chromatic (black lion, purple lion). The two groups described above (groups A and C-1) provided the data for four of the five series required here to provide for the remaining series (purple lion), another independent group of 45 Ss (group C-2) was required this group had to be given chromatic items exclusively and reaction to be provided with congruent chromatic items. Interspersed within a single series including the incongruent (purple lion) items. Hence, a special series of congruent chromatic items (similar to the tan lion series) had to be provided to fill out this series since the 10 available congruent chromatic items could not be to the same Ss.

Apparatus and procedure

The materials were produced as follows: The 20 basic stimulus forms were originally painted incongruent colors, appropriately shaded, using standard watercolors. Duplication of these forms various colors was accomplished through a commercial printing process. The originals were photoengraved onto a copper plate from which printed copies were then run off in each of six carefully chosen colors. Table 1 shows the specific hues used for each of the items in each of the three chromatic series. The assignment of hues in the incongruent series was manipulated in such a manner that no single hue was associated solely with incongruence or congruence.

Instead of timing by stopwatch, customary previous investigators, a precise and completely objective technique was used. By combining a modified tachyscope and voice key with a Springfield timer, it was possible to obtain a measure in hundredths of a second of the elapsed time between the start oi the exposure of the stimulus and S's first verbal response. Preliminary trials were given to train S to react promptly and to use the voice key properly tape recording of each S's record was made also so that E could get measures of the few trials in which the voice key was inadvertently activated.

S received the following instructions "I am giving you a test of your speed of perception I am going to show you a series of stimulus blots, and I want you to tell me *as quickly as possible* the first thing that each blot makes you think of. Although there are several possible responses to the blots. What I want is your *first* reaction."

The Ss were 135 unselected female undergraduates drawn from an introductory psychology course at Smith College. Adjustment scores for these ss were available since the MMPI had previously administered routinely in this course.

RESULTS

For individual time scores both the median and mean reaction tunes of the 10 items each series were computed for each of the 135 Ss. A limit to the possible effect of extreme scores was set by assigning an arbitrary maximum of 10 sec to reactions beyond that limit and to failures to respond

Table 3

Group Results for the Various Series, Reaction Times in Seconds

Group	Class I forms			Class II forms		
	Series	**Media**	**Mean**	**Series**	**Media**	**Mean**
A (*N* = 45)	black seal	1 015	1 158	black lion	1 025	1 225
C-1 (*N* = 45)	red seal	1 078	1 261	tan lion	1 018	1 212
C-2 (*N* = 45)				purple lion	1 155	1 438

Note: Group medians are based on each S a median reaction time for 10 items, group means are based on individual means.

Table 4

***U* Tests between Series with the Same Stimulus Forms in Congruent and Incongruent Colors**

Series compared	Individual median time scores			Individual mean time scores		
	U	z	*p*	*U*	z	*p*
black lion tan lion	1076 5	52	60	1074 5	50	62
red seal black seal	1335 0	2 60	0094	1374 0	2 92	0036
purple lion tan lion (*8 stems*)	1451 5 1421 5	3 54 3 30	0004 001	1469 5 1370 5	3 69 2 89	0002 0038
(*Norm series*) tan lion black seal	1126 0	92	36	1232 0	1 77	08

(rejections). Since the distributions of both median and mean individual time scores were asymmetrical, showing a high degree of positive skewness, nonparametric statistics were applied throughout to the group data.

Comparisons of Reaction Times, Independent Samples

The design of the experiment provided for the comparison of independent groups of Ss presented with the same 10 stimulus forms in congruent or incongruent color (see Table 2, vertical comparisons). Table 3 presents for each of the series the central of the individual time scores for each group. Table 4 presents the results of applying the Mann-Whitney U Test to the reaction-time data to determine whether the independent samples represent populations which differ in central tendency. For the formula used, see Siegel (1956, p 123).

The first experimental hypothesis is a directional one, namely, that each of the incongruent chromatic series (red seal and purple lion) produce longer reaction times than their congruent norm series (black seal and tan lion). As shown in Table 4, incongruity comparisons of these experimental series with their respective norms yield high values of z associated with two-tailed probabilities ranging from 009 to 0002. The statistical evidence, then, clearly supports this hypothesis and implies that most of the reaction times for both types of incongruent chromatic forms are higher than those of their congruent norms. Since the data based on median time scores yielded values of z with very low probabilities, we can conclude that chromatic incongruity slows up the S's general level of reacting rather than producing merely a few unusually long reactions.

Our second hypothesis is a nondirectional one, namely, that the reaction times for the incongruent achromatic series (black lion) will be the same as those in the congruent norm series (tan lion). That is the reaction times for this incongruent series will not be reliably longer (nor shorter) than the norm. That this hypothesis is confirmed is apparent from the low values of z (50) and high probability levels obtained.

Table 5
Wilcoxon Signed-Ranks Tests between Series with the Same *Ss* for Congruent and Incongruent Items

Group	Series compared	T	z	p
C-1 (N = 43)	red seal tan lion	245 4	1 75	006
A (N = 43_	black lion black seal	393 0	97	33

Note: Two *Ss* in each group were not included since they showed a zero difference in reaction time for the series compared

Although both of our hypotheses are thus supported by the results from independent groups, closer examination shows that only one of the three comparisons made (purple lion with tan lion) is the variable of congruity-incongruity completely isolated. In the other two comparisons (red seal with black seal and black lion with tan lion) the series being compared necessarily differ in the achromatic-chromatic dimension as well as in congruity-incongruity. Since this study was designed to include signs of incongruity which cut across the achromatic-chromatic dimension. This difficulty is an inherent one, the congruent mate of an incongruent item like *red seal* is necessarily achromatic, while the congruent mate of an incongruent item like *black lion* has to be chromatic. Since previous evidence indicates that, in general, chromatic blots are likely to produce longer reaction times than achromatic blots under time-pressure conditions (Siipola, 1950), the achromatic-chromatic variable may confound the effects of the congruity-incongruity variable. The influences of these two variables on reaction time would work in the same direction for one of our comparisons (red seal with black seal) and in opposing directions for the other comparison (black lion with tan lion). This complication in isolating the experimental variable occurs only when the design requires that the same stimulus forms be used in both the congruent and the incongruent series. Fortunately, our findings here can be checked by applying the alternative procedure of holding the Ss constant while using different stimulus forms for the congruent and incongruent series.

Comparisons of Reaction Times, Related Samples

Here we deal with the results of presenting to the same group of Ss one class of stimulus forms in incongruent color and a different class of forms in congruent color (see Table 2, horizontal comparisons). The use of this procedure requires that the two classes of forms be equated in response latency for the two norm series evidence to show that this requirement is satisfied is supplied by results in Table 4, which show that comparison of the latencies for the two norm series (tan lion and black seal) yields low values of z, the probabilities of a difference are 36 and 08 for median and mean time respectively here is restricted to median time scores where the evidence for equality of the norm series is quite strong. The Wilcoxon matched-pairs signed-ranks test was applied to the data for group C-1 and for group A to determine whether the reaction times of a given group were reliably longer for incongruent items than for congruent items. For the formula used, see Siegel (1956, p. 81).

The effectiveness of chromatic incongruity is retested here by comparing the red seal and tan lion series, both of which were presented to group C-1 as a single, continuous series with the congruent and incongruent items interspersed both of these series are chromatic, the variable of incongruity of the chromatic type (red seal) was experimentally isolated here. The results presented in Table 5 show that when each S serves as his own control and is exposed to a series of mixed chromatic forms, the incongruent items have reliably longer reaction times than the congruent items since the value of z obtained here for the related samples (2 75) is even higher than that obtained previously for independent samples (2 60) we can conclude that chromatic incongruity of the red seal type, without any possible confounding effects from the achromatic-chromatic variable, is effective in significantly increasing response latency.

The ineffectiveness of achromatic incongruity is retested here by comparing the black lion and black seal series, both of which were presented to group A as a continuous series. Since both of these series are achromatic, the variable of achromatic incongruity was experimentally isolated here. The results in Table 5 show that when each S serves as its own control and is exposed to a series of mixed achromatic forms, there is no reliable difference in reaction time for congruent and incongruent items (p = 33). The absence of any dependable effect of achromatic incongruity on reaction time, even when this variable is given a chance to work in isolation, is impressive, except for the absence of chroma, all of the conditions for group A (even the order of the 20 identical stimulus forms) were exactly the same as those applied to group C-I. To be effective, increasing response latency, form-color incongruity obviously must have chroma (hue) present as an essential ingredient.

Content of the Responses

The responses obtained in each of the five series were classified under the following categories for which the frequencies are given in Table 6:

correct response, one corresponding to the particular object intended by E in designing the stimulus-form, *other response,* any response other than the correct one, using the whole form, detail response, any response to a detailed area of the form, *rejection,* a complete failure to give any response whatsoever.

It is not surprising that the majority of the responses, even in the incongruent series, fell into the category of correct responses rather than into the categories reflecting symptoms of associative disturbance. As suggested in a previous study (Siipola, 1950, pp 374 ff), highly structured blots will not produce the high frequency of symptomatic changes in content which ambiguous blots produce. Some symptomatic responses did occur, however, and were more frequent in the incongruent series in addition to detail responses and relations. Included under other responses were the following, usually considered symptomatic of serious associative conflict. pure color responses (blood, fire), color-naming responses (purple), and farfetched or nonsensical responses ("blare" for banana).

The results in Table 6 supply evidence to establish a methodological point from the pilot study, we knew in advance that for the 20 basic forms in congruent colors (e.g. tan lion) about 90 percent of the responses would be correct responses designating the objects that E intended that S should perceive. But it could not be predicted m advance how often these basic forms would elicit correct responses when rendered in a different, incongruent color (e.g. purple lion). It was quite possible that the mere change in color would produce a marked reduction in correct responses with corresponding increase in the frequency and variety of other responses which might be either congruent or incongruent with the new color. The real danger lay in the possibility that a certain form in its new incongruent color might be perceived consistently as a new conceptual object for which the new color was really appropriate (e.g., lion, colored purple, seen as purple flower). Should an item of this kind be classed as a congruent or an incongruent stimulus? The answer is not simple, and fortunately we were spared the

Table 6

Frequencies of Various Types of Responses

Class I stimulus forms			
Form	**Responses scored correct**	**Frequency in each series**	
		Congruent (black seal)	**Incongruent (red seal)**
1	fork (pitchfork)	45	45
2	pliers (tongs, pincers)	36	42
3	frying pan (pan, skillet)	40	39
4	seal (walrus)	40	41
5	snake (cobra, serpent)	41	39
6	sword (dagger, knife, sabre)	45	42
7	elephant (— head, trunk)	39	38
8	squirrel	44	41
9	gun (pistol, revolver)	44	45
10	tree	44	45
	Total Frequencies		
	Correct responses	418 (93%)	418 (93%)
	Other responses	29	24
	Detail responses	3	7
	Rejections	0	1

Class II stimulus forms				
Form	**Responses scored correct**	**Frequency in each series**		
		Congruent (tan lion)	**Incongruent**	
			black lion	**purple lion**
11	tree (fir, pine, Xmas)	45	44	42
12	giraffe	39	40	42
13	lips (mouth, — imprint)	43	44	43
14	banana	44	42	42
15	violin (fiddle, guitar, bass,	44	43	42
16	viol, cello)	40	26	13
17	grapes	44	45	44
18	hand	41	44	43
19	cactus	45	44	39
20	fire hydrant (fireplug) lion	34	33	21
	Total Frequencies			
	Correct responses	419 (93%)	405 (90%)	371 (82%)
	Other responses	31	35	65
	Detail responses	0	6	6
	Rejections	0	4	8

Note: Only responses listed here were scored correct.

difficulties of dealing with all the complexities involved. We can be certain that our incongruent stimuli usually presented incongruent form-color combinations to the Ss since 88 per cent of all trials the stimuli presented the three incongruent series elicited the particular response defined by E in advance as incongruent with the color.

Table 6 supplies evidence on the adequacy of the 20 separate forms. Although all 10 Class I forms uniformly produced high percentages of correct responses in all series, only 18 of the Class II forms produced such uniform results. The two forms in question (grapes and lion) produced a majority of correct responses in two of the series but failed to do so in the incongruent chromatic series. In their incongruent chromatic form these two items functioned more like ambiguous stimuli than structured forms, producing much longer latencies and a larger variety of other responses, congruent as well as incongruent with their colors.

In order to supply for this atypical series (purple lion) data which would be strictly comparable to those for the other series, the results for this one series and its norm series were recalculated with the omission of the two incomparable stems. The remaining abbreviated series of eight items came out to the other series in degree of structuredness, providing 94 per cent correct responses. When the reaction times for this abbreviated series are compared with those for the norm series (see Table 4), application of the Mann-Whitney U Test still yields high values of z associated with probabilities below 004. Hence our conclusions concerning the purple lion remain unchanged.

Adjustment Scores Reach

We turn now to the secondary aim of this study, the relation of the adjustment maladjustment variable to the large individual differences in reaction time occurring in the various congruent and incongruent series. The hypothesis to be tested here derives from both Rorschach theory and the theory of hue-form incongruity. According to Rorschach theory, chromatic stimulus-blots, because of some affinity between color and affect, are uniquely effective in distinguishing between neurotically maladjusted Ss and adjusted S'. We have suggested the alternative hypothesis that it is hue-form incongruity in blots (rather than hue as such) which the critical and conflict-producing conditions necessary to symptoms of conceptual and behavioral disorganization, such as associative blocking and increased latency of response (Siipola, 1950, p. 381). The specific experimental hypothesis to be tested is that within a female college student population, neurotically maladjusted Ss in comparison to adjusted Ss, will give reliably longer reaction times to incongruent chromatic stimulus forms (red seal and purple lion series) whereas they will not give reliably longer latencies for congruent chromatic forms (tan lion series) or for achromatic stimuli of either type (black seal and black lion series).

Each of the three groups of 45 Ss (groups A, C-1, C-2) was divided into an adjusted subgroup and a neurotically maladjusted subgroup. The neurotic type of maladjustment is generally indicated on the MMPI by a high score one or more of the "neurotic" scales (Hy, Hs, D, Pt), a T score of 60 on any of these scales was selected here as the criterion for maladjustment since use of this score dichotomized the total group of 135 Ss. The individual time scores (median reaction times) for the adjusted and maladjusted ss were then compared for each of the series. The Mann-Whitney U Test was applied to determine whether the maladjusted ss produced reliably longer reaction times in any of the series.

Table 7

U **Tests between Median Reaction Times of Adjusted and Maladjusted** *Ss*

Series	U	z	p	Direction
Achromatic congruent (black seal)				negative[b]
Adjusted ($N = 23$) *vs* maladjusted ($N = 22$)	310 5	1 31	19	
Achromatic incongruent (black lion)				
Adjusted ($N = 23$) *vs* maladjusted ($N = 22$)	339 0	1 95	05	
Chromatic congruent (tan lion)				
Adjusted ($N = 19$) *vs* maladjusted ($N = 25$)	272 5	83	41	positive
Chromatic incongruent (red seal)				
Adjusted ($N = 19$) *vs* maladjusted ($N = 25$)	315 5	1 85	03[a]	positive
Chromatic incongruent (purple lion)[c]				
Adjusted ($N = 25$) *vs* maladjusted ($N = 19$)	313 5	1 80	036[a]	

[a] One-tailed test.
[b] A negative direction means that shorter reaction times are associated with maladjustment. For mean reaction times, $z = 2\ 42$, $p = 016$
[c] Abbreviated series of eight items

The results presented in Table 7 show that our prediction was correct. Only the incongruent chromatic series (red seal and purple lion) gave reliably longer reaction times for the maladjusted group, the values of z for these series, although not very high, are associated with one-tailed probability of less than 05. Striking is the fact that in the case of group C-1 (which had the congruent and incongruent chromatic forms interspersed in the same series) the very same maladjusted Ss reacted dependably more slowly than the adjusted Ss on the incongruent, but not on the congruent, items. Hue-form incongruity apparently presents S with a unique type of problem which is particularly difficult for the maladjusted S.

As important as the above finding is the unpredicted discovery that maladjusted Ss reacted reliably faster on the achromatic incongruent items (black lion), the value of z is higher here than for any of the other series. To show the relation of this unexpected finding to the predicted finding, a comparison of the adjusted and the maladjusted Ss as to the order of difficulty (median reaction times) of the various series is presented in Table 8. This comparison reveals certain interesting trends. (a) The order of difficulty for the various types of congruent and incongruent forms is different for maladjusted and adjusted ss (b) The fastest reactions of all are achieved by the maladjusted S when reacting to achromatic blots, especially if they are incongruent, the maladjusted S thus reacts faster than the adjusted S to both types of achromatic forms although this difference is reliable only in the case of incongruent forms (c) The slowest ructions of all are given by the maladjusted S when reacting to chromatic blots especially if they are incongruent, the maladjusted S thus reacts more slowly than the normal S to both types of chromatic forms although here again this difference is reliable only in the of incongruent forms (d) Varying the nature of the stimulus forms has a much greater effect on response latency for the maladjusted S than for the adjusted S.

Table 8

Order of Difficulty of the Types of Stimulus Forms for Adjusted and for Maladjusted *Ss*

Adjusted *Ss*		Maladjusted *Ss*	
Order	Median R T	Order	Median R t
Chromatic Congruent (tan lion)	1 015	Achromatic Incongruent (black lion)	935
Achromatic Congruent (black seal)	1 03	Achromatic Congruent (black seal)	995
Achromatic Incongruent (black lion)	1 035	Chromatic Congruent (tan lion)	1 055
Chromatic Incongruent (red seal) (purple lion)[a]	1 045 1 073	Chromatic Incongruent (red seal) (purple lion)[a]	1 10 1 15

[a] Abbreviated series of eight items

The relation of individual differences in reaction time to the adjustment-maladjustment variable is, then, entirely dependent on the particular kind of stimulus forms presented to the Ss with achromatic forms, the maladjusted S tends to react more rapidly while with chromatic forms he tends to react more slowly than the adjusted S. Combing the different types of stimulus forms within a single test (as is done in the Rorschach) could result in the canceling out of these opposite trends, thus reaction times could appear to be unaffected by the adjustment-maladjustment variable. Given these opposed trends, combining results of adjusted and maladjusted Ss may give a resultant which represents only what is common to both types of Ss, namely a relatively high latency for incongruent chromatic forms, as we found above when we combined results for the total sample of college students. The conclusions to be drawn from these complicated findings are first, that the exact relation of response latency to congruity-incongruity is dependent on the degree of adjustment of the population being tested, and second, that achromatic incongruent blots may be more effective in diagnosing maladjustment than chromatic incongruent blots since a distinguishing characteristic of the maladjusted S is his remarkable speed of response to achromatic incongruent forms. Since this latter finding was unexpected, however, replication is certainly needed before this should be adopted as a diagnostic recommendation.

DISCUSSION

The previously proposed theory of color-form incongruity (Siipola, 1950) still seems adequate to account for the major findings of the present study as they apply to the total unselected sample of female college students. The theory accounts for the primary finding here that chromatic incongruity of two basic types (red seal and purple lion) was effective in increasing reaction time over that of congruent norm series, whereas achromatic incongruity was ineffective. Since this finding was obtained with highly structured stimulus forms. It is clear that our theory of color-form incongruity does not need to be limited to apply to ambiguous blots only. In fact, it is possible that the more highly structured the forms, the more dependable will be the relation between color-form incongruity and response latency with highly structured forms more rigorous experimental control is possible. Here the reaction-time measure itself becomes more meaningful since it measures the time required to achieve a common product of common quality (the correct response) rather than the time taken to produce any one of a wide variety of responses of varying quality.

Although these results for structured forms seem to be contrary to those obtained by Lazarus and Oldfield (1955), the experiments are not comparable since, as we have indicated, their experiments were apparently done under relatively free conditions rather than time pressure. They reported (p. 370) relatively long latencies for structured forms (roughly 4 sec), while under time pressure we obtained very short reaction times (about 1 sec) and appropriately small differential effects (10 to 20 sec) between the various stimuli. Such minute differences would appear insignificant or could be entirely lost in the gross type of time scores obtained under free conditions.

Much of the confusion and controversy over the effects of such stimulus variables as color and congruity-incongruity on response latency is the consequence of comparing and interchanging results obtained under free and under time-pressure conditions. Our original and present experiments have been based on the assumption that the effects of a particular stimulus variable upon the speed of response can be measured only if that variable isolated and all other conditions (including the S's conception of his task) are held constant. This isolation can be readily accomplished by following, as we have done, the standard experimental approach in which reaction time is rigorously defined as the minimal time required for a specified response to a specific stimulus when S has the definite task of reacting as quickly as under such time-pressure conditions, we have found that the magnitude of the time scores obtained was appropriate to reflect subtle effects of stimulus variables Most other investigators, as shown by Baughman's recent review (1958), have used free conditions which allow the Ss to respond at their own widely different temps with any response that happens to please them. These investigators have almost uniformly arrived at the startling conclusion that variations in stimulus properties, notably colors, have no effect on reaction time. Only if time scores obtained under free and pressure conditions were interchangeable would we have the basis for a real controversy. That they are not has been shown by the fact that free and pressure conditions produce latencies of entirely different orders of magnitude which are affected differently by variables such as color (Siipola, & Taylor, 1952). Moreover, free conditions yield a score which represents an individual's tempo of reacting (rather than his minimal reaction time), and such scores have been shown to reflect gross individual differences m temperament and personality (Dunn, Bliss, & Siipola, 1958), rather than the relatively small effects of stimulus variables.

The theory of hue-form incongruity falls to account for all of our findings on the relation of the adjustment-maladjustment variable to the individual differences in reaction time. Although the theory offers a ready explanation of why the maladjusted S reacts abnormally slowly to incongruent chromatic forms, it fails to explain why he reacts abnormally quickly to incongruent achromatic forms. It now seems likely that the two seemingly opposite effects of incongruity may both express the same underlying process different (even reversed) symptomatic reactions have been found to have the same dynamic meaning under varying conditions (Siipola, Walker, & Kolb, 1955, p. 456) Reactions of both types may reflect a basically rigid, compulsive approach to reality testing (common in maladjusted college students) which places exaggerated emphasis on the accuracy of the match between the form of the stimulus and the object identified while neglecting the color. A person with this approach might welcome (be selectively sensitive to) the very kind of distortion of reality presented by achromatic incongruity (black lion) which makes all color meaningless by substituting a shade for a hue. At the same time, the kind of distortion present in chromatic incongruity (purple lion or red seal), which substitutes an unreal hue for a natural color, may represent the colorful world of unreality which such a compulsive neurotic might fear and defend himself against.

The results of this experiment suggest that some of the dynamic processes postulated in Rorschach theory to apply to amorphous blots may operate also in the perception of highly structured forms under rigorously controlled conditions of the laboratory. In this study, the S, in the presence of threatening apparatus rather than a friendly Rorschach tester, responded under strong time pressure to structured stimulus-forms which were presented mechanically in a slot of the machine—and he quickly gave as his first response the same one given by 90 per cent of the other Ss. Thus, instead of the usual rich variety of effects on response, all we obtained were slight variations in reaction time But precisely here, we believe, has a unique advantage of this approach. When reaction time is made the only possible dependent variable, it shows promise of providing an index which will summate in a single quantitative measure the effects of many complex phenomena associated with the free conditions of the Rorschach technique.

SUMMARY

The primary aim of the present study was to subject to direct experimental test previously promised theory concerning the effects of color-form congruity and incongruity upon reaction time. The specific hypotheses were (a) incongruent chromatic stimulus forms produce longer reaction times than matched congruent forms and (b) incongruent achromatic forms will fail to produce longer latencies than matched congruent forms. These hypotheses were tested under the following conditions the stimulus forms were highly structured (evoking a common response in 90 per cent of the instances), strong time pressure was imposed, and reaction time for S's first verbal response was precisely measured by use of a voice key and Springfield timer, 135 unselected female college students served as Ss.

A special feature of this research was limitation of the forms used as stimuli to only those which identified familiar objects possessing a single distinctive color. This made possible operational definition of the following basic types of color-form relationships (a) two types of congruity (black seal and tan lion), (b) two types of chromatic incongruity (red seal and purple lion), (c) one type of achromatic incongruity (black lion). The experimental design provided series employing these three types of incongruently colored forms each of which could be compared to a congruent norm series.

Comparison of the results for independent groups presented with the same stimulus forms in either congruent or incongruent colors supported both experimental hypotheses. Chromatic incongruity of the two types was effective in increasing reaction time over that of congruent norm series whereas achromatic incongruity was ineffective. These findings were checked by the alternative procedure of holding the Ss constant while using different, equated stimulus forms for the congruent and incongruent series, again the hypotheses were confirmed.

A secondary arm of this study was that of trying to relate the adjustment-maladjustment variable (as measured by the "neurotic scales" of the MMPI) to the large individual differences which occurred in the various congruent and incongruent series. The following trends were indicated: (a) Varying the nature of the stimulus form has a much greater effect on response latency for the maladjusted S than for the adjusted S (b) The maladjusted S tends to react more slowly than the normal S to both types of chromatic forms, but this difference reliable only in the case of incongruent forms (c) The maladjusted S tends to react faster than the normal S to both types of achromatic forms, but here again the difference is reliable only in the case of incongruent forms. These interesting trends need further confirmation by results obtained from Ss more severely disturbed than college students.

REFERENCES

Baughman, E.E. (1958). The role of stimulus in Rorschach. *Psychol Bull* *55*:121–147.

Berg, J., & Polyot, C.J. (1956). The influence of color on reactions to incomplete figures. *J Consult Psychol* 29:9–15.

Dunn, S., Bliss, J., & Siipola, E. (1948). The effects of impulsivity, introversion, and individual values upon association under free conditions. *J Pers* 19: 61–76.

Lazarus, R.S., & Oldfield, M. (1955). Rorschach responses and the influence of color. *J. Pers,* 23:356–372.

Siegel, S. (1956). *Nonparametric statistics.* New York McGraw-Hill,

Siipola, E. (1950). The influence of color on reactions to ink blots. *J. Pers* 18:358–382.

———— Kuhns, F. & Taylor, V. (1950). Measurement of the individual's reactions to color in ink blots. *J. Pers* 19:154–171.

———— & Taylor, V. (1952). Reactions to ink blots under free and pressure conditions. *J. Pers* 21:22–47.

———— Walker, N., & Kole, D. (1955). Task attitudes in word association, projective and nonprojective. *J Pers* 44:14–59.

Field Dependence in Young Anorectic and Obese Women

Harriet I. Basseches & Stephen A. Karp
(equal participants, listed alphabetically)
(1984). *Psychotherapy Psychosomatics* 41:33–37.

Abstract: *Bruch* and other clinicians working with patients suffering from eating disorders have noted substantial similarity between obese individuals and those with anorexia nervosa with regard to difficulties in achieving autonomous functioning. Although research has substantially supported this view for obese persons, some studies of anorectics have portrayed them as no different from or even more autonomous than normally weighted controls. In an attempt to clarify this discrepancy, the present study evaluated field dependence, a psychological measure reflecting autonomy, among 16 subjects with anorexia nervosa, 16 obese subjects, and 16 normally weighted controls. The three groups consisted of females between 12 and 24 years, matched for age, IQ, and socioeconomic status. The anorectic and obese groups, while no different from each other, were both significantly more field dependent than the normal controls. The results are viewed as supportive of the Bruch position, stressing similarity of the two eating disorder groups in their limited progress toward autonomous functioning.

Clinical and research interest in obesity has been extensive and sustained for a considerable period of time. More recently, however, there has been growing attention paid to another type of eating disorder, anorexia nervosa. The issue of autonomy versus dependence has been proposed as a critical factor in the personality development of sufferers from both of these disorders. While there appears to be substantial agreement as to dependence among obese persons (particularly those with a developmental history of obesity), the literature offers conflicting evidence on autonomy of persons with anorexia nervosa.

Bruch (1957, 1970, 1975), in her clinical observations and theoretical formulations, sees essential similarities among persons with the two types of disorder. She assesses both obese and anorectic individuals as experiencing severe difficulty in the attainment of autonomy, although anorectics continue the struggle for autonomy while obese individuals are likely to have ceased such a struggle. Bruch (1975) describes the obese person as manifesting "serious deficits in initiative, autonomy, experience of control and self-regulation … [obese persons] are deficient in their sense of separateness … and they do not feel self-directed but helpless under the influence of external forces …" Describing anorectics, Bruch (1970) notes a comparable sense of ineffectiveness and helplessness. In her experience, anorectics see themselves as acting only in response to demands from others.

In a quite separate, but extensive series of investigations, Witkin et al.(1962) have studied the ramifications in personality of performance on a series of perceptual tests of a psychological characteristic identified as field dependence. Among these tests are the Embedded Figures Test, which requires a subject to locate a series of simple geometric figures embedded in more complex figures, and the Rod-and-Frame Test, which requires a subject in a dark room to adjust a tilted luminous rod to the upright while it is embedded in a tilted luminous frame. Subjects have typically displayed individual differences in ability to perform these tasks.

Of particular relevance for the present research are the many findings that certain symptom groups, as a whole, perform atypically on tests of field dependence. For example, alcoholics (Witkin et al., 1959; Karp et al., 1963, 1965a,b; Karp and Konstadt, 1965), diabetics (Karp et al., 1969), asthmatic children (Fishbein, 1963), catatonics (Janucci, 1964), and patients with a hysterical character structure (Zukmann, 1957) have been found to be significantly less efficient in disembedding (less "field independent") than control groups, whereas paranoids (Janucci, 1964; Powell, 1964), and obsessive-compulsive characters (Zukmann, 1957) have been found significantly more field independent.

More directly bearing on personality, numerous studies (reviewed by Witkin and Goodenough, 1977) find persons who are more field independent to display significantly greater autonomy in interpersonal relations than field dependent persons.

Based upon the similarity of Bruch's (1957) characterization of obese persons and the descriptions by Witkin et al. (1962) of psychologically undifferentiated (field dependent) individuals, Karp and Pardes (1965) studied field dependence in groups of obese and normally weighted women. Obese women were significantly more field dependent than women in the control group, thus providing experimental evidence in support of Bruch's clinical observations. These results have since been confirmed for adults by McLaughlin (1975) and by McArthur and Burstein (1975), but not for children [Costanza and Woody, 1979). Garner et al. (1976) used a modification of Rotter's Locus of Control Scale (Rotter, 1966) to evaluate autonomy in obese and control subjects. Obese subjects were significantly more external than normals (i.e., they were more likely to perceive control as residing in others rather than themselves). However, two other studies of locus of control in obese subjects found them no different from normals (Gormanous and Lowe, 1975; Karpowitz and Zeis, 1975).

While Bruch's views on problems of autonomous functioning among those with anorexia nervosa receive support from other clinicians (see e.g., Brown, 1975; Tamagna, 1973), research on this issue, though sparse, provides contradictory evidence.

For example, in the Garner (1976) study cited above, anorectics were no different from controls in locus of control. Additionally, Smart et al. (1976) found a group of 22 anorectic females to be "independent" on Cattell's 16PF Questionnaire. In the sole study of field dependence in anorectics, using only three subjects (a fourth refused to be tested) and no controls, Sours (1969) found all three subjects to be field independent, although a later report by that author in 1980 describes anorectics as field dependent. Thus, what little research evidence there is tends to suggest that anorectics are no less autonomous than normally weighted controls and, perhaps, are more so.

The present study aims to attempt clarification of the contradictions between clinical and research findings on the autonomy of anorectics by studying field dependence among obese, anorectic, and normally weighted young women.

METHODS

Subjects

Subjects for the study were 48 white females between the ages of 12 and 24 years, all of average intelligence or higher. They were divided into three groups of 16 subjects each, based upon diagnosis of anorexia nervosa, obesity, or neither of these. The three groups were matched for age, intelligence (Altus Information Test) (Altus, 1948], and socioeconomic status (Index of Social Position) (Hollingshead and Redlich, 1958).

The anorectic group consisted of young women who met the criteria for acceptance into an ongoing research therapy project conducted at the National Institute of Mental Health, as follows: (A) Age of onset is less than 30 years. (B) Anorexia accompanied by weight loss of at least 25% of original body weight. (C) A distorted, implacable attitude towards food, eating or weight that overrides hunger, admonitions, reassurances, and threats: (1) The denial of illness with a failure to recognize nutritional needs. (2) Apparent enjoyment of losing weight with overt manifestations that food refusal is pleasurable indulgence. (3) A distorted body image of extreme thinness with overt evidence that it is rewarding the patient to achieve and maintain that state. (4) Unusual hoarding or handling of food. (D) No known medical illness that could account for the anorexia and weight loss. (E) No other primary psychiatric disorder, with particular reference to primary affective disorder or schizophrenia. (F) Amenorrhea. (G) At least two of the following: lanugo, bradycardia (persistent resting pulse of 60 or less), periods of overactivity, episodes of overactivity, vomiting (may be self-induced).

Eleven of the anorectic subjects were participants in the NIMH program of treatment. The remaining five were recruited from outpatients of therapists and physicians. The members of the obese group were selected on the basis of the American Academy of Pediatrics Triceps Skinfold Standard (Garn and Clark, 1976) as those falling beyond the 85th percentile of the Standards chart. Persons for whom there was a medical disorder directly responsible for the obesity were excluded. Subjects were recruited from a variety of sources including public and private high schools and colleges, local mental health clinics and weight reduction groups. The control group consisted of young women who met neither the criteria for anorexia nervosa nor those for obesity. Nine of them had been screened as normal volunteers and were residing temporarily at the National Institutes of Health. The remainder were recruited from local high schools and colleges.

Tests

In addition to the screening instruments already mentioned (Altus Information Test, Index of Social Position, medical diagnosis regarding obesity and anorexia nervosa), all subjects were given the Embedded Figures Test (Witkin et al., 1971).

The Embedded Figures Test, a measure of field dependence, consists of 12 complex geometric-like figures, embedded in each of which is a simple geometric figure to be located by the subject within a 3-minute trial. Score for the test is the mean amount of time taken to locate the simple figures. Reliability of the test ranges from 0.85 to 0.95. Evidence for the validity of the test as a measure of autonomy is extensive and has been summarized by Witkin and Goodenough (1977).

RESULTS

Means and scores and standard deviations for the Embedded Figures Test, and each of the three measures (IQ, age, and Index of Social Position) for which the groups were matched are reported in Table I. To compare the three groups on Embedded Figures Test performance, a one-way analysis of variance was carried out. This yielded an F of 5.56 which, with 2 and 45 d.f., is significant at better than the 0.01 level of confidence. To locate group differences more specifically, two t tests were carried out. Comparing an aggregation of the two eating disorder groups with the controls, the normal controls differed significantly from the anorectic and obese subjects ($t = 3.30$, d.f. = 45, $p < 0.01$), being more field independent than the symptom groups. The anorectic and obese groups did not differ ($t = 0.41$, d.f. = 30).

DISCUSSION

The present results are consistent with the view that obese and anorectic individuals have similar difficulties in functioning autonomously. Both of the eating disorder groups were significantly more field dependent (implying less progress toward autonomous functioning) than the normal controls.

The present results are consistent with and supportive of Bruch's formulations of similarity between the two eating disorders with regard to autonomy. Both groups function at a markedly less autonomous level than do normal controls. The present results may also be considered in terms of prior findings on autonomy among anorectics. Our results stand in contrast to those of Sours (1969) cited above, who found three anorectic subjects to be field independent. Similarly, our results are not consistent with those of Smart et al. (1976), who found anorectics "independent" on Cattell's 16PF Questionnaire. It may be noted, however, that a study by Thomy [1971] found no relationship between the Cattell independence factor and field dependence.

ACKNOWLEDGMENTS

We wish to express our indebtedness to the staff of the Anorexia Nervosa Project, Section on Experimental Therapeutics, at the National Institute of Mental Health and to the George Washington University Center for Academic and Administrative Computing.

REFERENCES

Altus, W. (1948). The validity of an abbreviated information test used in the army. *J. Consult. Psychol.* 12: 270–275.

Brown, F. (1975). Disturbances and psychosexual development of adolescent girls. *Mount Sinai J. Med.* 42:216–222.

Bruch, H. (1957). *The Importance of Overweight.* New York: Norton.

——— (1970). Psychotherapy in primary anorexia nervosa. *J. Nerv. Ment. Dis.* 150:51–67.

——— (1975). Obesity and anorexia nervosa: psychosocial aspects. *Aust. N.Z. J. Psychiat.* 9:159–161.

Costanza, P. & Woody, E. (1979). Externality as a function of obesity in children: pervasive style or eating-specific attribute? *J. pers. soc. Psychol.* 37:2286–2291.

Fishbein, G. (1963). Perceptual modes and asthmatic symptoms: an application of Witkin's hypothesis. *J. consult. Psychol.* 27:54–58.

Garn, S.& Clark, D. (1976). Ad hoc committee to review the ten-state nutrition survey: trends in fatness and the origins of obesity. *Pediatrics* 57:443–456.

Garner, D., Garfinkel, P., Stancer, & H., Moldofsky, H. (1976). Body image disturbances in anorexia nervosa and obesity. *Psychosom. Med.* 38:327–336.

Gormanous, G., & Lowe, W. (1975). Locus of control and obesity. *Psychol. Rep.* 37:30.

Hollingshead, A. & Redlich, F. (1958). *Social Class and Mental Illness; A Community Study* New York Wiley.

Janucci, G. (1964). Size constancy in schizophrenia. A study of subgroup differences; unpublished PhD diss., Rutgers University.

Karp, S.; Konstadt, N. (1965). Alcoholism and psychological differentiation: long-range effect of heavy drinking on field dependence. *J. Nerv. Ment. Dis.* 140:412–416.

——— Pardes, H. (1965). Psychological differentiation (field dependence) in obese women. *Psychosom. Med.* 27:238–244.

——— Poster, D. & Goodman, A. .(1963). Differentiation in alcoholic women. J. Personality 31: 386–393.

——— Winters, S. & Pollack, 1. (1969). Field dependence among diabetics. *Archs Gen. Psychiat.* 21:72–76.

——— Witkin, H. & Goodenough, D. (1965a). Alcoholism and psychological differentiation: effect of achievement of sobriety on field dependence. *Q. J. Stud. Alcohol* 26:580–585.

——— ——— ——— Alcoholism and psychological differentiation: the effect of alcohol on field dependence. *J. Abnorm. Psychol.* 70:262–265 (1965b).

Karpowitz, D. & Zeis, F. (1975). Personality and behavior differences of obese and nonobese adolescents. *J. consult. clin. Psychol.* 43:886 (1975).891.

McArthur, L.; Burstein, B.: Field dependent eating and perception as a function of weight and sex. *J. Personality* 43: 402–420 (1975).

McLaughlin, J. (1975). The differentiation of obese women into developmental and reactive types. unpubl. PhD diss., George Washington University.

Powell, B. (1964). A study of the perceptual field approach of normal subjects and

schizophrenic patients under conditions of an aversive stimulus; unpubl. PhD diss. Columbia University.

Rotter, J. (1966). Generalized expectancies for internal versus external control of reinforcement. *Psychol. Monogr.* 80:1–28.

Smart, D.; Beumont, P.; George, G.; Some personality characteristics of patients with anorexia nervosa. *Br. J. Psychiat.* 128: 57–60.

Sours, J. (1976). The anorexia nervosa syndrome: phenomenologic and psychodynamic components. Psychiat. Q. 43: 240–256 (1969).

——— (1980). Starving to death in a sea of objects: the anorexia nervosa syndrome New York: Aronson.

Tamagna, E. (1973). Anorexia nervosa: struggle for control during adolescence. *Clin. Proc. Child Hosp. Natn. Med. Cent.* 29:88–97.

Thomy, V. (1971). Relationships among three factors reflecting independence: field independence, UI 19, and Q IV; unpubl. PhD diss., George Washington University

Witkin, H., Dyk, R., Faterson, H., Goodenough, D. & Karp, S. (1962). *Psychological Differentiation.* New York: Wiley.

——— Goodenough, D. (1977). Field dependence and interpersonal behavior. *Psychol. Bull.* 84: 661–689.

——— Karp, S. Goodenough, D. (1959). Dependence in alcoholics. *Q. J Stud. Alcohol* 20:493–504.

——— Witkin, Oltman, P. Raskin, E., & Karp, S. (1971). *Manual For The Embedded Figures Tests* (Consulting Psychologists Press, Palo Alto).

Zukmann, L. (1957). Hysteric compulsive factors in perceptual organization; unpubl. PhD diss. New School for Social Research.

PRESENTATIONS AND SELECTED PUBLICATIONS

Hearing What Cannot Be Seen: A Psychoanalytic Research Group's Inquiry Into Female Sexuality

Harriet Basseches, Paula Ellman, Susan Elmendorf, Elizabeth Fritsch, Nancy Goodman, Fonya Helm and Shelley Rockwell[1] (1996). *J. Amer. Psychoanal. Assn.*, 44(Supplement):511–528.

Advances in the theoretical understanding of female psychology are not easily integrated into psychoanalytic practice. This paper reports on a study of female psychology and clinical practice by a group of seven female psychoanalysts. Through discussing the literature and case vignettes, we discovered a lag between current theoretical ideas and our clinical practice. The group identified an anachronistic emphasis on penis envy functioning as "bedrock." This report addresses how the group facilitated individual members' integration of theory and practice, and how this integration affected work with patients. We found that as we became open to considering a wider range of potential dynamic meanings of penis envy and female bodily concerns, we were able to explore a richer, and often surprising unfolding of vicissitudes. The discussion highlights some technical issues with this approach.

While Freud's ideas about feminine psychological development are often debated, they have had a profound impact on psychoanalysts as well as on

---

1 Harriet I. Basseches, Paula L. Ellman, Susan S. Elmendorf, Elizabeth Fritsch, Nancy R. Goodman, Fonya L. Helm, and Shelley Rockwell. Members, New York Freudian Society.

the culture at large. Freud (1925, 1931, 1933, 1937) portrays the female as imprisoned and propelled by her envy over the superiority of the male genital. From this perspective, the analysis of a female will inevitably uncover penis envy and culminate with the view that penis envy is "bedrock."

A burgeoning body of literature rejects this classical Freudian picture as phallocentric.[2] These writers propose that early on, little girls experience genital sensations and develop a narcissistically valued sense of femininity. They also form psychic representations of the female genitalia and generate fantasies and anxieties about them. This literature emphasizes concepts associated with primary femininity, often challenging Freud's view that penis envy is "bedrock." Mayer (1995) observes that while primary femininity represents a significant theoretical advance, it has not been "adequately incorporated into everyday clinical work" (p. 35). By discussing concepts from the literature side by side with case material, our research group was surprised to discover the extent of the lag in our work. This study represents an attempt to bridge theory and practice.

In a brief review of the early and recent literature, this paper documents that more than sixty years ago, some analysts anticipated contemporary ideas of female development. The report then presents the research findings: identification of the lag, exploration of the difficulties in changing technique, and subsequent shifts in the analytic work. Vignettes from two cases illustrate these changes. The discussion addresses the tenacity of the lag, the role of the group in integrating theory and practice, and the implications of the shift for technique.

---

2 Freud constructed working hypotheses that were not always aligned with others of his ideas. His powerful metaphor of "the first ego as a body ego" (1923) supports the notion of a central female bodily sense as the organizational core for the female.

LITERATURE REVIEW

Early Literature

Although Freud's view of the centrality of penis envy and the castration complex dominated the early writings on female sexuality, some analysts tried to present another perspective. On December 3, 1924, Abraham wrote to Freud: "… I have recently wondered whether in early infancy there may be an early vaginal awakening of the female libido, which is destined to be repressed and which is subsequently followed by clitoral primacy as the expression of the phallic phase …" (Abraham and Freud, 1965, p. 375). Freud (in 1924) replied, "… According to my preconceived ideas on the subject, the vaginal share would tend to be expressed anally. The vagina … is a later acquisition by separation from the cloaca …" (Abraham and Freud, 1965, p. 377). Nine years later, Freud (1933) stated, "… It is true, that there are a few isolated reports of early vaginal sensations as well, but it cannot be easy to distinguish these from sensations in the anus or vestibulum; in any case they cannot play a great part …" (p. 118). In 1937 Freud declared, "… [W]ith the wish for a penis … we have … reached bedrock, and thus our activities are at an end. … [T]he biological field does in fact play the part of the underlying bedrock …" (p. 252).[3]While analysts agreed about the importance of penis envy in women, Horney (1926) and Jones (1927) pointed out that penis envy can serve as a defense against oedipal wishes. A number of early analysts concurred with Abraham's view that the little girl develops an early female identity and body image based on her kinesthetic knowledge of an interior genital (Brierley, 1932; Horney, 1926; Jones, 1927; Klein, 1928; Muller, 1932; Muller-Braunschweig, 1926). And some clinicians observed

---

3 Freud is using the word "biological" loosely here to mean unanalyzable. Freud was influenced by the idea of the inheritance of acquired characteristics (Ritvo, 1965) and seems to have believed that the clitoris was a vestigial penis.

"female" fears and fantasies about the inner genital: fear of penetration (Horney, 1924); fear of the destruction of internal organs and the capacity for motherhood (Klein, 1928); anxiety about violation by an overpowering father (Muller-Braunschweig, 1926); and dread of the "masochistic triad … castration-defloration-parturition" (Deutsch, 1930). Brierley (1932) posited "… two lines or directions of displacement of cathexis, namely, a nipple-penis-faeces-child line and a mouth-anus-vagina line" (p. 435). The seeds were sown for what was later to become a significant revision in Freud's hypotheses about women.

Recent Literature—Expanding Ideas of Primary Femininity

Recent writings about female development and conflict do not disregard the presence of penis envy, but emphasize the centrality of primary femininity, a concept articulated by Stoller (1976). From this perspective the little girl draws on early body experiences to create psychic representations of her body ego. These images, in turn, have an impact on her drive/defense constellations. Over the last two decades, there has been an elaboration of these ideas. Writings have focused on the girl's awareness of both inner and outer genital sensations, representations of the female genitalia, and associated anxieties.

Some clinicians describe the little girl's early bodily experiences. Girls become aware of inner and outer genital sensations through masturbation (Lax, 1994), the flexing of perineal muscles (Richards, 1992), and closely linked urethral and anal feelings (Bass, 1994; Kestenberg, 1982; Lax, 1994). Delineation of these kinesthetic experiences adds new dimensions of what girls want—that is, the wanting of their own pleasure.

Psychoanalytic observations of children also confirm the little girl's knowledge of her genitalia. Galenson and Roiphe (1976) document genital awareness in boys and girls between 15 months and 19 months. Kestenberg (1982) designates an inner-genital phase of development for girls between infancy and the phallic phase. Characteristic of this period is the young girl's interest in distinguishing inside from outside. Erikson's (1950, 1974) and Mayer's (1991) observations of girls' building of and responses to block designs also suggest that from an early age girls are grappling to form representations of their inner genital. There is evidence that adult women do form mental representations of the inner genital. Kalinich (1993) proposes that adult female analysands displace representations of their inner genital onto mental functioning. Krausz (1994) and Lerner (1976) report on female analysands who defend against awareness of their inner genital through fantasies of being invisible and diffuse.

Lerner (1976) claims that the mother's failure to label her daughter's genitalia contributes to the girl's denial, resulting in a conviction that "[t]he vulva (including the clitoris) is not important, must not be spoken of or thought about, or should not exist" (p. 276). By not naming what the girl has, the mother deprives her daughter of "permission" to be "a sexually operative and responsive female" (p. 270). Lerner argues that the traditional castration complex results more from the mother's failure to label what the girl has, than from "the fact that the clitoris is a smaller (and thus inferior) organ compared to the penis" (p. 277).

Recognition that girls get pleasure from genital sensations and form mental representations and fantasies about their genitalia makes it possible to conceptualize women as having uniquely female genital anxieties. As punishment for libidinal strivings, girls fear threats to their inner space, i.e., that it will be violated, taken away, or sealed off (Kulish, 1991; Mayer, 1995; Richards, 1992, 1996; Wilkinson, 1991). Clinicians point out that the little girl's confusion over vaginal, urethral, and anal sensations fosters anal-stage regressions, and concomitant anxieties about loss of control and incapacity to hold on to contents (Barnett, 1996; Kalinich, 1993; Shaw, 1995).

The model of female development set forth in these writings presents the girl as having knowledge and conflicts about "what she isn't and hasn't [as well as about] … what she is and what she has" (Mayer, 1995, p. 32). These dual anxieties play off each other and contribute to rich and varied movements within and between compromise formations.

FINDINGS: IDENTIFYING THE LAG AND MAKING A SHIFT

The research group, comprised of seven female psychoanalysts, met weekly over one year. The group reviewed literature on female development and sexuality, and discussed vignettes from each analyst's psychoanalyses with women, twenty-five in total. Reading the more recent literature solidified the group's theoretical thinking and dramatized the extent of the lag between theory and clinical technique. Early on, we discovered our collusion with Freud's phallocentric perspective in concert with our patients' self-assessments.[4] There is always the question to what extent the patient's associations are influenced by the analyst's bias. In clinical vignettes we were experts at identifying the female castration complex. We documented two familiar constellations of the female body self. First, patients suffered from a sense of shame about being defective or damaged. Using concrete images, female analysands complained that their body parts were too big, too small, or misshapen. They spoke of defective mouth, waist, breasts, or genitals. In displacements, analysands viewed themselves as incompetent in their careers, academic work, or in relationships with spouses, lovers or children. Second, patients tended to view activity as masculine. When they perceived and expressed bodily urges in an active way, they talked about "having a penis"

---

4 Grossman and Stewart (1976) point out that the patients who have a narcissistic character disorder tend quickly to concur with interpretations of penis envy which "confirm their worst fears of being worthless" (p. 208).

or "penetrating a boyfriend." Even specifically female functions, such as pushing out a baby, breast-feeding or managing a household, were often imbued with phallic meaning. As discussions of the literature and vignettes evolved, the group realized that at times images of damage and activity might not be simply evidence of the castration complex and penis envy, but also serve defensive functions. As already noted, Horney (1926) and Jones (1927) had set forth this idea in the 1920's. Almost fifty years later, Grossman and Stewart (1976) emphasized the importance of treating penis envy as "manifest content, the significance of which will only emerge in the analysis" (p. 207). Also elaborating on these ideas, Tyson (1994) stated, "… penis envy represents a complicated compromise formation involving aspects of gender identity, pathological object relations, defenses, narcissism, and self-esteem" (p. 456).

Yet, participant analysts' theories and identifications with their own personal analysts and clinical supervisors did not yield easily to integrating the newer ideas of primary femininity into clinical practice. They felt uneasy about "moving away" from these "inner authorities" (Grossman, unpublished). Buttressed by the recent literature and the group's interest in expanding their horizons, they began to try out different ways to intervene. One member of the group reported her dream, a dream full of joy (and conflict about the joy) at the discovery of an exquisite new flower with a beautiful inside shape. The group resonated to this image and the difficulty in accepting its obviously feminine message. The dreamer revealed not only her delight in the dream, but also the punishing way she began to use interpretations of penis envy to diminish her discovery. The "new flower" came to represent a broader understanding of the participating analysts' female patients and their own feminine identities and conflicts.

Analysts reported somewhat timidly on early attempts to experiment with new types of interventions. Over time, they became more comfortable giving language to what had now been analyzed into consciousness. Yet, seeking new ways to address patients' feminine fantasies and conflicts continued to stir up both excitement and anxiety. One analyst reported feeling "knocked off her analytic position" as she shifted from focusing on her patient's wish to deny penis envy to looking at the patient's wish to deny interest in her feminine space.

The following clinical vignettes illustrate the efforts of group members to intervene in ways more consistent with current theories of female psychology.

Case 1. Ms. Q., a thirty-five-year-old single woman, entered treatment with an inability to establish a satisfying partnership with a man. She saw men and women as having hopelessly irreconcilable differences. As her analysis progressed, she developed a viable relationship with a man, but remained fearful of being overwhelmed by him.

She began the following session with a mild complaint that the analyst had been "bossy" in the previous session:

P. You think I should want a relationship and be living with my boyfriend in six months. You don't know how much I like my splendid isolation. I love my apartment. My boyfriend is the one who brought up the idea of living together.

A. Perhaps we could understand more about the importance of having your own place. What is it that your apartment reflects of you?

P. It reflects my love of travel, fine things, style.

A. And what do you think a place you shared with your boyfriend would reflect?

P. I would get diluted—like having paintings on the walls that are not me. That is disconcerting. My boyfriend even said, "I am really beginning to like your photographs. If we lived together, I might sell some of my paintings," and I replied, "Oh no, you have worked so hard to acquire them."

A. Your thoughts remind me of your fantasy that to share a place with a man means you would be "overwhelmed." And you are seeing me right now as a man who would overwhelm you. You felt I didn't understand you or your viewpoint in the session yesterday.

P. I feel so relieved. That is the first feeling of relief I have had. [She becomes tearful and falls silent.]

A. In your view, perhaps a man shouldn't give up his things.

P. That was why I thought my boyfriend was gay. He wanted help in redoing his office. My boss never asks for direction. He is never collaborative. The connection with a man leaves me diminished....

P. [Nearing the end of the hour] This is a chock-full session. I'm extremely anxious. I have the feeling somehow this is something I've never gotten to with you before—how difficult is it to think about being in a relationship.

The analyst understood Ms. Q.'s associations to her apartment as referring to her inner feminine space. Previously, when the patient had spoken about her apartment and her pleasure in its museum-like quality, the analyst had thought of the apartment as a phallic equivalent. Certainly, one of this patient's conflicts involved her wish to be like father. In this hour, the analyst heard the associations of the apartment differently. Recalling recent readings on the female's narcissistic investment in her genital (e.g., as described by Krausz, 1994, and Kubie, 1974), the analyst encouraged the patient to elaborate on protective feelings about her "inner space."

Ms. Q.'s concerns about her space, whether and how it would be filled, were at the center of her feminine identity concerns. She felt strong and invulnerable in her determination not to yield or share her space. But her "splendid isolation" within her apartment/body was threatened by the paternal transference. When misunderstood by the analyst, she felt overwhelmed. The patient seemed relieved when the analyst interpreted the paternal transference: "You are seeing me right now as a man who would overwhelm you." The patient's view that the session seemed "chock-full" reflected her evolving capacity to open herself to a man.

In a session a few weeks later, Ms. Q. began by recounting her fury with her boss who refers to women in demeaning ways. She then observed her difficulty holding on to her sense of outrage.

P. With my boss, I feel humiliated because I don't have a penis. I remember Dad would go in the bathroom and be peeing and talking to me at the same time. I felt curious about what he was doing.

A. You speak about your curiosity about your father in the bathroom. I wonder what happened to your awareness and curiosity about your body and what you have. You have a vulva, a vagina, a urethral opening....

P. When I was a little girl, I remember asking my mother, "What is this blister next to my vagina?" My mother said that once she had left me in diapers too long and it was "an ammonia burn." She said, "Hair would grow over it and you won't see it anymore." I remember seeing a blue stain on my mother's underwear. I used to wonder if blood was blue in your body and then became red. I think she douched and that caused the blue stain. I'm suddenly remembering being at my grandfather's house and a black woman came up to the porch with a knife wound in her arm. And Grandfather said, "You're bleeding like a stuck pig." That makes me think of my boss and his comments about women. I felt curious about this black woman and seeing her blood and what color it was. And I remember thinking my Grandfather was upset she was getting blood on his porch.

In this example, the analyst's intervention focused on repressed aspects of the girl's bodily experience *vis-à-vis* her father. The patient shifted from an initial feeling of humiliation in relation to the man, due to her penisless condition, to a state of excited curiosity. The patient's heightened interest in what her father was doing in the bathroom appeared to involve a defense against her awareness of a matching interest in her own body. The analyst's inquiry elicited in the patient a flood of speculations about the female body, tinged with anal and urethral concerns. In previous sessions, the analyst had interpreted the patient's fixed voyeuristic interest in men from the viewpoint of penis envy. Now, influenced by the study, the analyst felt freer to explore the defensive use of this focus and to experiment with explicit language to delineate the female genital.

The analyst's intervention led to an important piece of reconstruction. On several occasions the patient had told the analyst about this "memory" of discovering a "blister" on her vulva. Up to this point, the patient had used this "memory" as confirmation of her mother's neglect. In this session, the "memory" was illuminated in a new way. It appeared that Ms. Q. was recounting a question to her mother about her clitoris and her mother's failure to label this part of her anatomy. Clitoris, thus, had become "blister," something to be covered by hair and forgotten. On reflection, the analyst realized that when she had named parts of the female genitalia, she also had omitted any reference to the clitoris. Her intervention may well have triggered the memory of the mother's omission. This screen memory seemed to contain an element of experience with the mother (the clitoris remaining unnamed) as well as the accompanying sense that her mother forbade her to find pleasure in this part of her body (Lerner, 1976; Tyson, 1994). Confirmation of this hypothesis in subsequent sessions supports Lerner's (1976) theory that "incomplete, undifferentiated, and often inaccurate [naming] … of female genitals prevents the growing girl from achieving pride in femininity, and may lead to anxiety and confusion regarding her sexuality" (p. 282).

Although the analyst's intervention referring to the female genitalia was abrupt and interrupted Ms. Q.'s further associations to her father, the patient's pressured responses demonstrate a deep connection between her feeling of being demeaned/castrated and her mother/analyst's inadequate "naming" of her clitoris. The most important castration for Ms. Q. as it emerged in this session was the misnamed clitoris. The bloody images and memories that followed give a hint of her primitive anxieties about her genitalia. The preoccupation with male demeaning behavior may help Ms. Q. contain the equal if not greater anxiety about what her body actually possesses. If she can complain about the devaluation by men, she can express some of the fear and disappointment in herself without fully grappling with it, a compromise formation. Here is an example of the phallic castration complex as a symptom, defense, and gratification. In addition, this symptom serves to ward off a more intimate relationship with her analyst.

Case 2. Ms. T. is a twenty-five-year-old woman in the fourth year of her analysis. She began to speak of a fantasy of having malformed genitals. In one hour, she spoke of conflicts over her exhibitionism.

P. You think I'm provocative? I worry about being sexy, strong and hurtful.… I remember telling you I'm anxious. Having something valuable and showy is not okay. Something is wrong with my genitals. When I look at myself I always see a bump. It does not look feminine.… Other women don't have a bump. It's too much. I try to hide it. It doesn't look feminine enough. I feel humiliated not having a penis and not having an adequate vagina.…

A. Your vagina, your labia, and your clitoral bump are not adequate?

P. Labia and vagina are fine. I don't know all these words. It's all unclear to me, what's what. I'm the one who keeps it unclear. I touch the bump and it's like a penis, a not adequate penis, and then my vagina is not adequate.

A. You can't feel good about whatever you have.

P. I remember when I was a young girl and I dressed up and my Dad took me out. That felt good. [She then recalled childhood memories of feeling ashamed of her genitals.]

In a following hour, Ms. T. began questioning her professional and interpersonal capacities.

P. I'm anxious about my adequacy. I have talked before about the adequacy of my female genitals. Yesterday I looked at myself and was embarrassed. If I had a boyfriend, would he be pleased or would I disappoint him?

A. What did you see?

P. A bump, a bump protruding. It's inadequate, not feminine … I notice now how large my hips are … I like that, but I wish I didn't care. I don't like the fact that larger is more feminine.

A. Larger genitals, larger clitoris, is not more feminine?

P. It pushes out, like a penis.

A. If you have something, it must be a penis. It can't be feminine. If it is more than other women have, it must be masculine.

P. I believe men prefer voluptuously big women.

A. And so with your genitals, you can't look at yourself as more femininely developed.

P. I worry that I will disappoint a boyfriend. I enjoy telling my father, not my mother, about my dates. My mother seemed especially distant last night, and I asked if she was okay. She's not happy with her job, and I love working at the newspaper. I felt I was hurting her feelings by telling her of my happiness. I don't want to lose her.

A. Especially to your success.

On one level, Ms. T.'s fantasy of the "bump" is an expression that something is "wrong" with her genital. She feels defective and wishes for a penis. Ms. T.'s inaccurate naming of the clitoris as a "bump" appears to reflect her belief that this pleasurable organ is "unfeminine" (Lerner, 1976, p. 270).

In this vignette, the analyst listened to the patient's associations with an ear toward the material that "penis envy" might be keeping obscure. Rather than assist Ms. T. in accepting her lot in life as a "castrated man" and her ineffectual pursuit for compensation, the analytic work moved toward uncovering the layers of her experience.

In the second hour the analyst interpreted the defensive nature of Ms. T.'s penis envy. After Ms. T. had stated her belief that men prefer "voluptuously big" women, the analyst pointed out that Ms. T. cannot seem to look at herself as femininely developed. The threat of her oedipal longings emerged both in displacements and more directly (Richards, 1996; Shaw, 1995). Shaw writes, "… resolution of … symptoms … hinged on an integrated understanding of the ways … [the patient's] … sense of genital damage not only expressed her phallic envy … but also defended against her guilt and anxiety about having a pleasurable and valued genital that could be aroused and penetrated …" (p. 325). Ms. T.'s wishes to gain her father's love and usurp her mother's place were accompanied by fears of losing her mother.

For Ms. T. there is an uncertainty about the nature of her genitalia. The fantasy of the bump is a symptom that substitutes for a piece of disavowed reality. Bass (1991) notes, "The study of disavowal continually demonstrates a partial detachment from reality marked by a non-synthesizeable oscillation between absence and presence" (p. 322). Ms. T.'s bump fantasy represents a regression from the acknowledgment of anatomical differences between the sexes. It keeps alive her omnipotent wish to be both male and female (Fast, 1979; Kubie, 1974), and thereby contributes to her "worry about being sexy, strong, and hurtful." By labeling the genitalia, the analyst interfered with the patient's omnipotent wish. Yet, in spite of the analyst's intervention, Ms. T. was invested in maintaining her disavowal of the reality of anatomical differences: "I don't know all these words. It's all unclear. … I'm the one who keeps it unclear."

Earlier in the work, the analyst had been frustrated with the immobility of the patient's "penis envy" construction. Exploration of the patient's defensive use of penis envy facilitated the patient's awareness of both oedipal strivings and fantasies of omnipotence.

DISCUSSION

The identification of the lag between theory and clinical practice raises questions. Why has there been such a tenacious lag? Once participants in this study recognized the problematic position they had maintained, how did the group facilitate their new integration of theory and practice? And what are the technical implications of this shift?

The persistence of the lag arises from powerful identifications that shape psychoanalytic thinking. While Freud's "masculine" perspective about the female body and experience has been disputed, his ideas about feminine development have been a mainstay in the identity of psychoanalysts. Not only do analysts have strong identifications with Freud, but also with their personal analysts and clinical supervisors. It is difficult to scrutinize and revamp these highly invested ideas without intensive self-examination. Through discussion of the literature and clinical material, the group project facilitated this process. It is persuasion of a scientific community that produces changes in its tenets and language (Kuhn, 1964).

The reification of Freud's phallocentric theory (a boy's version of femininity characterized by the absence of a penis) may have occurred because it lessens anxiety about anatomical differences for analysts and patients of both sexes (Bass, 1991; Bernheimer, 1991; Young-Bruehl, 1994). Bass (1991) points out, "The unacceptable reality is not the absence of the penis, but the genital distinction" (p. 313). Indeed, both Bass and Bernheimer argue that the psychoanalytic theory of female development based on the phallic castration complex "disavows" sexual differences and therefore functions as a fetish. The fetishist's "fundamental fear is that women are intolerably, uncannily other" (Bernheimer, 1991, p. 3). To enable the female analysand to come to terms with what she "has" and "has not" requires the analyst and patient to lift the fetishistic veil hiding her mental representations and conflicts about her genitalia.[5]We observed our patients' tendencies to form explanations in very concrete terms. Upon reflection, we realized it had been easy to join them in this kind of literalism to reduce complex layers of material to a traditional view of penis envy and the castration complex. In exploring the female's sexual fantasies and conflicts, we were aware of the temptation for analysts to overlook Waelder's (1936) principle of multiple function as well as the principle of synecdoche (Sharpe, 1937).[6] In addition, the analyst can lose sight of the idea that images and metaphors have many meanings (Grossman and Stewart, 1976), and that body images can become embedded in the context of object relations, which appear in psychoanalyses as transferences.We wondered whether our reluctance to give up relying on penis envy interventions might be because this focus can function as a phallic equivalent with its clear, penetrating interpretations. Our struggle to allow space for a new theory seemed to echo our female analysands' difficulty opening their minds to the discovery of a feminine space. Young-Bruehl (1994) notes that there is a tendency to choose either "feminine" or "masculine" to describe particular images or fantasies (p. 390). In adding a lens of primary femininity through which to view the patient's material, we were cognizant of the danger of substituting a feminine theory for a masculine theory. Young-Bruehl cautions, "If Freudian psychoanalysis is phallocentric, any theory aimed at correcting for its bias runs the risk of bias in the opposite direction, a compensatory bias" (p. 384). We were also aware that just as a phallocentric theory might influence the patient's material, so might a primary femininity perspective, especially if the analyst were riveted to this position.

---

5 Many societies show evidence of difficulty in acknowledging girls and women as sexual beings with female fantasies and conflicts. Resistance to seeing and accepting anatomical differences between the sexes is reflected in such religious and cultural practices as the hiding and covering of women, especially their heads and hair.

6 The part stands for the whole.

How did the group facilitate a shift in our thinking? Once research participants became convinced of the considerable lag between current theory and their clinical practice, the group functioned to encourage experimentation and confront resistance. Similar to our work with patients, we challenged each others' reluctance to exploring material relating to primary femininity, i.e., to "looking," acknowledging, and giving words to "what was there." We interpreted the ways that one or another of us seemed "fixed" on an idea or avoided hearing something. The group supported disclosure in a nonjudgmental way. As we gradually integrated concepts of primary femininity along with the paradigm of penis envy and the phallic castration complex, the group offered new ego ideals and alternative identifications. The study also stimulated further self-analysis, for investigating female psychology was as important personally as it was clinically and professionally to this group of women analysts.

This paper demonstrates the value of drawing on the theoretical constructs of primary femininity, as well as of penis envy and the phallic castration complex. In each case presented, the analyst's shift in focus to a primary femininity perspective facilitated the emergence of oedipal themes that had previously remained unanalyzable. This approach also elicited memories and fantasies of early body experiences and early object relations in the transference. In the work with Ms. Q., the transference intensified as the analyst began to use her thinking about primary femininity. There was a struggle (i.e., the analyst's "bossiness") over who would yield to whom, who would provide the feminine holding space. The analyst's acceptance of the patient's criticism enabled Ms. Q. to reveal more of her anxiety about sharing her "splendid isolation." Ms. T. had been caught in an impasse formerly understood as intractable penis envy. With the added dimension of primary femininity, the analyst was able to hear the more complex situation of her oedipal conflicts as well as the primitive confusion about her genitalia.

By naming the female genitalia the analyst addressed each patient's defense of disavowal, and as Lerner (1976) suggests, gave the patient permission to "look," to elaborate on mental representations and fantasies about "what she does have." This labeling may also have facilitated the patient's capacity to lift into consciousness formerly repressed representations and fantasies about her genitals. Freud (1915) states that "a presentation which is not put into words ... remains therefore in the *Ucs.* in a state of repression" (p. 202). In *The Words to Say It*, an autobiographical account of her analysis, Cardinal (1983) recognizes the importance of words for bringing into consciousness and claiming "unnamed" parts of her body.[7] The analyst's words enabled Ms. Q. to gain access to heretofore hidden fantasies about her female anatomy. The analyst's naming of the genitals led Ms. T. to renewed efforts to disavow delineation of her female parts in order to maintain a fantasy of being both male and female. Participant analysts observed a tendency to make more active and challenging interventions when exploring issues of gender identity and sexuality with their female analysands. At times patients felt directed and pursued. They often appeared startled by the analyst's labeling of the female genitalia, and occasionally experienced this naming as seductive, thereby heightening the homosexual transference. The analyst's increased activity may reflect an eagerness to correct an earlier, masculine bias. As analysts more fully integrate concepts of primary femininity along with penis envy, there may be a decrease in the level of activity, as well as a refinement of interventions to encourage patients to oscillate more freely between perspectives.

---

7 Referring to her anus, she writes, "Then I understood therewas an entire area of the body which I had never accepted and which somehow, never belonged to me. The zone between my legs could be only expressed in shameful words and had never been the object of my conscious thought" (p. 240).

CONCLUSION

The findings of this study demonstrate the usefulness of expanding the analyst's listening to include two theoretical paradigms: penis envy and the phallic castration complex, and primary femininity and its derivatives. All psychoanalysts face the challenge of integrating new ideas into technique each time they read or hear a stimulating paper, receive consultation, or develop new insights. Relinquishing the narrow view of penis envy as "bedrock" and the traditional understanding of the phallic castration complex enables the analyst to gain a more analytic stance from which to explore the metaphoric and defensive layers of the patient's material. While patients were often surprised by the change in focus, several analytic impasses were broken, demonstrating that penis envy is not "bedrock." The idea that something, anything, can be "bedrock" and therefore unanalyzable is essentially unanalytic. We join writers such as Grossman and Kaplan (1988) in stressing that clinical work be grounded in technical concepts that are psychoanalytic in nature. The recognition of the ever unfolding and multilayered vicissitudes of compromise formations is as essential to understanding female sexuality as it is to all psychoanalytic discovery.

REFERENCES

Abraham, H.C. Freud, E.L., Eds. (1965). *A Psycho-Analytic Dialogue. The Letters of Sigmund Freud and Karl Abraham 1907–1926*. New York: Basic Books.

Barnett, M.C. (1966). Vaginal awareness in the infancy and childhood of girls. *J. Am. Psychoanal. Assoc.*, 14:*129–141*.

Bass, A. (1991). Fetishism, reality, and The Snow Man. *Amer. Imago*, 48: *295–328*.

———— 1994). Aspects of urethrality in women. *Psychoanal. Q.*, 63:*491–517*.

Bernheimer, C. (1991). Castration as fetish. *Paragraph*,14:*1–9*.

Bernstein, D. (1990). Female genital anxieties, conflicts and typical mastery modes. *Int. J. Psychoanal.*, 71:*151–165*.

Brierley, M. (1932). Some problems of integration in women. *Int. J. Psychoanal.*, 13:*433–448*.

Cardinal, L. (1983). *The Words to Say It.* Cambridge, MA: Van Vactor Goodheart.

Deutsch, H. (1930). The significance of masochism in the mental life of women. *Int. J. Psychoanal.*, 9:*48–60*.

Erikson, E.H. (1950). *Childhood and Society.* New York: Norton.

———— (1974). Once more the inner space: letter to a former student. In *Women and Analysis*, ed. J. Strouse. New York: Grossman.

Fast, I. (1979). Developments in gender identity: gender differentiation in girls. *Int. J. Psychoanal.*, 60:*443–453*.

Freud, S. (1915). The unconscious. *S.E.*, 14.

———— 1923). The ego and the id. *S.E.*, 19.

———— 1925). Some psychical consequences of the anatomical distinction between the sexes. *S.E.*, 19. Freud, S.(1931). Female sexuality. *S.E.*, 21.

———— 1933). Femininity. *S.E.*, 22.

———— (1937). Analysis terminable and interminable. *S.E.*, 23.

Galenson, E. & Roiphe, H. (1976). Some suggested revisions concerning early female development. *J. Am. Psychoanal. Assoc.*, 24(Suppl.).:*29–57*.

Grossman, W.I. & Kaplan, D.M. (1988). Three commentaries on gender in Freud's thought: a prologue to the psychoanalytic theory of sexuality. In *Fantasy, Myth, and Reality: Essays in Honor of Jacob A Arlow, MD*, ed. H.P. Blum, Y. Kramer, A.K. Richards A.D. Richards. New York: Int. Univ. Press, 1990, pp. *339–370*.

———— Kaplan, D.M.& Stewart, W.A. (1976). Penis envy: from childhood wish to developmental metaphor. *J. Am. Psychoanal. Assoc.*, 24:*193–212*.

Horney, K. (1924). On the genesis of the castration complex in women. *Int. J. Psychoanal.*, 5:50–65.

Horney, K.(1926). The flight from womanhood. *Int. J. Psychoanal.*, 7:324–339.

Jones, E. (1927). The early development of female sexuality. *Int. J. Psychoanal.*, 8:438–451.

Kalinich, L.J. (1993). On the sense of absence: a perspective on womanly issues. *Psychoanal. Q.*, 62:206–228.

Kestenberg, J. (1982). The inner-genital phase prephallic and preoedipal. In *Early Female Development: Current Psychoanalytic Views*, ed. D. Mendell. New York: Spectrum.

Klein, M. (1928). Early stages of the Oedipus complex. *Int. J. Psychoanal.*, 9:167–180.

Krausz, R. (1994). The invisible woman. *Int. J. Psychoanal.*, 75:59–72.

Kubie, L.S. (1974). The drive to become both sexes. *Psychoanal. Q.*, 43:349–426.

Kuhn, T. (1964). *The Structure of Scientific Revolutions*. Chicago: Univ. Chicago Press, 1970.

Kulish, N.M. (1991). The mental representation of the clitoris: the fear of female sexuality. *Psychoanal. Inq.*, 11:511–536.

Lax, R. (1994). Aspects of primary and secondary genital feelings and anxieties in girls during the preoedipal and early oedipal phases. *Psychoanal. Q.*, 63:271–296.

Lerner, H. (1976). Parental mislabeling of female genitals as a determinant of penis envy and learning in women. *J. Am. Psychoanal. Assoc.*, 24:269-283.

Mayer, E.L. (1991). Towers and enclosed spaces: a preliminary report on gender differences in children's reactions to block structures. *Psychoanal. Inq.*, 11:480–510.

———— (1995). The phallic castration complex and primary femininity: paired developmental lines toward female gender identity. *J. Am. Psychoanal. Assoc.*, 43:*17–38*.

Muller, J. (1932). A contribution to the problem of libidinal development of the genital phase in girls. *Int. J. Psychoanal.*, 13:*361–368*.

Muller-Braunschweig, C. (1926). The genesis of the feminine super-ego. *Int. J. Psychoanal.*, 7:*359–365*.

Richards, A.K. (1992). The influence of sphincter control and genital sensation on body image and gender identity in women. *Psychoanal. Q.*, 61:*331–351*.

———— (1996). Primary femininity and female genital anxiety. *J. Am. Psychoanal. Assoc.*, 44(Supp.).:261–281.

Ritvo, L.B. (1965). Darwin as the source of Freud's neo-Lamarckianism. *J. Am. Psychoanal. Assoc.*, 13:*499–517*.

Sharpe, E.F. (1937). Dream Analysis. New York: Brunner/Mazel, 1978.

Shaw, R.R. (1995). Female genital anxieties: an integration of new and old ideas. *J. Clin. Psychoanal.*, 4: *297–314*.

Stoller, R.J. (1976). Primary femininity. *J. Am. Psychoanal. Assoc.*, 24(Suppl.).: 59–78.

Tyson, P. (1994). Bedrock and beyond: an examination of the clinical utility of contemporary theories of female psychology. *J. Am. Psychoanal. Assoc.*, 42:*447–467*.

Waelder, R. (1936). The principle of multiple function. In *Psychoanalysis: Observation, Theory, Application*, ed. S.A. Guttman. New York: Int. Univ. Press, 1976, pp. *65–80*.

Wilkinson, S.M. (1991). Penis envy: libidinal metaphor and experiential metonym. *Int. J. Psychoanal.*, 72:*335–346*.

Young- Bruehl, E. (1994). What theories women want. *Amer. Imago*, 51: *373–396*.

CHAPTER 16

Into the Second Century: One Theory or Many? The Fit between Practice and Theory; Introduction to L. Rangell's Presentation

Journal of Clinical Psychoanalysis 6:461–464.
See below, p. 28 in this volume.

In today's world Freudian psychoanalysis has come under serious question both in regard to its therapeutic usefulness and its validity as a theory of human psychology. Its value is questioned even as the numbers who practice its tenets and the numbers who benefit from them both increase. There is great pressure from a society in which "quicker and cheaper" supplant "careful and long lasting." There is pressure to match from the mental health community. Within our own psychoanalytic community, the pressures seem no less. The currently proliferating schools of thought provide for some a wealth of possibility, but for many others, a sense of confusion about which path to follow.

We are coming to the end of our first century. The New York Freudian Society has a continuing intent to examine our intellectual base as it relates to our clinical work. We state in our *Bulletin* the following:

The New York Freudian Society and Psychoanalytic Training Institute was founded in 1959 to provide training and a collegial community for psychoanalysts from many disciplines. Since 1993, the Society has been a Component Society of the International

Psychoanalytical Association. Its purposes are two-fold: first, to offer those who are qualified an opportunity to belong to, and participate in, an active institutional structure, and second, to offer those who are qualified the opportunity for psychoanalytic study. The Institute, sponsored by the Society, offers a full course of training in adult, child, and adolescent psychoanalysis.

Committed to the basic principles of Freud's profound discoveries, we identify ourselves in an historical context that began with that revolution in the understanding of the human mind and that continues in a creative and productive evolution. We are working together to contribute to that evolution by our participation in the psychoanalytic movement, responsive to the need always to value, refine, increase, and share our intellectual inheritance.

We believe that an effective professional life is dependent upon a vital spirit of inquiry, stimulated by the exchange of experience, insight, and ideas. It is in the implementation of that belief that the Society and Institute find their substance [Foreword].

This conference is designed to give us two separate but related opportunities. The first, to listen to the words of one of the most distinguished of our seminal thinkers in Freudian psychoanalysis, Dr. Leo Rangell, as he shares with us his perspective acquired over more than fifty years of observation and participation in the psychoanalytic enterprise.

Following Dr. Rangell's presentation, we will have the pleasure of hearing a discussion of his paper by Professor Charles Hanly, familiar as one of the strongest proponents in the IPA for the welcoming of independent institutes from North America into the IPA.

In the second part of the program we will have the opportunity to hear three stellar psychoanalysts, each distinguishing themselves among the newer generation of important thinkers in the Freudian tradition: Drs. Hanly, Gail Reed, and Owen Renik.

They will give us clinical material from their own practices. Their work will showcase a range of technical approaches about which Dr. Rangell will then comment. His assessment will let us hear his understanding of these cases through the filter of his theory. We will then be treated to a dialogue among the panelists, and between the panelists and the audience.

For a moment, let us return to Dr. Rangell's theoretical point of view. Dr. Rangell has published very many articles and books in which he has developed his line of thinking (see full bibliography at the end of this issue). The breadth of his reach in articulating Freudian theory and charting new areas within that basic frame is astonishing. He has combined a dedication to the principles developed by Freud and his successors with a steady advancement of the boundaries of the theory. In particular, he has emphasized unconscious processes, the structural model, the ego psychology of Hartmann and Rapaport, the technical approach of Fenichel, and at the center of all, a focus on intrapsychic conflict and the role of anxiety.

In some instances, Rangell has created further clarification of existing theory, as for example, in his integration and unification of Freud's first and second theories of anxiety (1955, 1968a). At the same time, ever mindful of his learning from his patients and the process of closely observing clinical data, he has continually added new and original conceptualizations, such as his early, brilliant description and delineation of the psychology of poise (1954a), and his later systematic development of a theory of action (1989) within the structural model.

Rangell has studied the individual not only in his inner states but in his interpersonal social milieu as well. Within the individual, he has described an ongoing "unconscious intrapsychic process" (1969a), within which he demonstrates a complex sequence involving unconscious as well as conscious choice leading to action. In developing that line of thought, he has gone on to describe the "unconscious decision-making function of the ego" (1969b, 1971a) as a central ego activity. Turning to the functioning of the superego, Rangell, from his studies of group phenomena, has made the original contribution of "the syndrome of the compromise of integrity" (1974), which he regards as being as ubiquitous as neuroses in human life. Stressing the question of autonomy, Rangell pursues thorny and critical issues not often the fare of psychoanalytic study, such as the relative freedom of ego will (1986), and from these the problems of integrity and responsibility in human behavior.

Dr. Rangell has twice been the President of the International Psychoanalytical Association and twice the President of the American Psychoanalytic Association, five years apart. He is Clinical Professor of Psychiatry at UCLA, and Clinical Professor of Psychiatry (Psychoanalysis) at UC San Francisco. He has been awarded every prize to be won within the psychoanalytic spectrum.

And now, it is with great pleasure and respect that I introduce the distinguished Dr. Leo Rangell.

REFERENCES

New York Freudian Society and Psychoanalytic Training Institute (1996–1997), *Bulletin*, Foreword.

Rangell, L. (1954). The psychology of Poise—with a special elaboration on the psychic significance of the snout or perioral region. *Int. J. Psa*, 35:313–32.

———— (1955) On the psychoanalytic theory of anxiety—a statement of a unitary theory. *J. Amer. Psa. Asso.*, 3:389-414.

———— (1968). A further attempt to resolve the "Problem of Anxiety". *J. Amer. Psa. Asso.*, 16:371–404

———— (1969). A Choice-Conflict and the decision-making function of the ego: A psycho-analytic contribution to decision theory. *Int. J. Psa.*, 50:599-602, and ibid (1971) *Psa. Study of the Child*, 26:425–452.

———— (1969). The intrapsychic process and its analysis—recent line of thought and its current implications. *Int. J. Psa.*, 50:65–77.

———— (1974). A psychoanalytic perspective leading currently to the syndrome of the compromise of integrity. *Int. J. Psa.*, 55:1–12.

———— (1986). The executive functions of the ego—an extension of the concept of ego autonomy. *Psa. Study of the Child*, 41:1–37.

CHAPTER 17

The Dynamic Surface of Psychic Realities in The Psychoanalytic Situation: Implications For Technique

With Nancy R. Goodman, PhD.(both senior authors)
Presented at IPA Congress, July 27, 1999.

Abstract: Current views of the analytic surface are considered and expanded to capture the concept of a dynamic surface. The authors propose utilizing the dynamic surface to acknowledge the ever-changing movement and flow of the psychic reality that is occurring in the psychoanalytic dyad during the psychoanalytic process. The authors also maintain the continued value of retaining the more static idea of analytic surface to mark what occurs at particular moments in the analytic space.

The paper includes a selected review of the literature from Freud's coining of the term, surface, to more current applications. Clinical material is presented along with an assessment of that material, highlighting the flow that occurs as analyst and analysand work. A discussion follows to consider the questions raised. By proposing the idea of the dynamic surface, the authors invite the development of a new paradigm for tracking the continual unfolding of fantasy derivatives in a shifting series of compromise formations. Implications for technique are considered.

INTRODUCTION

This paper explores a conceptualization of the "dynamic surface" to augment the historical term, analytic surface, with special focus on the understanding of what takes place in the psychoanalytic dialogue. Mindful that the analytic aim is to alleviate the patient's suffering through analytic understanding, this paper examines the dynamic surface in the interaction of the analytic dyad, as the vehicle to that goal. The interaction is attended for its properties in influencing the uncovering of the psychic reality of the patient.

Concentration on the shifts in direction and depth that occur as analyst and analysand speak invites the construction of a new paradigm (Kuhn, 1962) with implications for the study of and theory building about psychoanalytic technique. The dynamic surface is envisioned as a shifting panoply of multiply determined phenomena which evolve in the psychoanalytic situation. Out of a fluid ever-changing flow, particular surfaces form and appear for momentary analytic attention. Any particular surface is embedded in the dynamic surface and is invariably connected to other surfaces which will move into positions of attention as the analysis, and even the session, progresses.

Clinical material is used to clarify the way the dynamic surface functions. Each analyst/analysand pair tends to enter the communication field with certain patterns that create distinctive surfaces and eventually gravitate toward inclusion of aspects of the material that other couples might have chosen in a different sequence. A variety of surfaces are contained in patient's material at any moment; and depending on the analytic dyad, a particular aspect becomes selected for focus. The authors' sense is that some overlapping number of analysts would arrive at a similar set of core fantasies, whatever their selected route.

LITERATURE REVIEW

Surface is an old concept in psychoanalytic thought. Freud referred to the surface many times in his writings. Indeed, Guttman's Concordance lists 91 references to it in the Standard Edition (Paniagua, 1991). Freud used the term primarily in connection with the topographical theory (Freud, 1900), which divided the mind into the systems Conscious, Preconscious, and Unconscious. Freud most frequently referred to the surface to distinguish the patient's conscious awareness from that which was unavailable in the unconscious. The surface was recognized to be continuously shaped by the unconscious forces pushing forward from the deeper layers of the psyche.

Fenichel brought the idea into the realm of technique and into the arena of the dialogue occurring between analyst and analysand when he recommended that "[O] ne should always start the interpretation at the surface" (1941, p. 44). The metaphoric imagery involves a picture of the topographic model with layers of hidden and forbidden knowledge rising to the surface. Although this advice became embedded in the teachings of analytic technique, the concept remained unexplored in the literature. For example, a review of the literature from 1920-1986 (Mosher, 1987) yielded only two references, one in 1974 and the other in 1985 that dealt with the idea of surface.

In the past few years, however, there has been a renewed interest in application of the concept, surface, to understanding elements of the analytic situation. Paniagua (1991) postulates that there is not in fact "one" surface at play in analysis; but rather, there are three: the patient's surface, the clinical surface, and the workable surface. The patient's surface refers to aspects of the patient's presentation that are conscious to him or her. The clinical surface is what the analyst sees.

Paniagua defines the clinical surface as a combination of both objective, observable perceptions about which fairly consensual agreement could be reached by similarly trained analysts and also attribution of meanings to those perceptions.He considers the workable surface to be that aspect of the clinical surface that is accessible to the patient.

It is the workable surface where Paniagua proposes that the active, interpretive process actually takes place. Presumably, the workable surface is the part of the material close enough to the patient's surface to be acceptable to the patient's apperceptions.

In another recent paper, Levy and Interbitzen (1990) point out that theoretical orientation may have an impact on technical approaches. These theoretical leanings function as "different analytic surfaces that can orient the analyst in his listening and intervening" (pp. 374-375). The theoretically defined surfaces of Merton Gill (the transference), Paul Gray (the defensive), Anton Kris (continuity of thought and affect), and Evelyne Schwaber (careful empathic attunement) are described. Each of the analysts mentioned makes intervention choices influenced by the way their theory organizes perception of analytic material and analytic surfaces.

These articles have essentially used surface as a dimension of the psychoanalytic situation or to indicate a place in the patient's psyche which is identified by the analyst as a useful place for directing analytic interventions.

Poland (1992) takes the concept of surface into the realm of the dyad viewing the communication system in the analytic space as one created by analyst and analysand. To Poland, "the surface [is] an artificial aspect of the unitary living phenomenon" (p. 385), and "…refers to the variegated, that is diverse and multicolored, alive and shifting, multiple-meaninged and multiple-leveled boundaries of the uniquely analytic dyadic engagement" (p. 384).

In this view, the concept of the surface of the patient's mind is enveloped within a concept that includes the mind of the analyst as well, calling it (after Viderman, 1974), the analytic space.

Spence, et al. (1994) conduct research attempting to monitor activity occurring in the analytic space. To these authors, the analytic surface becomes "manifest material," and the analytic space becomes the location in which the analytic work is done. The analytic space may be "entered" and at times "shared" by the two participants, analyst and analysand, and also not entered and not shared.

CLINICAL MATERIAL

The authors' goal in presenting clinical material is to demonstrate the dynamic surface as it evolves between analyst and analysand. Over a number of weeks, a female analysand, Susan, talked about her difficulties finding chairs that were just right for her. In preceding sessions, she had been speaking of conflicts as a child around room-sharing with her sister in particular, they had fought over who got to use various surfaces such as the dresser top, the desk, and the floor space. The genetic material had led to her expression of similar transference concerns with her analyst. The topic of this hour, the chairs, was multiply determined with layers of id, ego, and superego derivatives (Waelder, 1936). The vignette provides an example of the way in which the analyst and analysand attend to some of these derivatives as they work in the analytic space they create.

Session:

Susan, a 23-year-old graduate student, introduced the topic of the chairs with a description of a conversation with her mother who had seen chairs she was sure Susan would like. Susan did not like them and spoke for awhile of her difficulty disagreeing with her mother and saying "no" to her.

At a pause, the analyst used some of the analysand's language in commenting: "It feels too much to let your mother know your taste is different." Following the analyst's comment, the patient filled out an imagined picture of her mother's hurt and feelings of deprivation if she were to disagree and respond truthfully.

Susan presented further examples of encounters in which she did not speak up and eventually wondered if her analyst was hating listening to these details.

The analyst responded with a transference interpretation. "You wonder if I am interested in knowing what you truly think, what your taste for details is?" The patient moved on to speak of a feeling of being aimless, particularly in her search for the dining room chairs.

She proclaimed with real feeling her frustration, "What I'd like to say is: How come the stupid world does not make chairs I like?"

The analyst repeated her statement, and Susan continued describing the disappointing chairs and her determination to find what she wants

The analyst asked "And, what is the image of what you are wanting?"

Susan: "Tall chairs, not curvy or round or short, and I'll never find exactly what I want, and no one can help find them, [deep sigh] so I look at things and I try to convince myself I like them but I don't."

After replying with "mmmms" to the patient's sound of pain and frustration, the analyst stated: "And this is a familiar feeling for you?"

Susan: "Yes, it is," recalling occasions of shopping and of receiving presents as a child and a feeling of being cheated. She then wondered if the analyst found her and her concerns silly.

Analyst: "I wonder if you are worried that I could not understand your painful disappointment and frustration; perhaps you're wondering if my understanding will never be quite right, like the chairs."

When asked, the analyst described her own style in this session as unique in some ways to this patient and in other ways typical of the analyst's patterns of attention to flow of associations, affect, and transference images. When going over the session, the analyst became aware of how she and Susan had developed a way of working together with Susan's concrete, reality-bound stories. The patient introduces material in this way, eventually allowing the emergence of newly conscious ideas and affects.

Indeed, this particular session was followed by analyst and analysand continuing to move to other images, wishes, and fears interconnected to the story of the chairs.

OBSERVING THE FLOW OF THE DYNAMIC SURFACE

The authors' goal is to illustrate the path of the dynamic surface by describing the way the analyst and patient move through this session. The patient brings in a topic, the chairs, as she tells her analyst about a conversation with her mother. The analyst makes a clarification inviting the patient to stay with the imagery. The effect is to deepen the patient's fantasy activity, as she imagines her mother's hurt. The patient spontaneously shifts to an expression of transference concern. The analyst then follows with a transference interpretation.

All of these moves bring the patient to express greater affect in reports of painful aimlessness. Again, the analyst reflects back the patient's words, at which point the patient presents a new affect, her relentless persistence. The analyst then selects one element to investigate further, the image of the object of Susan's search. In turn, the patient provides a more vivid fantasy and deepening of painful affect. The analyst shows affect of her own (the "mmmm's") and follows with a question inviting genetic material. As she elaborates the memories, the patient shifts back to the transference leading her to wonder if her analyst finds her silly. The analyst again stays with her patient's shift interpreting derivatives of the fantasy now developing in the transference.

Standing back somewhat further, more theoretical descriptions can be made. The patient and analyst are working to elaborate features of fantasy derivatives with increased clarity, and with the patient experiencing more affect and more here-and-now awareness of the transference. Each member of the dyad, consciously and unconsciously, activates shifts and responds to shifts. At times the patient puts a spotlight on a particular image, theme, or affect; and at times, the analyst does so. Etchegoyen (1991) likens this process of interpreting to the process of hypothesis construction, data collection, and further hypothesis adjustment. Both experience near and theoretical descriptions of the session speak to movement.

The path of the dynamic surface develops as both analyst and analysand respond to internal pressures and aspects of the other's speaking. The patient presents a flow of associations manifesting elements of her dynamic psychic constructions. The analyst chooses some element on which to focus, that choice determined by many factors including hypotheses about the patient's conflicts, favored theoretical conceptualizations, style, and activated unconscious pressures. In response, the patient reveals more of the components of the active compromise formations. It is the interpenetrating mutuality of responses which allows the patient's psychic reality to present itself for reflection and working through.

DISCUSSION

We have defined the dynamic surface as an everchanging multiply determined entity which evolves over time. Within the flow of the dynamic surface one may focus on particular surfaces delimited within specific periods of time or on types of surfaces making up the entity. Various psychoanalytic models are helpful for labeling these specific surfaces. For example, the structural model (Freud, 1923) and the proposition of multiple function (Waelder, 1936) alert us to id, ego, and superego derivatives. The theory of compromise formation (Brenner, 1976) brings our attention to drive-defense and accompanying affects. Preferential surfaces of analysts may be theory related (Levy & Inderbitzen, 1990) or stylistically determined and help identify places of attention.

Gardner (1991) has written how analysts "oscillate," "leap, and "romp" between "poles" of their interests. He writes, "One finding may lead to the other and usually does but never the same way and never with the same accents and rhythms (and the music is always more telling than the words" p. 859). We assert in this paper that learning how to think about the "music" of psychoanalytic work calls for a new paradigm for enhancing the study of technique. A new paradigm invites us to view issues differently. By looking at the topography of the dynamic surface, technique can concentrate on movement and help reveal how fantasy derivatives continually intersect with reality (Arlow, 1969) to create psychic reality. In regard to the analytic dialogue, concentration on movement reveals the path analyst and analysand build together to uncover the patient's psychic reality. Both Poland (1992) in his use of analytic space and Renik (1993) in his explication of intersubjectivity advocate a need to bring theory of technique into concert with the communication system (at all levels of consciousness) of the analytic pair.

Recent research by the Washington, DC Psychoanalytic Research Group (Goodman, et al., 1993) on the analysts' inner experience during moments before speaking studied analysts' patterns of attention. Analysts were found to work along a continuum of consciousness as they sorted through patient associations, their own associations, and the words they spoke to their patients. There was a continual feedback loop of information taking place as analysts caught up with emerging knowledge.

Indeed, Freedman (1994) has postulated that a halt in the usual rhythmicity of analytic attention is an indicator that a 'de-symbolizing' countertransference is occurring and must become a symbolizing counter transference to allow the analysis to progress. A way to detect this unproductive countertransference is to watch for, not particular contents, but for loss of rhythmicity.

Entering a new concept to our already full analytic lexicon may raise the question, why keep the term, surface, and why add the term, dynamic surface. Traditionally, the term, surface, was used to designate the most conscious part of an individual's psyche or a target toward which the analyst directed an intervention. This descriptive use carries an intuitive conviction for patients and analysts alike. As such, the idea of surface as something that becomes available at a particular time has a phenomenological value and seems to resonate with a fantasy about how thoughts and feelings arise. Using surface as location is experientially compelling but lacks explanatory power about why and how it has appeared.

We have defined the dynamic surface as a system of interconnected pressures in which the integral features of change and movement occur over time. Tracking these changes can be put to the task of explaining vicissitudes of the individual psyche and vicissitudes of the analytic dialogue.

Imagine a kaleidoscope. The patterns produced in a kaleidoscope are brought about by movement. We can think about a pattern appearing at any one time, about elements in that pattern, and also about the changes occurring over time. Delimited surfaces are embedded in the flow of change that evolves over time. The kaleidoscope is a metaphor that epitomizes together the dynamic surface and the delineated surfaces within it. Psychoanalytic study of both brings technique closer to the actualities of how analysts and patients work together.

CONCLUSION

The term, surface, has continued to interest analysts because of its intuitive descriptive power and its ability to help identify aspects of the analytic situation. We have chosen to add the word, *dynamic,* to the concept of surface, calling it "the dynamic surface." We put forward this new concept for the following reasons:

"It adds explanatory power to the understanding of the way different surfaces appear at specific times, and it opens us to a new paradigm in which *movement* is the primary data for observation and study. The dynamic surface fits with contemporary thinking about the multitude of motivations which are active at all times in psychic realities. By applying this concept to the psychoanalytic dialogue, theory of technique is expanded to include the variables of change and flow.

REFERENCES

Arlow, J.A. (1969). Unconscious fantasy and disturbances of conscious experience. In *Psychoanalysis: Clinical Theory and Practice,* Madison, CT: Int. Univ. Press.

Brenner, C. (1976). *Psychoanalytic Technique and Psychic Conflict,* Madison, CT: Int. Univ. Press.

Etchegoyen, H. (1991). *The Fundamentals of Psychoanalytic Technique,* London: Karnac Books.

Fenichel, O. (1941). *Problems of Psychoanalytic Technique,* Albany, NY: *Psychoanal. Quarterly.*

Freedman, N. (1994). Discussion of Panel Presentation on how psychoanalysts work: A report of research on the inner experience of the psychoanalytic research instrument. Division 39 of the American Psychological Assn. Spring Meeting, April 15, 1994.

Freud, S. (1900). The Interpretation of Dreams. *S.E.* 4.5. (1923). The ego and the id. *S.E.* 19.

Gardner, M.R. (1991). The art of psychoanalysis: On oscillation and other matters. *J. Amer. Psychoanal. Assn.* 39:851–870.

Goodman, N.R. et al. (1993). In the mind of the psychoanalysis: Capturing the moment before speaking. The 38th Congress of the IPA. Amsterdam.

Kuhn, T.S. (1962). *The Structure of Scientific Revolutions.* Chicago: U. of Chicago Press, 2nd. ed. 1970.

Levy, S.T. & Inderbitzen, L.B. (1990). The analytic surface and the theory of technique. *J. Amer. Psychoanal. Assn.* 38:371–392.

Mosher, P.W., ed. (1987). *Title Key Word and Author Index to Psychoanalytic Journals 1920–1986.* NY Psychoanal. Assn.

Paniagua, C. (1991). Patient's surface, clinical surface, and workable surface. *J. Amer. Psychoanal. Assn.* 39:669–685.

Poland, W. S. (1992). From analytic surface to analytic space. *J. Amer. Psychoanal. Assn.* 40:381–404.

Renik, O. (1993). Analytic interaction: Conceptualizing technique in light of the analyst's irreducible subjectivity. *Psychoanal. Q.* 62:553–571.

Spence, D.P. et al. (1994). Monitoring the analytic surface. *J. Amer. Psychoanal. Assn.,* 42:43–64.

Viderman, S. (1974). Interpretation in the analytic space. *Int. Rev. Psychoanal.* 1:467–480.

Waelder, R. (1936). Principle of multiple function: Observations on over-determination. *Psychoanal. Q.* 5:45-62.

CHAPTER 18

The Riddle of Femininity: The Interplay of Primary Femininity and the Castration Complex in Analytic Listening

Elizabeth Fritsch, Paula Ellman, Harriet Basseches, Susan Elmendorf, Nancy Goodman, Fonya Helm and Shelley Rockwell

(2001). *International Journal of Psycho-Analysis*, 82(6):1171–1182.

This study elucidates the application of an analytic attitude to questions of gender and sexuality. The paper reports on a study group's exploration of the relative heuristic use of two important organizing concepts in analytic work with female analysands: primary femininity and the phallic castration complex. A tendency to cling to one position over the other skews analytic listening. Two cases are presented of women struggling to consolidate positive feminine identifications and, to that end, working through conflicting feminine identifications and defenses against a resolution of the awareness of gender differences. Analytic listening requires a view of each psychic construction as a layer to be understood in its own right yet as a cloak soon to reveal the next layer—a different construction. The study includes observations on perverse fantasies in women.

Theory offers a guide to our analytic listening and yet presents significant obstacles to maintaining an analytic attitude. Freud suggested that the science of psychoanalysis follows from its art. He argued that the analyst must be able to 'swing' from one mental attitude towards another and spoke of the inherent tension between the technique and the research of psychoanalysis (1912, p. 114). Our study group became interested in studying the effects of our theories about female development on our listening. In a previous paper (Basseches et al., 1996), we discussed our discovery of a significant lag between current theories of female sexuality and development and the application of these theories in our work. Despite our intellectual acceptance of contemporary views of female development, we found it difficult to assimilate fully these ideas in the clinical situation. Our study group functioned to facilitate individual members' further integration of theory and practice and to examine how this integration affected our work with patients.

With the implications of primary femininity more in the forefront of our work, we became aware of the problem of substituting a feminine theory for a masculine theory. Young-Bruehl speaks of this danger: 'If Freudian psychoanalysis is phallocentric, any theory aimed at correcting for its bias runs the risk of bias in the opposite direction, a compensation Bass (1994, p. 384).' Mayer has also noted the 'polarity' that can develop as 'current reconsideration of female gender identity … [is] advanced in terms either of the phallic castration complex or of primary femininity' (1995, p. 33). In our previous study we noted a heightened tendency to interject interventions when exploring issues of gender identity and sexuality with female analysands. Our increased activity involved both an eagerness to correct an earlier phallocentric bias and an effort to test out our evolving conjectures.

This earlier work led us to investigate the interplay of primary femininity and the phallic castration complex in our analytic listening. We sought to examine the relative heuristic use of these two organizing concepts in our ongoing analytic work. Clinging to one position over another in an analysis skews analytic listening, where oscillations in material occur, and more importantly where clinical data is layered and the uncovering of one layer serves to reveal the next for further exploration. Using a study group format, we examined the emergence of compromise formations involving primary femininity and those involving the castration complex in the analyses of several female patients.

The study group offers salient advantages for the examination of the analyst's activity. There is an opportunity to sample work with a range of listening styles and activity levels in the analyst as well as with a variety of patients. By introducing multiple clinical perspectives, a group exploration allows scrutiny of material that might otherwise remain embedded in a particular analyst-patient dyad. Schlessinger and Robbins, discussing the advantages of using the continuous case seminar for investigative purposes, observe 'the large number of alternative propositions' that can be subject to group criticism' (1983, p. 26). The group challenges the analyst to elaborate his/her thinking and activity.

Our study group is composed of seven female psychoanalysts who studied and worked together over the course of twelve years. Investigations into the area of female sexuality occurred over a period of three years in which material from the analyses of women were presented to the study group. Additionally, the group studied early and current psychoanalytic writings in the area of female sexuality. These ongoing meetings generated ideas that were subject to further scrutiny and development.

As the study group applied the construct of primary femininity, we questioned whether to focus exclusively on material relating to the patient's body representation (including her representation of her genitals and relative investment in her body) or to expand our enquiry to a consideration of the patient's identifications. Does the term primary femininity refer to a construct of self as female and feminine or to a sense of self specifically derived from her female body? Elise (1997) discusses a number of conceptual complexities in the term primary femininity. She suggests that we differentiate between the sense of femaleness and primary femininity. She argues that we should term the sense of self derived from the female body 'the sense of femaleness' and reserve the term primary femininity to refer to feminine gender identifications and identity. However, she observes, 'a primary sense of femaleness can never in reality be separated from social meanings of gender' (1997, p. 514). We found this separation to be arbitrary and in practice impossible and included a consideration of identifications in our examination of the patient's conflicts about her femaleness. Our discussions of the patients' conflicts over their feminine identifications included not only the early psychic representation of the female body ego and later layering of defenses and compromise formations, but also the later feminine identifications influenced by the developmental disturbances that each patient faced.

LITERATURE REVIEW

'Freud declared…with the wish for a penis … we have … reached bedrock, and thus our activities are at an end … the biological field does in fact play the part of the underlying bedrock' (1937, p. 252). He believed the difficulty that made women unanalyzable was their refusal to give up their wish for the penis. Although Horney (1926) and Jones (1927) wrote of penis envy as a possible defense against oedipal wishes, other early writers wrote of the girl as developing an early female identity and body image based on kinesthetic knowledge of her genital. These writers did not influence mainstream analysts' adherence to Freudian tenets. Only in the 1960s and 1970s did writings on feminine development begin to take hold. Numerous clinicians have described the little girls' early bodily experiences and their awareness of inner and outer genital sensations (Lax, 1994; Richards, 1992; Bass, 1994, Kestenberg, 1982). Psychoanalytic observations of children suggest girls form representations of their inner genital (Erikson, 1950, 1974; Mayer, 1991; Galenson and Roiphe, 1976) and develop uniquely female genital anxieties. Lerner attributes the source of anxiety to failure to create mental representations with correct verbal labelling, giving 'permission' to 'be a sexually operative and responsive female' (1976, p. 270). Other authors emphasize the female genital anxieties in terms of threats to inner space as punishment for libidinal strivings (Kulish, 1991; Lax, 1994, Mayer, 1995; Richards, 1992, 1996).

Attempts have been made to examine the interrelationship that penis envy phenomena have with female genital anxiety. Torok (1970) contends that the penis itself is not involved with penis envy. Lerner asserts that 'it is not the actual or perceived superiority of the penis which leads the girl to envy it, but rather the anxiety-provoking nature of her own genitals that predisposes her towards penis envy' (1988, p. 47). Here envy of the male genital is seen as secondary or defensive to the more primary female genital anxiety.

Other writers bring a broader perspective to clinical phenomena that would have been historically understood as penis envy. Their effort is to integrate feminine identification processes with penis envy and castration complex. Tyson annotates text that initially appears as 'bisexual' analytic material. She asserts that core gender identity is established before the child comes to terms with differences between the sexes. She writes, 'The child tends to identify with aspects of both parents … This follows rather than precedes core gender identity' (1994, p. 455). She moves away from penis envy as a cliched understanding of the patient's sense of inadequacy, and illuminates the contribution of the girl's superego functioning and the effects of the loss of her idealized relationship with her mother. More emphasis is placed on pre-oedipal conflicts over the expression of aggression. Lax (1995) emphasizes the early conflicts in identification processes, the guilt over the identification with forbidden unfeminine character traits that causes a woman to feel unwomanly because of unintegrated mother-father roles.

As early as 1932, Brierley noted, 'it is possible to distinguish two lines or directions of displacement of cathexis, namely, a nipple-penis-faeces-child line and a mouth-anus-vagina line' (p. 435). More recently, Mayer (1995) proposed two perspectives as two developmental lines, each with its own affective mode. She contends that a successful analysis depends on understanding the contributions of both developmental lines. The two developmental tasks for the woman involve her coming to terms with what she is not and has not, and what she is and has. Each is built on its own fantasy of a danger. Mayer suggests that the different affect/defense configurations involve responses to anxiety manifested as inhibition (dynamics of primary femininity), and responses to depressive affect manifested as enactments of wishful fantasy (dynamics of penis envy). She attempts to integrate two perspectives to arrive at a balanced understanding of complicated compromise formations.

CASE STUDIES

In our study, we found that keeping multiple strands of development in our listening led us to focus on a pivotal question: how does the woman come to terms with the differences between the sexes? Our listening became subtly attuned, less either/or, our focus more keenly on the question of fantasies and compromise related to the question of gender. Our work became more aligned with the viewpoint of Grossman and Kaplan who assert that 'a psychoanalysis of sex and gender involves an understanding of the costs and gains of becoming one sex or the other, along with their conflicted ideals of gender' (1988, p. 365). We became impressed by the importance of perverse defenses in working with questions of sex and gender with our female analysands. Two case studies of female patients working with female analysts will be presented to illustrate this development in our work. The cases are both of women who expressed disinterest in an intimate relationship with a man.

CASE 1: MS A

MS A is a 34-year-old, married, professionally successful woman with intense and pervasive somatic preoccupations. Until recently she had expressed little concern with having her own baby or in having an intimate relationship with her husband. Her marriage to an older man with adolescent children was, in part, an attempt to stave off the challenges of adult womanhood; she is competitive with her husband's children and resents his devotion to them. Recently she has become poignantly aware of what she has missed in life because of her self-absorption, a kind of somatic encapsulation. Over the course of the following sessions, Ms A grapples with her conflicts and anxieties regarding her feminine and masculine identities (oedipal conflicts which are imbued with femininity concerns and phallic compensatory fantasies expressed in terms of identificatory processes).

The conscious event which appears to have stirred this sequence was Ms A's observation one evening of a close friend and husband walking by, deeply engrossed with one another. Her friend did not notice her. She intuited that this friend was pregnant, though she had no actual knowledge. Ms A felt envious, jealous, betrayed and outraged at being 'left out and left behind'. Up to this point in the analysis the patient had been remarkably removed from thoughts about becoming a mother or ideas about her analyst as a mother. Now, the pain of imagining her friend's happy marriage and pregnancy was palpable. Her associations included the memory that she could not leave the house while her mother was there: "I felt that I should always sit with her, but then how could she go out dancing, when I'm sitting on the sidelines?" The realisation that her parents 'danced' and left her behind was a distinct break in a fixed idea that she and her mother were merged, stuck in a 'sickbed' together. The shared feminine identity of sickness and impaired functioning of mother-daughter was challenged by her real-life observation and the memory of her mother's dancing.

In the next session, Ms A reported a dream: *she was pregnant but bleeding. The patient wondered: was it minor 'irregular bleeding' or would she lose the pregnancy, and would she be disappointed?* The 'bleeding pregnancy' captures the ambivalence Ms A feels about her stage in life: is she a young girl starting out in her life full of promise or a fully mature woman with her own baby. Her associations included a 'confusion' regarding her identity: is she her father's daughter or wife? She then reported extreme controllingness and denigration towards her husband, perhaps to defend against oedipal anxiety.

Several sessions later, she noted a psychoanalytic journal in the analyst's office. As with the "mother who dances," she felt surprised and shocked. She observed, "Oh, you are a real psychoanalyst." While she felt betrayed and envious, she also expressed relief that the analyst had a life apart from her. Her usual complaints were of a mother who had no life other than her children and her headaches. The next hour, her anxiety heightened; she wondered whether she and the analyst were locked into a 'sickbed grip' (as the analyst did not take the 4 July holiday off), both too sick to go out. At the end of the hour she reported the most disturbing idea, one which 'put her in a tizzy'; she thought of the analyst's 'wonderful secret relationship' with her husband, perhaps a reference to the analyst's upcoming vacation. While the intimacy of the 'parental couple' was agonizing to her, it also permitted her to begin to shift her feminine identity away from devoted sickness and closer to sexual longing.

In the next hour she reported a dream. *She was gripping a fast-moving car; her husband was there but not together with her. Her grip was tenuous, and she ruminated about how to let go.* The analyst interpreted this dream as a reaction to her having felt her grip loosened on the analyst as her 'sickbed mother'.

In the following hour, Ms A reported another dream. *She was instructing a woman, a beautiful assistant and colleague to her husband, how to degrease a brisket with a turkey baster. The woman did not have a baster, went out to get the baster but the store was closing.* The analyst questioned: 'Who was this dumb woman?' Ms A remembered reading and laughing with friends about a woman trying to impregnate herself by squirting sperm into her vagina with a turkey baster. Ms A is contemptuous and triumphant. She is the real woman who knows how to cook. She is more adept at using tools that squirt.

COMMENTARY ON MS A

This analytic sequence demonstrates a forward and backward movement in Ms A's difficult femininity. Her struggles with multiple identifications are the 'stuff' of the conflict between primary femaleness and phallic castration concerns; in these vying identifications we witness the living out of these processes and conflicts. The conflicts are at both a pre-oedipal and oedipal level. Because her feminine identity is imbued with a 'sick mother' much of the analytic work is directed at this distortion, to challenge and separate the more healthy strands from the destructive. Ms A has used her phallic identifications as a defense or haven from this difficult sense of her femaleness. Hence the analyst has the job of holding all three issues in mind: to respond and bring to light both the phallic and primary feminine strands of her identification, but also the distorted elements in relation to her mother which have colored her entire development.

Ms A's observation of her friend's intimacy with her husband and possible pregnancy evoked in her powerful feelings of envy and betrayal as well as emotional and sexual longings. It led to her reporting memories of her mother 'dancing' which challenged her fantasied mental merger with her mother. Similarly in observing the analyst's journal and feeling the upcoming summer break, she allowed herself to imagine a healthy sexual union between husband and wife. This is material for a more nurturing vital femininity. Of course, it is not so simple. In between the observation of friend/mother and analyst is the dream of pregnancy and bleeding, Ms A wonders if she would be disappointed if pregnant and 'irregular bleeding' led to miscarriage. The dream implies a competitive urge, to have what her friend, analyst and mother do, yet even so the 'illness' remains. The term 'irregular' implies that the pregnancy is not normal; perhaps incestuous, alternatively pregnancy experienced as an illness. Normal, feminine life passages become deeply confused for her. After her wedding (five years before) she reported several dreams in which the wedding ceremony was transformed into a bar mitzvah. For Ms A the normal active 'exchange' of intercourse is transformed into illness and undifferentiation. The masculine identification 'rescues' her from her frightening ill maternal and feminine identification. Her inability to imagine her mother's/ friend's/analyst's sexuality also implies an extraordinary claim or possession of the mother and a profound retreat from the oedipal disappointments. At a deep level there is confusion between life and death, good and bad, specifically for Ms A in that illness is 'preferred' over health.

The dream of the next hour gives reason to be hopeful as it provides evidence of psychic change; she reports *a 'tenuous' grip on a fast-moving car and wonders how to let go.* The interpretation—she has loosened her grip on the analyst as her sickbed mother—addresses the ill internalized mother. In the next hour the problem of her triumphant phallic strivings becomes clearer. We see the intertwining of the conflicted femininity and the false phallic solution to her envy of her mother›s success and her feelings of betrayal. In this dream she emerges as the superior cook to her husband's beautiful but stupid assistant: she is 'in the know' about degreasing a brisket.

This old-fashioned dish (one of her mother's favorites) gives away the pathetic nature of her triumph in that it is not truly her own (generation's) creation but a recycled version of her mother›s cooking. Her superior use of the tool, a turkey baster, indicates her use of the phallus as a compensatory illusion supporting her triumph over mother/analyst, dodging the experience of envy, loss and mourning. The turkey baster might also represent the power of the female genital to procreate, an object that women wield in the matriarchal kitchen (Richards, 1998). Her triumph is established on a conglomerate image of herself as of two generations, and as male and female. This dream is a response to the earlier progress in 'loosening'; we see an increased hold on her devitalized femininity. The sad irony is that in 'having it all' she has nothing of real substance or satisfaction.

This sequence offers an instance of the intertwining that takes place in early female development, and the frequent finding in analytic work that our female patients' earliest feminine experience has been developmentally compromised. The clinical sequence is illustrative of the pressures and conflicts involved with achieving a more differentiated level of feminine functioning. As Ms A moves towards more complexity and a more direct experience of her disappointment and pain, she counters this with a myriad of defensive solutions involving an effort to subvert the analytic breakthrough. This clinical example gives witness to the importance of separating and understanding both feminine and phallic contributions to our patients' femininity.

CASE 2: MS Q

Ms Q entered her analysis at the age of 35 with relative professional success. However, she felt very anxious that she might lose her position as an executive assistant to her powerful yet erratic boss. On balance, Ms Q took pleasure in her life. She had many friendships, loved gardening and entertaining, and was affectionately regarded by others. She had not had a serious relationship with a man for many years and expressed no interest in dating. She reported this with a curious blandness.

In the transference with her female analyst, Ms Q developed strongly affectionate feelings for her analyst together with the wish to exclude the analyst's husband. The oldest of five children, the patient had often been in the position of her mother's confidante and chief helper as her father busied himself with his career and frequent business trips. As her analysis progressed the patient became aware of her pleasure in being her mother's companion in her father's absence. She came to recognize the feeling of injury when her father returned at the end of a day or after a trip to his position of household head. She harbored deep resentment about these demotions.

In a session two months into the analysis, Ms Q described her reactions to having taken a parking spot she identified as belonging to her analyst's husband. She had observed his car in another spot and played with the assertion that he had left his space for her. The next day she began her session by noting she had her keys in her pocket, like 'a third leg'. She went on to say she had 'a lot of thoughts. I've been thinking about you. I think you like me and I really like you. I was reading *Psychology Today*. The therapist has to wait one year after ending therapy before dating his patient. Well, we won't date. I was wondering if we would be friends. What got me thinking was the thought that you know me better than I know myself'. She then reported more thoughts after the session the previous evening including the fantasy that the analyst›s husband had gone out to buy pizza for his wife. Then she wondered if her hair dye had left a stain on the couch and was 'tickled' by this thought. After these thoughts, she said, "Why am I noticing everything? It's like I have huge pores. It›s schizophrenia. I just wish I hadn›t had those thoughts last night. They're distracting. I couldn›t figure out why your husband had parked across the street. I know it's behind closed doors."

The analyst said, "It sounds like you felt disappointed as you left your session."

The patient went on, "Why do I worry about these things?"

The analyst interpreted, "You had many questions about your place in your family. Here you took my husband's place but then had to leave. But you held on to a pleasing thought that you had left your mark with your hair dye."

A pivotal point in the analysis occurred two years later when the analyst became pregnant. The patient touched on the possibility of the analyst's pregnancy for several weeks. She let on she knew but let there be an air of doubt about this. She seemed content to toy with the idea. Finally, she asked the analyst to confirm her observation. The patient was able to understand this period of activity as an effort to keep herself from re-experiencing the shock of her mother's pregnancies, a confirmation of her father's sexual link to her mother and furthermore the baby's disruption of her close tie with her mother.

This analytic experience led to Ms Q beginning a relationship with a man. The relationship matured but she felt a deep reluctance to live with him. She described her 'splendid isolation'. She spoke about her pleasure in her home with its museum-quality pieces. The analyst sought to understand more about the meanings of taking a man into her space and the anxieties about being overwhelmed and spoiled by a man. The patient described her fears of sharing her space: "I would get diluted—like having paintings on the wall that are not mine." The patient identified the analyst's interest in her investment in her space and their developing understanding that she sought to protect herself from longings and disappointment for the paternal figure as helpful. She ultimately went on to live with her boyfriend.

COMMENTARY ON MS Q

Ms Q has the fantasy that her analyst's husband left his parking spot for her and that she has a third leg. Ms Q, with her longing to move closer to her analyst and wish to become a friend, has a fantasy of taking the phallic position. Her closeness to the female object includes the fantasy of possessing the penis and being like her father. Her bodily secretions (hair dye) had left a stain and she is stimulated by this thought, she feels 'tickled'.

The analysis takes Ms Q one step beyond her declaration of penis envy. She recognizes the regressive characteristic of her fantasy of taking the husband's place. She says she 'notices everything' and her position vis-à-vis her analyst is 'schizophrenic'. She is aware that, in fact, she is shut out, outside the closed doors of the parental relationship. At the same time this is the reality she struggles to disavow. She acknowledges her effort to not see the analyst's pregnancy, the evidence of the marital relationship. She describes the shock of reality, the shock of the generational reality and the emerging reality of her body's female genitals. She is shocked by the father's sexual link to her mother, the generational reality, and the fact that she is not her mother's partner. The shock is also the gender reality, that men impregnate women and that she, too, is impregnable.

It is in the context of these 'reality shocks' that Ms Q begins to be available as an adult woman for a relationship with an adult man. She is reluctant to give up what she calls her 'splendid isolation'. What is this splendid isolation? She describes her museum-quality pieces and her pleasure in her space. She feels fiercely protective of her space. Just what is she attempting to protect, to stave off? She expresses her identification with her father who enjoyed a splendid isolation from her mother and from her. But her splendid isolation also expresses her female genital anxiety. Richards (1996) categorizes these fears as fear of penetration, fear of loss of pleasure and fear of loss of fertility. In this splendid isolation is a space with her museum-quality pieces: her valuable body parts where there is no space for a man. Here she is protected from her genital anxieties. Within her protected space she may also fantasize a merger with her mother because it is dissipation that she speaks of fearing.

Ms Q is frightened of her own submissive urges to give herself over to a man in the way she gives herself over to her mother. 'I would be diluted … if we lived together. I might sell some of my paintings … Having paintings on the wall that are not me.' She fears the dissolution of her identity. Perhaps it is because of the intention to hold on to both genders that the relationship with a man poses a threat to her self-expression. She consciously thinks she must protect herself from the disappointing man (her father). To admit a man with the hope of gratification nullifies the perverse illusion of no gender and generational differentiation and would open her up to experiencing female genital anxieties.

Ms Q has been able to identify with the healthy ego strengths of her mother and father. She has the capacity in her sturdy identifications to analyze her regression to a negative oedipal compromise formation from oedipal anxiety, including her female genital anxiety and her expression of penis envy. She tries to recognize that she is without the penis, without her mother and the loss that is contained here for her. Her further analysis will entail the loss of the fantasied illusion of closeness with her mother and exclusion of her father yet allow for the gain of a more realistic closeness as an adult woman with an adult man.

DISCUSSION

Freud observed that 'throughout history people have knocked their heads against the riddle of the nature of femininity' (1933, p. 113). Indeed, in current theoretical formulation about the psychological development of females there is a dialectic. Some writers continue to assert the centrality of the phallic castration complex (Brenner, 1982; Rangell, 1991). Another group emphasizes that penis envy is primarily defensive against female genital anxiety (Torok, 1970; Lerner, 1988). In the middle are those who declare that a girl's psychosexual development is feminine and involves components of the phallic castration complex and female genital anxieties (Lax, 1995; Mayer, 1995; Richards, 1996). Our efforts to correct the neglect of anxieties about the female genital and to follow the implications of primary femininity need not exclude the analysis of derivatives of penis envy. But, in practice, how does the analyst proceed?

The clinical material presented here confirms the view that psychic material involving derivatives of penis envy or female genital anxiety has multiple developmental determinants and stems from varying defensive solutions. Penis envy may relate to an effort to merge with the pre-oedipal mother or alternately to a wish to pleasure the oedipal mother. The turn to a wish for a phallus may involve an effort to move away defensively from female genital anxiety involving oedipal level conflicts. And/or it may serve as a protection against the terrors of merger with the pre-oedipal mother. Compromise formations may involve attempted solutions to the terrors of female genital anxiety: of penetration, losing pleasure or losing fertility. The multiplicity of determinants of conflict and the opportunistic use of defenses creates this shifting template of analytic data.

Our study documents our patients' concreteness in their explanations of their bodies. Something is 'deformed' or 'nothing is missing' or 'something is missing'. The analyst may also be tempted to this kind of literalism and reductionism so that the panoply of complex feelings is reduced to a single idea, the phallic castration complex. As we tolerate ambiguity and discern multiple functions in material related to sex and gender, we work with an analytic attitude. Schafer writes, the analytic attitude will be evident in the analyst's making a more modest as well as sounder claim, namely that a point has now been reached in the analytic dialogue where reality must be formulated in a more subtle and complex manner than it has ever been before (1983, p. 8).

Working analytically, we see salient individual differences in our patients. When our approach is grounded in technique that is psychoanalytic, our work does not have a 'one size fits all' quality. The patients Ms A and Ms Q present important contrasts in their relationship to their femininity. Each has significant obstacles to establishing an adult genital relationship. For Ms A, the distorted elements of her early identifications with her mother undercut her interest in a feminine self. There are vitiated elements in her view of femininity, e.g. the fantasy that females are defective or females are disabled. Without clarification of such fantasy the vitality of femininity is sapped. This is consistent with Birksted-Breen's (1996) observation that the phallic attitude, in part, is an escape from the 'frightening feminine'. Birksted-Breen writes that 'the feminine which is felt lacking … is an image of the mother able to find pleasure and value in her own body and able to attract father' (1996, p. 130). By contrast, Ms Q has a strong identification with the positive elements of her mother's femininity. She experienced her mother as able to attract her father and as taking pleasure in her body. It is her defensive effort to protect an isolated feminine space and the disappointment in her father that has limited her development as an adult woman.

As we listened to our female patients keeping both possibilities of the castration complex and anxieties related to fuller feminine functioning in mind, we became more alert to our patients' reluctance to relinquish fantasied triumphs over the realities of gender. Our female patients at times sought a perverse fantasy solution to the untenable reality of sexual differentiation: they disavowed realities that disturbed them and created illusions that obscured the differences between the sexes and generations. Departing from Freud's categorical distinction between perverse and neurotic processes, Grossman (1993) proposes that both 'neurotic' and 'perverse' defenses are commonplace. He suggests that neurotic defenses contend with wishes whereas perverse defenses help the individual avoid the consequences of perception. Grossman agrees that neurotic wishes alter reality and that reality is constantly constructed with neurotic distortion. However, he argues that perverse defense is an effort to disavow a reality that has been registered.

Recognizing this distinction has important consequences for the clinical situation. In Grossman's view, when perverse defenses are operative, the analyst may find it necessary to take a stand with respect to the demands of reality. Also drawing on Freud's late work on fetishism to understand a much wider range of clinical phenomena, Bass (1997) relates the mechanism of disavowal to the difficult work with the 'concrete' patient. The concrete patient creates defensive substitutes to avoid reality. Bass argues that the difficulty of working with the concrete patient is due to the patient's efforts to disrupt the processes of analysis which introduce unacceptable, differentiated realities. Reed, in writing about perverse enactments, discusses the technical requirements in working with patients who rely on disavowal. She suggests focusing on the abrupt shifts away from anxiety to illusion as well as on the patients' efforts to bring the analyst into an aim of maintaining illusions (1997, p. 1177).

One way to understand the development in both analytic cases reported in our study is that the analyses successfully challenged the patients' efforts to establish protective illusions. The telling comment of Ms A, "so you're a real psychoanalyst," revealed her heretofore hidden disavowal of the disturbing realities around her. At this moment in her analysis, she was faced with the shattering of an illusion. Her analyst is a real analyst and, implicitly, a real woman and a real wife and not hers to have. Nor is the analyst able to protect her from the realities that perplex and trouble her as in her observation that pregnant friends have husbands that impregnate them. The fact that Ms A is now making these observations which threaten her somatic encapsulation suggests the analysis is moving and may free her to inhabit a more genitally oriented world.

After Ms A gets closer to a theme of more differentiated female functioning, she has a dream about instructing others as to how to degrease a brisket with a turkey baster. The dream puts forth her wish to be both female and male (Kubie, 1974) as well as a simultaneity of penis envy and female genital anxiety. She cooks beautifully but with a masculine implement, a turkey baster. The dream contains her anxieties over successful feminine functioning as well as her sense of loss and limit about not having a phallus. This dream corresponds to the patient's recurrent dream in which she changes her wedding ceremony into a bar mitzvah.

Ms Q also only gradually comes to terms with the disappointments and untenable aspects of her negative oedipal position. She makes efforts bit by bit to contend with the disappointing, even devastating, realities she encounters in the analysis. She observes that she has a third leg but not the real thing: the analyst's husband is the one who gets to be behind the closed doors. She plays with the possibility of the analyst's pregnancy before reluctantly acknowledging its reality. A fuller acknowledgement through the analytic process of the implication of these truths and a differentiation between herself and her married, pregnant analyst led to important shifts in her emotional life.

We propose that work with a troubled femininity may require particular technical attention to the use of disavowal to maintain illusions about 'having it all'. The wish to be both sexes (Kubie, 1974) may well be matched by the effort to obscure the implications of gender differences. We use the term perverse defense in the way that Grossman (1993) suggests: an effort to disavow a registered reality with illusion. While these defenses might also be understood with more familiar ways of thinking—such as narcissistic fantasy solutions—we found value in the subtle shift in our thinking and intervention that occurred as we paid attention to the ways patients skirt reality through simultaneously both looking and not looking. Particularly given the protected nature of the analytic situation, we can easily miss this form of defense.

Our study group previously identified a lag between contemporary psychoanalytic views of female development and the technical interventions in our clinical work (Basseches et al., 1996). While some lag between theory and practice will always exist, the lag we identified was pronounced and distorted our ability to work with some conflicts presented by our patients. Our listening became more attuned to the ways women were speaking about their interior spaces and their anxieties about their bodies.

Our present investigation takes up Mayer's (1995) challenge to "rethink old and familiar observations" in the light of current revision of theory. As we listened to our female patients keeping both possibilities of the castration complex and anxieties related to feminine functioning in mind, our attention turned to their perverse fantasy solutions to the riddle of femininity. The woman's sense of femaleness is imbued with many distortions and illusions that must be addressed before the vitality of femininity can emerge. It is imperative that we avoid formulaic interpretation in our work with distorted or disavowed femininity. Listening to the patient's thoughts involves viewing each construction as a layer to be understood and as a help in revealing the next layer, likely to be a different construction. The analyst, as if holding a prism, must be able to view the analysand's feelings and ideas first one way and then another to catch various rays of light.

REFERENCES

Bass, A. (1994). Aspects of urethrality in women. *Psychoanal. Q.*, 63: 491–517.

——— (1997). The problem of 'Concreteness'. *Psychoanal. Q.*, 66:642–682.

Basseches et al. (1996). Hearing what cannot be seen: a psychoanalytic research group's inquiry into female sexuality. *J. Amer. Psychoanal. Assn.*, 44 (S): 511–528.

Birksted-Breen, D. (1996). Unconscious representation of femininity. *J. Amer. Psychoanal. Assn.*, 44 (S): 119–132.

Brenner, C. (1982). *The Mind in Conflict.* New York: Int. Univ. Press.

Brierley, M. (1932). Some problems of integrating in women. *Int. J. Psycho-Anal.*, 13:433–448.

Elise, D. (1997). Primary femininity, bisexuality, and the female ego ideal: a reexamination of female developmental theory. *Psychoanal. Q.*, 66: 489–517.

Erikson, E.H. (1950). *Childhood and Society.* (Second Ed.) New York: Norton.

——— (1974). Once more the inner space: Letter to a former student. In *Women and Analysis*, ed. J. Strouse. New York: Grossman.

Freud, S. (1912). Recommendations to physicians practicing psycho-analysis. *S.E.* 12.

——— (1933). New Introductory Lectures on Psycho-Analysis. *S.E.* 22.

——— (1937). Analysis terminable and interminable. *S.E.* 23.

Galenson, E. & Roiphe, H. (1976). Some suggested revisions concerning early female development. *J. Amer. Psychoanal. Assn.*, 24(S): 29–57.

Grossman, L. (1993). The perverse attitude toward reality. *Psychoanal. Q.*, 62:422–436.

Grossman, W.I. & Kaplan, D.M. (1988). Three commentaries on gender in Freud's thought: a prologue to the psychoanalytic theory of sexuality. In

Fantasy, Myth, and Reality, ed. H. P. Blum, Y. Karmer, A. K. Richards & A. D. Richards. New York: Int. Univ. Press, 1990, pp. 339–370.

Horney, K. (1926). The flight from woman-hood. *Int. J. Psycho-Anal.*, 7:324–339.

Jones, E. (1927). The early development of sexuality. *Int. J. Psycho-Anal.*, 8:438–451.

Kestenberg, J. (1982). The inner-genital phase—prephallic and preoedipal. In *Early Female Development: Current Psychoanalytic Views*, ed. D. Mendall. New York: Spectrum.

Kubie, L. (1974). The drive to become both sexes. *Psychoanal. Q.*, 43:349–426.

Kulish, N.M. (1991). The mental representation of the clitoris: the fear of female sexuality. *Psychoanal. Inq.*, 11:511–536.

Lax, R. (1994). Aspects of primary and secondary genital feelings and anxieties in girls during the preoedipal and early oedipal phases. *Psychoanal. Q.*, 63:271–296.

——— (1995). Freud's views and changing perspectives on femaleness and femininity: what my female analysands taught me. *Psychoanal. Psychol.*, 12 (3):393–406.

Lerner, H. (1976). Parental mislabeling of female genitals as a determinant of penis envy and learning inhibitions in women. *J. Amer. Psychoanal. Assn.*, 24:269–293.

——— (1988). *Women in Therapy*. Jason Aronson: New Jersey.

Mayer, E.L. (1991). Towers and enclosed spaces: a preliminary report on gender differences in children's reactions to block structures. *Psychoanal. Inq.*, 11:480–510.

——— (1995). The phallic castration complex and primary femininity: paired developmental lines toward female gender identity. *J. Amer. Psychoanal. Assn.*, 43:17–38.

Rangell, L. (1991). Castration. *J. Amer. Psychoanal. Assn.*, 30:3–23.

Reed, G. (1997). The analyst's interpretation as fetish. *J. Amer. Psychoanal. Assn.*, 45:1153–1181.

Richards, A.K. (1992). The influence of sphincter control and genital sensation on body image and gender identity in women. *Psychoanal. Q.*, 61:331–351.

——— (1996). Primary femininity and female genital anxiety. *J. Amer. Psychoanal. Assn.*, 44:261–282.

——— (1998). Discussion of the 'Riddle of Femininity'. Division 39 meeting, Boston, MA.

Schafer, R. (1983). *The Analytic Attitude.* New York: Basic Books.

Schlessinger, N. & Robbins, F. (1983). *A Developmental View of the Psychoanalytic Process: Follow-up Studies and Their Consequences.* New York: Int. Univ. Press.

Torok, M. (1970). The significance of penis envy in women. In *Female Sexuality: New Psychoanalytic Views*, ed. J. Chasseguet-Smirgel et al. Michigan: Univ. Michigan Press.

Tyson, P. (1994). Bedrock and beyond: an examination of the clinical utility of contemporary theories of female psychology. *J. Amer. Psychoanal. Assn.*, 42:447–467.

Young-Bruehl, E. (1994). What theories women want. *Amer. Imago.*, 51: 73–396.

CHAPTER 19

A Foreign Language: Voice for the Forbidden Thought

Presented at FEPAL Meeting, 26th October 6, 2006.
Latin American Congress of Psychoanalysis, Lima, Peru.

The issue of people being analyzed in a language other than their native language has been surprisingly neglected. In the year 2006 it is doubly surprising. This report of such a case occurred many years ago but offered a phenomenon of such interest that it has continued to intrigue me. I found myself wanting to explore it further to see if I could understand more about it. I treated a woman from a different culture from my own. The patient used my language, English, as the mode for communication. This appeared as no hardship for her because she was fluent in English, and I did not speak her Asian language.

What I discovered was that she was able by her own account to say the most explicit and anatomically correct statements to do with sexual organs and sex; she was also able to report a dream with overt sexual meaning, and to speak in general with a frankness and directness that she claimed was completely alien to speech and modes of communication in her native language.

I had seen and do see many people from other cultures in treatment even though I, unfortunately, speak only English fluently. On reflection, that may not be as surprising as it might at first appear, since I live in Washington, D.C., a community that is an international center, where many organizations and academic settings draw from a global pool of participants. I soon realized, however, that although language, and even more often, cultural issues, emerged in various of these other therapies, none revealed the same phenomenon in such bold relief. With regard to language facility, that first young woman would be labeled as a polyglot multilinguist in that she learned languages other than her native language later in life. Others, who learned more than one language simultaneously as a young child in contrast to a polyglot, are simply called bilingual or multilingual.

There are many interesting observations to be made about multiple languages and cross-cultural psychoanalytic therapies. This paper will cover the following set of questions: First) What understanding may we derive from that early case about meanings and effects of multiple language facility on therapy? Second) What are some of the meanings and effects from therapies with other multilingual persons that may or may not resonate with this first case? Third) In what ways was treatment with multilingual patients distinguishable in terms of such factors as content, process, transference and countertransference from a therapy in which both partners, analyst and patient, are fluent in the same language or languages? This latter question raises another important consideration, what does this reveal about patient-analyst match?

LITERATURE REVIEW

A literature search revealed a paucity of the phenomenon that I had discovered. A few papers addressed cross cultural issues and psychoanalysis (Basch-Kahre, 1984; Devereux, 1963; Jackson, 1968; also, Stoller & Herdt, 1982). Of those of a cross-cultural nature, Basch-Kahre (1984) was the only one to speak directly about language (the others offering interesting material relevant to more general cultural factors not to be addressed here today). Basch-Kahre (1984) reported transference and countertransference difficulties in working with a person from another culture which she described as "a mutual feeling of estrangement" (p. 62) afflicting both analyst and analysand; with somewhat of a leap, she conceptualized this as a regressive experience of "stranger anxiety" reminiscent of the 8- to 9-month-old. Basch-Kahre also labeled the spoken language of the psychoanalysis mother tongue for the analyst but not the analysand, as "alien" to the analysand, cut off from the naturally occurring emotionally colored sensorimotor experiences encoded in his childhood language. Further, Basch-Kahre suggested that this linguistic alienation, no matter how well the analysand may have learned the adopted language of the analyst, removed the patient not only from memories but symbolization. The resulting linguistic communication was called in the language of the psychoanalysis "operational" i.e., logical, secondary process thinking devoid of sensorimotor meaning and symbols. In labeling the initial problem as an example of stranger anxiety and the resulting consequences conceptualized in cognitive terms, Basch-Kahre bypasses explicit reference to unconscious conflict as playing a key role. This problem could only be overcome by the analyst's attentiveness and mastery over her own alienated feeling through self analysis and interpretation for the analysand.

Interestingly, Basch-Kahre's use of the term, operational, resonates with Joyce McDougal's (1985) moving discussion of patients who do not have words for their feelings and psychic images creating a block in their ability to communicate in analysis.

The most exhaustive text to explore a broad range of topics connected with multilingual issues and psychoanalysis is the book, *The Babel of the Unconscious* (1993, Amati-Mehler, et al). Their review of the literature highlights a selection of important writings, including the Ferenczi paper to be discussed shortly, but seems to have bypassed the cross-cultural papers mentioned earlier. The authors cite examples of polyglot analysands who used the later "foreign" language defensively. They reported that the newer language provided a way for the analysand to stay away from conflictual material encoded or carried in the language of the mother tongue. At the same time as the authors mention examples of the defensive use of the foreign language, they also stress that the new language can in some instances contribute an adaptive pathway for development, sometimes resolving and sometimes bypassing early conflicts.

In recognizing repeated examples of splitting along linguistic lines, the authors discuss different conceptualizations and uses of the term, splitting, most notably those of Freud, Bion, Klein, and Winnicott (Amati-Mehler, et al., pp. 251-264). Their effort was to de-pathologize the inevitable splitting that they found demonstrable in multilingual patients, no matter what the level of personality organization. They wanted to focus rather on the idea of undoing splits and creating integration, often observed in therapies. Acknowledging that some writers consider "the very condition of multilingualism [if not the] cause, albeit potential, of a split," Amati-Mehler, et al. "believe that the splitting processes lean on and in a certain way exploit the different linguistic registers as a means for organizing and expressing themselves." (p. 264)

The Babel of the Unconscious book is encyclopedic. Sandor Ferenczi's paper, however, entitled "On Obscene Words," (1911) seemed especially relevant to my case. Ferenczi discussed the motoric and hallucinatory quality of words for the young child learning language. Quoting Freud, he explained, "Children treat Words as objects" (p. 140). "… at a certain stage of development, this concreteness, and with it probably a strong tendency to regression, applies still to all words. (p. 140). Ferenczi demonstrated that an inhibition occurs during development from infancy through latency years, brought about in connection with "the Oedipus-complex" that precludes ease of speaking obscene words. While perhaps not forgotten entirely, these thoughts are carried in the child's mind like a "foreign body"

(p. 145), undisturbed by ongoing language development toward abstraction. Such words and images, when they reemerge at puberty, have taken on a shamefulness (replacing the earlier pleasurable affects). Along with the shame, however, Ferenczi suggested: "When uttering an obscene word one has the feeling that it is almost equivalent to a sexual aggression"…, [and give] "the definite feeling of initiating an act. (p. 141). He pointed out that "delicate allusions to sexual processes, and scientific or foreign designations for them, do not have this effect, or at least not to the same extent as the words taken from the original, popular, erotic vocabulary of one's mother tongue …" (p. 137), the language of early childhood.

In this connection, "The Babel of the Unconscious" cited an article by E. Krapf (1935). Krapf described "a patient who used English in order to keep the relationship on a purely intellectual level, while he had a great fear of talking to… [the analyst]… about sex in his own mother tongue." (Amati-Mehler, et al., p. 50)

Buxbaum (1949) reported work with polyglot patients who expressed their conflicts by controlling which language they used in their analytic work. Buxbaum spoke both languages. For two of the patients, the second language was used as a mechanism of repression that also "saved them from having to resort to long periods of complete silence and was therefore valuable in their treatment." (p. 286) Buxbaum noted that "verbalizing experiences in the language in which they occurred makes them become real; speaking of them in any other language renders them unreal [which emphasizes the magic quality speech can have]" (p. 286)

The ideas highlighted stress the extent to which individuals in general, and those with multiple language possibilities in particular, may inhibit or even silence their speech. Giving an example of nonverbal communication as a solution to that which may not be said, Malawista (2000) describes a case in which nonverbal, body movement in the form of a conversion symptom, became an important vehicle toward understanding of work between a polyglot patient and a monolingual analyst.

When I presented an earlier version of this paper, an attendee from the audience who was deaf and from another culture volunteered ideas that expanded consideration of the role played by multiple languages in a person's psychic economy. She explained with the help of a remarkable interpreter that she "spoke" through sign language with great feeling about the disjointedness and complications of her experience. She contrasted her early language learning in a family of hearing parents in that other culture with her more recent learning of sign language since living in the United States. The sign language newly connected her with the "culture" of the deaf world. She seemed to feel that the two "worlds" were not easily integrated, reminding us again to be in tune to inevitable linguistic splits and cultural adjustments.

THE CASE OF MS. A.

A petite, Asian woman, exquisitely dressed, and very feminine but with a firm handshake as strong as a burly man, greeted me in my office. Her English showed no trace of accent. She sought treatment because of an upsetting end to a relationship. I soon learned of a highly accomplished young professional whose private life was a mercurial mosaic of brief, passionate liaisons with American men. There was a sense of high drama, the pain she experienced quickly masked and, as it turned out, soon bundled up into a flight into health in the form of work. Less than a month into the treatment, apparently more comfortable emotionally, she suddenly informed me that she was called away for three weeks for work. We met only twice more after that interruption, when she explained that she was doing well and had to leave the area in connection with her professional responsibilities. I did not see her for another year and a half when, with some surprise, I heard from her of her interest in returning to therapy. She came back for two years of twice-weekly psychotherapy, with the idea that she would allow herself to stay awhile and learn more about herself. During that second therapy effort, Ms. A., as I will call her, shared genetic material that she had clearly found too disturbing to speak about in our earlier brief encounter. Hers was an educated family. Her capable mother, however, was described as not only submissive but downtrodden and passive, unable to protect her daughter from the men of the family.

I want to focus on the linguistic issues and mode of communication. Ms. A. began a session explaining that a message her mother had left for her had made her very angry at her mother. "I called her back to tell her of my irritation but in our culture even telling her I was angry is not the same [implying, as it would be here in the United States]. Feminine speech is more delicate. There is a gender difference in speech."

My thoughts: I understood her to be telling me not only the obvious that her Mother was a target of her anger—but also that being female in her culture was a handicap to her freedom to express aggressive and critical feeling; further, I imagined that she was forecasting that she would have similar feelings towards me, in the transference, and maybe, a similar delicacy of expression.

She went on to recall an event that had occurred when she was 13 or 14. Her brother, then 22, was on leave from graduate school in the United States. She had been talking on the telephone to a girlfriend and not helping to prepare the dinner. Her brother said to her, "You think food drops from heaven." She apologized but apparently not sufficiently to satisfy her indignant brother. He brandished a knife at her, which evoked no protest from her mother. She recalled being so frightened that she ran out of the house, toward the railway station. Her (younger) sister ran after her to reassure her that it would be safe to come home now. As she recalled it, she did return home, and that later there was no further discussion.

My thoughts: So much seemed to be condensed in this sequence! She seemed to be explaining (in part) why she was angry with her mother for not taking her side, protecting her. That perhaps she felt like the Princess who did not have to do scullery drudgery like Mother making the dinner. But her "comeuppance" administered by the so-much-older brother was violent and frightening, and carried a moral authority. The evoking of a knife, suggested the violence of a man; the metaphor of a knife as the weapon that frightened her, suggested not only her fear of the power of the phallus, but also possibly castration anxiety. And again, metaphorically, she would be "cut off" from her Mother, "cut off" from her grandiose ideas of being of a higher status than her mother, and punished with bodily harm. Further, she was also telling about her choice of defense, flight (with a hint of escape through travel, i.e., the railroad station); with a little stretch, knowing that she had later come to the United States where the brother had gone, I also thought, could this be a hostile identification with her brother, an early hint of a future course, turning passive into active?

In a later session, Ms. A. told of a dream that she had had that she said she found amusing. She was sitting cross legged in a circle with a group of women. Each one had her own penis in full erection between her legs. Further associations beyond her amusement were not forthcoming and she never mentioned the dream again.

My thoughts: Her apparent pleasure in the dream seemed to underscore her wish for phallic power; my counter transference association was of her being a member of a guild of Amazonian-like women. Her inability or unwillingness to consider her associations made me think about the inhibitions that lay behind the apparent directness of her communication of the dream itself.

In another session, she said that a person from her country, when speaking, tends not to specify the person being referred to, other than as male or female.

My thoughts: Was she telling me that in her mind, her native language supported her wish that there be no gender differentiation? In an hour during which she shared shocking information that she had been sexually abused by her father, she said of her feelings. "I could cry at the drop of a pen.

My thoughts: Again, so much seemed condensed in that sentence. Linguistically, there was something unsettling about the slightly altered idiom. Her use of English ordinarily was so seamless that I would have expected her to have said the more usual expression: "at the drop of a hat." Yet, the particular word selected, "pen," could clearly be considered phallic imagery, especially in conjunction with the topic of her father's sexual abuse. For a penis to drop, what might that mean? And then, her understandable grief, but nevertheless unclear specifically over what.

She remarked further that she could be more direct in English than in her native language. Ms. A. described an incident at work where the task as she understood it was to brainstorm together with a more senior male colleague of her nationality. He was someone with whom she felt very collegial, as an ally, even a comrade, but with a definite hint of flirtation. On this occasion he remarked, following something she had just said: "Where did that come from? Are your hormones acting up or something?" She felt hurt and annoyed by this. When she described something as sexual harassment, that would deflate the sexual feeling (which she apparently felt toward this person), and she had mixed feelings about doing that. If you stand up for yourself, would you feel something sexual is lost? She returned to the idea of her father's sexual abuse, how he would sit and watch her, as a teenager, in the bath.

I thought, she seemed to be getting close to the idea of her conflict over her sexual excitement with her father and with a current displacement figure in the man at work.

In that hour, I wondered more about why it was easier to speak in English about these concerns, why she felt she could be more direct? She tried to illustrate what she meant. In a language other than her native tongue, such as English, she feels free to say dirty jokes and speak of penises without a blush. She continued by recalling a recent occasion when she was with a Spanish-speaking group (incidentally, letting me know as she had so many other times of her erudition). She had told the members of the group that the word in her native language for "testicles" means "golden balls" in Spanish. The group began to chant to her "golden balls," repeating it in her own language. She became so embarrassed that she blushed.

I thought, here was the explicit example of the release from inhibition that she permitted herself, when speaking in a foreign language. She could speak obscene words, as directly as men important to her from her own culture were perceived as acting; she could say without a consequence of shame the aggressively infused sexual ideas concerning men's bodies, the way she felt men from her own culture could speak and act toward women's bodies and their sexuality. But in her own language, she again felt the inhibition and the shame.

A few months later, she was speaking as usual in English and switched to her native language to say (later translated at my request): "The most important thing is for us to get together and get to know each other more."

I thought, to be direct about feelings of tenderness, intimacy, and perhaps sexual feeling toward the analyst was not so safe, as if issues to do with her feelings toward a woman were to be avoided in the shared language and this time permissible in the delicate, feminine form of her own native language. The timing of this admission coincided with a time when I made the recommendation that she consider deepening the work and undertaking psychoanalysis. Unfortunately, it was not too long after her admission of a wish for greater closeness to the analyst that a "flight" that ended the therapy occurred. Suddenly and irresistibly she was in love with a solitary romantic-sounding man from the United States. She decided quite quickly to quit her prestigious job and go with the man to a distant country. They were planning to bike, backpack, and ostensibly to do research together in preparation for a book—adventurous and dangerous activity.

My thoughts: It seemed that the intensity of the transference and the suggestion of the emergence of a negative oedipal configuration became frightening to her. I was unable to interpret her anxiety over her wishes for closeness, sexual and aggressive feelings towards me sufficiently to discourage her flight. As direct as she was in English, the transference seemed to require her to hold back from clearly voicing her feelings toward me, as if we had been speaking together in her native language, her mother tongue. In a way, she was able to continue her avoidance of facing her conflicts by silencing the language of the therapy altogether.

In the foreign language (so perfectly rendered that it was only when it came to a subtle idiom was it detectable that her fluency was not complete), in that language she could be active, outspoken and sexually bold more like the men of her home culture. Nevertheless, despite her sexual and professional adventurousness in a foreign land and language, her sexual arousal, and true inclinations toward intimate connection remained in a sense locked in her native language.

Some years later, I learned about her when another patient reported taking over a high level international job stationed in the United States from a person of Ms. A's full name and description. I gathered that at some point the relationship with the man had ended (as so many had in the past) and that she had been able to reenter her former workplace, but only to again leave precipitously to go to another job, this time in Europe. If that was in fact Ms. A., it seemed that she had returned to the area (and not to the therapy). She was continuing to keep on the move both professionally and personally without fully engaging. It seems she was still running away from the threat of the knife through her enactments but also through her use of foreign languages to keep her conflicts at bay.

Hearing about a person whom I thought might be her renewed my feeling of sadness that this was so. My hope was that perhaps the therapy had been "good enough" for her to risk renewing a therapy with someone else, who could have helped her further to understand her conflicts and make it safe for her to integrate her linguistic divide.

CONTRASTING VIGNETTES

The Case of Ms. B.

A contrasting group of people would be called multilingual rather than polyglot. Four of these patients, who are women, had mothers from another culture and learned the mother's language in close succession with learning English. Each was raised in America and had a sense of herself as American; the mothers, in contrast, clearly maintained a sense of self tied (although presumably ambivalently) to their original countries and not to America.

Obviously, there are many factors to be understood in these therapies, one at twice per week, one at three times per week, one at four times per week, and one at five times per week, but I believe they shared in common a difficulty in establishing a relatively comfortable identification with their mothers, leading to a variety of difficulties, including separation from mother, consolidation of their own sexual and female/ womanly sense of self, and establishing a relatively successful love object choice. You perhaps are noting that I proffered a somewhat similar suggestion about the polyglot young woman described in some detail above in terms of her unresolved feelings toward her mother which I saw as central to her difficulties.

In psychoanalytic work, we rely on language as the main vehicle of transmission carrying an enormous variety of meanings both conscious and unconscious. Yet it may be more than a fortuity that early language acquisition and one's native language are referred to as "the mother tongue." If such an idea has validity, language will be particularly vulnerable to expression of early disruptions in the mother-child dyads that then create the conflictual underpinnings coloring later inevitable developmental identifications, conflicts and accomplishments.

The following is an example of hearing echoes of these conflicts in terms of language, in material from the work with one of the multilingual patients.

Pt.: "My sense of confidence 'evaporated'. Oh, what am I trying to say? It makes me think of a word that is not in English." [says the word in the non-English language, which sounds quite close to vaporated, with a different sounding ending]. She goes on, "It's a machine that is not found in this country that my mother used it the last time we were in, [Let's call it, X]. She used it to get the stains out of a dress. It was amazing. Oh, the word I meant just now was E-vaporated! That happens to me. Often, I can't think of the word I want in English [something the analyst had not particularly noted as happening] and when I am in X, I often struggle to find the right word and say it wrong and fear I will seem foolish.

That reminds me, my Mom learned English on her own from listening to TV and radio back in X when she was a teenager. Although she speaks English quite well of course with an accent that everyone thinks is cute she often says things that sound almost right but aren't. For example, the other day she said, "The proof is in the puddle." So close but yet so wrong, losing the essential meaning of the idea! In her its cute, but I worry often when I speak that I'm saying the wrong thing, that I've learned from her to do that too and don't know. But if I do that, it just sounds stupid."

In contrast to this vignette, Ms. B's ambivalent transference toward the analyst seemed to be expressed in a more global way, in terms of her ambivalence toward the psychoanalysis. She would alternate endlessly between devaluing the analysis along with doubts about her need for treatment, coupled with her expressed idealization of the analyst in a variety of ways. Language was addressed only with respect to her own running assessment of her performance in analysis; how superficial or not she was being in her expression of topics that mattered, how prolific she was being in her quantity of production, i.e., how much she talked—which she rightly noted was in a pretty steady stream most of the time.

With regard to the topics Ms. B. addressed, she oscillated from glowing reports to disappointments and criticisms, which she in turn would regret and undo. Childhood and immediate family, however, were consistently painted in the rosiest of hues. To the analyst, it seemed as if the patient said, metaphorically, that Mother was amazing in making stains disappear; that the daughter was trying to do the same in the psychoanalysis—make the stains disappear—but she wasn't sure that psychoanalysis was the right machine; that when she tried to or felt compelled to follow her mother, she felt foolish and doubted everything, which made her feel badly about herself and guilty for her negative feelings toward her mother. The repeated questioning of the analysis while putting the analyst on a pedestal aptly captures her dilemma, which I felt was confirmed by my counter transference. So often, I felt a strong pull toward being nurturing and encouraging like a non-critical Mom at the same time as I felt the sting of the persistent jabs of her devaluation for what I was "putting her through" in the analysis.

While I would wish to say more about this patient and the many others who displayed aspects of their conflicts through their uses (and misuses) of English as the language of the therapy, time for this presentation is running out. Instead, I will try to collect some observations for consideration.

DISCUSSION

I have raised several questions in this paper. The first focused on that early case and the discovery that led me to entitle this paper: "A Foreign Language: Voice for the Forbidden Thought." Certainly, Ms. A. demonstrated the split that many writers (Amati-Mehler, et al., 1993 Basch-Kahre, 1984; Buxbaum, 1949; and Paul, 2000) have identified in polyglot and multilingual patients. This split for defensive purposes served her in much the ways that Buxbaum reported in her patients and Krapf did in his. In my patient's case it seemed that a more comprehensive way to think about her linguistic conflict solution was as a compromise formation which allowed her to bypass strictures possibly derived from internal directives unconsciously associated with her mother against her forbidden thoughts and impulses. At the same time, she could keep her painful affect in check, and go, unfrightened and unashamed, on her verbal, adventures and triumphs, as long as she was frolicking in foreign territory. Unfortunately, it seemed that her solutions could not hold sufficiently to last, so that she was repeatedly compelled to enact her having to run away from love and work (and as it turned out, from therapy). Ferenczi's explanation of the way obscene words adhere to the language of childhood, unchanged in structure, meaning, and action right into adulthood with only the affective valence changing from positive to negative, goes a long way toward our understanding of Ms. A's behaviors. It is not difficult to speculate on the advantages of alternative avenues of expression that a multiple linguistical range could provide.

A second question focused on whether it made a difference in the therapy, if secondary languages were acquired later in life (polyglot) or at the same time as one's first language acquisition. There were, of course, many differences between the two cases described above. But the striking difference between the two vignettes in terms of language factors was in the quality of the split. In the case of Ms. A., the polyglot patient, the barrier to integration was fenced by the two languages, whereas, in the case of the second, multilingual patient, her conflicts bridged the languages in such a way that she suffered the symptom in both languages.

The third point centered on the uniqueness of process, transference and counter transference problems that might emerge in a monolingual therapist working with multilingual and polyglot patients as compared with a therapist who matched the language facility of the patient. This latter topic deserves not one separate paper, but two! So briefly, I would say the following: Empathy and understanding is always a challenge and never can be taken for granted. One of the hallmarks of our work is not to "presume" that we "know" what the patient intends, be it movie, book or feeling state. So too is it axiomatic that anything can be used defensively (Brenner, 1982) or adaptively for that matter. At the same time, several of the multilingual and polyglot analysts who have addressed these issues (Krapf [1935] in Amati-Mehler, 1993; Flegenheimer, 1989) have demonstrated the great benefits of linguistic competence in the languages of their patients to their understanding of unconscious symbolic meanings. Flegenheimer gave an example of a slip in the second language that had a significant meaning in the first but not in the second language. On the other hand, he suggests that he might have been able to understand the general meaning if not the specific symbols anyway through an understanding of the transference.

With regard to patient-analyst match, Kernberg (2000) addressed issues pertaining to gender of patient and analyst. He concluded that.

"gender makes not only one but many differences, but… not [in] accord with the conventional common sense view of the influence of the actual gender of both participants on the treatment… Transferences override… the actual gender full deployment… depends on the analyst's skill, experience and relative freedom from conventional assumptions" (p. 881).

Along with Kernberg, Vaughan & Roose (2000) concur that "… patient-therapist match … must be treated first and foremost as evidence of important transference-counter transference signal." (p. 897)

Conclusion and Suggestions for Further Investigation

For both the multilingual and the polyglot patients, multiple languages share an expression of conflicts in ways that at times seem similar and at times different from other patients who do not have the same broader possibilities for expression. The basic concerns for the analyst are unchanged: to experience primarily, although not exclusively in the transference and countertransference dialogue an understanding of the important conflicts and accompanying fantasies that are unique for each patient, and then to work with the patient step by step for emotional understanding of what is transpiring.

Perhaps this understanding might better be achieved for the polyglot or multilingual patient by matching such a person with a comparably endowed analyst. I have a regret that I am not in a position to offer such a possibility and be able, like Buxbaum and others were able, to engage with my patients in their mother tongue as well as in their adopted language. Yet, as Vaughan and Roose (2000) have told us, the literature does not support the concept of the "good match"; what remains is the careful work to understand the transference and countertransference. Perhaps, the concept of the "good enough analyst" is an acceptable idea for now.

REFERENCES

Amati-Mehler, J., Argentieri, S., & Canestri, J. (1993). *The Babel of the Unconscious.* Madison, CT: IUP.

Basch-Kahre, E. (1984). On difficulties arising in transference and countertransference when analyst and analysand have different socio-cultural backgrounds. *I.R.P.,* 11:61–67.

Brenner, C. (1982). *The Mind in Conflict.* NY: IUP.

Buxbaum, E. (1949). The role of a second language in the formation of ego and superego. *P.Q.* 18:279–289,

Devereux, G. (1953). Cultural factors in psychoanalytic therapy. *J.A.P.A.,* 1:629–655.

Ferenczi, S. (1911). On obscene words. Chapt. 4 in *First Contributions to Psychoanalyses.* NY: Brunner/Mazel, 1952, Reprinted 1980, pp. 132–153.

Flegenheimer, F.A. (1989). Languages and psychoanalysis. The polyglot patient and the polyglot analyst. *I.R.P.,* 16:377–383.

Jackson, S.W.(Reporter) (1968). Panel: Aspects of culture in psychoanalytic theory and practice. *J.A.P.A.,* 16:651–670.

Kernberg, O.F. (2000). The influence of the gender of patient and analyst in the psychoanalytic relationship. *J.A.P.A.,* 48:859–883.

Malawista, K. (2000). Unpublished case.

McDougall, J. (1985). *Theaters of the Mind.* NY: Basic Books.

Reppen, J. (Reporter) (2000). Panel: Development of affect in bilingual patients. *I.J.P.,* 81:153–155.

Vaughn, S.C. & Roose, S.P. (2000). Patient-therapist match. J.*A.P.A.,* 48:885–899.

Stoller, R.J., & Herdt, G. (1982). The development of masculinity: cross-cultural contribution. *J.A.P.A.* 30:29–59.

CHAPTER 20

How Far Can the Frame Be Stretched Without Breaking: What Helps the Patient, and is it Psychoanalysis?

Presentation, 2008.

My basic training and the organization of my thinking has been Freudian. Within the Freudian tradition questions have always arisen that have created rethinking of an analyst's perspective, mine included. It is thus disturbing that new ideas in our field are often presented as antithetical to Freudian thought, presented as a "new" school of psychoanalytic theory seen not only as oppositional to Freudian thought but as requiring a wholesale rejection of the Freudian point of view. But Freudian thought is neither monolithic nor static. It has been evolving since Freud was at the helm and is continuing in contemporary Freudian theorizing. While some ideas are obviously incompatible, many of the evolving concepts can appropriately be viewed as expansions of the Freudian conceptual framework. In that sense, I strongly agree with Rangell (1990) in his one unified theory approach. I would also add Harry Smith's caution (2001, 2003) that analysts misunderstand the words and theories of others in the service of their own use of concepts.

The word "frame" found in the title of my talk reflects several of its many meanings. When I just spoke of the "framework" of Freudian theory, I meant frame as in the Dictionary definition "anything composed of parts and united together; a structure; especially, the constructional system that gives a [matter] its model and strength." Another meaning that is familiar to us all, however, is the expression that we analysts have for the cluster of necessary elements that surrounds an analytic session. To rely again on Webster's Dictionary: "an enclosing border." It is the combination of those two definitions to which I refer. More days of analytic work than not, I struggle with the question, am I breaking the frame when I respond in some way that seems to me to be stretching my own sense of the limits I have previously established to reach a patient: have I overreached?

You might say, "Oh, you are talking about countertransference and enactments," a thought to which I would agree; but the question goes further, to another level of concern. Is this still psychoanalysis? To which I could add, is this still *Freudian* psychoanalysis, bringing together the two meanings of "frame" to which I have alluded?

My talk today interweaves those two threads—the coherence of my underlying psychoanalytic theories and the implications in the clinical setting of my evolving work mode as expressed with different patients—and at different stages of the work with the same patient. My work has begun to be infused with more recent theoretical ideas which broaden my Freudian-Brennerian-Paul Gray model. While my essentially Freudian ideas continue to act as the foundation of my listening, I have found myself shifting the acoustical ear of my thinking to include consideration of Kleinian, Bionian and later object relations theorists who focus on the here and now. Further, the vicissitudes of pathological narcissism increasingly play a central role. The result is that I oscillate between a one person and two-person point of view. I will try to explicate how my thinking has changed, and how, therefore, my practice seems to have evolved based on my experience with patients.

For me, the preferred analytic frequency is five times a week. In reality, this goal has been difficult to achieve for personal and professional commitments which call me from the office more than I would wish. Therefore, fairly early in my work, I abandoned it and settled on a maximum of four times per week for those in psychoanalysis. This was a standard I seemed better able to maintain. That has worked for candidates and for some patients not in the field. For others—at the moment I am thinking of three patients for whom three times a week was all that they could tolerate—I have accepted their expressed needs and rhythms.

To complete the picture, I have two patients who had an interesting progression with regard to frequency: both started on a once weekly basis, and each built up slowly, first to twice a week, then three, then four. In one case, after six years of successful work focused on her intense ambivalent attachment to an intermittently abusive mother and passive but successful businessman father, the patient allowed herself to become engaged to be married and move from the area. For the period before she left, she chose to continue on the couch even though we were then only meeting once a week. Her conscious wish to continue in that mode centered on her comfort in the familiar. My willingness for her to continue on the couch at whatever the frequency provided a containing function (Bion; Winnicott), and I see our work as a pre-analysis preparation that has allowed her to successfully transition to a full analysis with a colleague in another city.

For the other patient who continued to work on the couch no matter what the frequency, the therapy is on-going. This patient, for whom separations have played a palpable, perhaps retraumatizing, role, was able to marry after many years of intense treatment. Once married, however, he undertook a series of self -destructive acts—threesome sex, accosting a woman at work with a sexual overture which led to his losing his high paying job, followed by a long period of passivity. The period of passivity was similar to an earlier point two- and one-half years into the therapy. At that earlier time, having completed business school and passing the licensing exam on the first try— both worthy accomplishments—he failed to get a job for a year and stepped up perverse sexual activity. That earlier sequence coincided with my return from summer break. There has been a phoenix-rising-from-the-ashes quality about his rebirths or reinventions of himself after each of these protractedly difficult periods. The first one clearly followed a separation from the analyst AND a success on his own. The second might be thought of similarly. But the point I wanted to mention here is that during this second period of passivity, he slowly reduced the treatment time (on the grounds of money and negativity toward the treatment) until he was at once a week, still on the couch. And without a job, he was again paying a reduced fee as he had during business school. Now, in the process of resurrecting himself, he is outwardly positive toward the treatment but continuing once a week. I have chosen to extract one theme, his bumpy road to independence and self-reliance. Although the reduction of number of sessions per week is clearly multiply determined, I believe that he is trying to master his sexualized dependence on the analyst mother, whom he cannot live without, but does not want to live with, because he finds too painful that he is not her chosen partner. He seems to say through his actions that he cannot give her up, but he must. And that the only way he knows to stay with her is to be the helpless, dependent but resistant one. This has entered the analytic space largely through actions not words. I, the analyst, give him the space to play with the ideas by cooperating with his actions and watching for the opportunities to speak to the meanings to make the actions hopefully less necessary.

I have two more obvious deviations from an expected treatment frame to mention. In one, the change in the frame involves use of the telephone. After an extended consultation period, the patient had begun an analysis at a very reduced fee when her circumstances precipitously changed and she was forced to leave the area because of unavoidable family commitments. For a period of many months, she was moving around to locations far from me and other analytic therapists. We began to speak on the telephone three times a week, wherever she was. This arrangement went on all told for seven years! At that point, she was finally able to move to an area where she could settle, and which held promise of the availability of analytic therapists.

Finally, we were able to consider terminating. This work seriously stretched my own sense of a frame for treatment, and yet, it felt vital to proceed. Although we continued our focus on analyzing, in my mind my major function was to provide object constancy and stability—critical indeed for someone for whom chaos could have otherwise been the outcome.

The second case, however, is the one which precipitated my particular interest in writing about these matters to clarify my ways of working. I see this patient four times a week. She travels close to an hour each way. Previous to me, she had found it difficult to settle on a satisfactory therapist since having had to move from her former location because of her husband's professional opportunity. She had worked well with an (idealized) therapist she had had to leave, and no one she tried since seemed to fit, until she met me. Her selection of me and desire for analysis had a quality of desperation; she thought this was her last chance. The patient, Ms. Q, as I shall call her, is a woman well on in years who presents as a tragic figure, a Sisyphus forcing herself to push the rock up the mountain against a tide of anxiety. She feels profound shame for how little she has and can accomplish and hides behind a sweet charm to "appear normal," while inside she feels waves of anger, particularly when she experiences herself as treated unjustly. Almost any task feels "too much" for her even if, according to her, it is easy, but her ambitions and duty push her on. At the same time, she is consumed by envy and resentment, starting with her mother, who according to the patient, has not enough interest in my patient's plight to pay attention and understand her.

She functions from crisis to crisis, ostensibly getting no relief when things go better than she expects. While she can acknowledge when something went well, it is quickly submerged into the next crisis, which escalates her anxiety to fever pitch, proving yet again that "she can't handle" whatever the "It" is.

A theme of the work from early on was her grappling with feelings that she needed to quit her job, which is too much in addition to "her job" of coming to psychoanalysis. Much, although not all, of the timing of the work-related job is under her control. She chafes at those elements that are out of her control, but even the aspects that she herself determines, once they are set, become oppressive external demands. Getting rid of the job sometimes shifts to ridding herself of "her" analysis; she must have the job because "it is structure," and she cannot handle both. Thus, she puts pressure on herself in my presence and in effect on me, to make a decision, to act; to choose, but also to get rid of something unwanted or unbearable. I have not only been accused of saying the wrong thing but also of not talking, leaving her all alone to grapple and suffer, of not supporting (in the helpful way that the therapist in the old place used to). But then, she has called me back and left a message on my voice mail not to leave her. Leon Wurmser (2007) in *Torment Me but Don't Abandon Me,* has written about such patients with great empathy, characterizing them as troubled from very early traumas, with complementarily pressing conflicts and sometimes diagnosed as borderline with strong narcissistic and masochistic elements.

With Ms. Q., there have been many stretches of the frame. Here are three. The first involves the use of the telephone. Ms. Q, after an initial period of apparent pleasure and excitement about undertaking the analysis, began to complain about the trip by subway: Being in the presence of strangers left her feeling excruciatingly exposed. She solved this by choosing to drive herself to her appointments, which involved a reclaiming of an inhibited skill according to the patient, driving on superhighways. Again, she was at first exhilarated, but that soured, and she complained about her dread of leaving the house, of how harrowing the trip was, until she proposed making a plan to speak with me by phone one day of the four. I acquiesced. While at first, she did not take up the opportunity, there came a time when she "could not bear to drive in," and another time, she "could not bear to leave her house," and at another time, she "had a doctor's appointment on the same day, and could not bear to drive to her analysis as well." I just accepted what she said and only mildly inquired whether there was something in the previous session that had not gone as she would have wished, or whether I had said something to offend her—all denied. She claimed that she felt very connected with me when we spoke on the phone and that she got a lot out of it. As yet that has not been analyzed successfully, and she still does occasionally create an excuse to use a phone session, although less frequently.

She told me during one of those phone sessions that it was difficult to tell me but she feared that "her analysis would take a very long time and that I would leave, that is, retire, before she was done." I thought that she felt the need to say that to me out of my sight. More recently, in a session she said that I seemed to her to lean in too close to her, and it made her uncomfortable." Thus, I see the continuum from too (physically) close to too far away getting enacted by her in her words and actions; and that the phone is being used for 'hearing, not seeing,' a situation she experiences on the couch and which she feels needs more of her own control. One might say that her handling of the distance and seeing of each other represents identification with the aggressor, a sadomasochistic enactment and an object relationship with a maternal transferential figure.

A second stretch of the frame involved my manner of greeting this patient. Ms. Q. informed me one day that the way I approach and greet her in the waiting room, turn and walk back into my therapy room made her feel as if I did not care if she came in to the room at all: that she could just get up from her seat and walk out of the office and I would not care or even notice. I said to her, "I wonder if you see me waiting for you standing at my chair until you enter the room and lay down on the couch." She said, "No." (I then recalled how she does not look at me again once we have greeted in the waiting room, enters and kind of backs up to the couch.) For her, I changed my greeting pattern. Instead of preceding her, as I usually do with patients, and walking back to my chair to wait, I waited in the hallway for her to pass, and followed her into the room. After some weeks of this, she said, "You don't have to do that. Once I spoke about It—I don't know—the feeling just seemed to go away, and I don't mind anymore."

My third example is one in which I change another aspect of my manner, my verbal activity. During the early course of the treatment, which now stands at two and half years, I listened silently with occasional clarifications, for example, showing how she seemed to feel something in two ways. At first, she seemed to think about my clarifying remarks and add new information. After a while, she told me that I did not help and support her like her former therapist had. While the former therapist had not told her what to do, the patient felt she gave her choices. Further, she said that she could not remember what I said and that she had stopped listening and did not feel connected to me nor I to her. I was startled as I had experienced myself as doubling my efforts to "tune in," perhaps even trying too hard to attend. One day, she said that she did not like being on the couch and that she would sit in the chair. She did, and stole glances at me, but mostly looked away. I became more active and said that she treated me as if I were "chopped liver," an expression meaning "nothing much and not worthy," and that I was confused by her saying that I was unconnected, when I felt I was paying attention to her as much as I was capable of. She laughed and the next day went back on the couch, assuring me that I was not chopped liver. At the time, I thought but did not say that the way she was treating me seemed similar to the way she felt her mother often treated her. My reason for acting "in" the transference rather than interpreting it was my experience that she could best understand soup and dumplings—to use Freud's expression according to the patient, and that I could better serve her just then by being role responsive—to use Sandler's term.

I am trying to convey the way I move from my basic stance of listening and procedural actions, from a position of being thoroughly interested, attentive, but fundamentally guided my own rules of therapy conduct—as in Freud's technique papers—to a stance that is influenced by my attunement to the patient. In my view, her narcissistic issues trump her conflictual issues for now. I do not believe I am talking about abandoning abstinence and neutrality. My view of abstinence and neutrality feel solidly within contemporary Freudian thinking and rely on Loewald's thought (1989) that what counts is the underlying intentions of the analyst and her attitude of valuing that frame for the work. I would say the same for self-disclosure, as referenced in my "chopped liver" comment. I say what I feel, and it is a disclosure of my analytic self entirely within the frame of the analytic exchange.

I realize that all my stretches of the frame can be discussed under the rubric of enactments of the transference-countertransference variety. Here, the question of intersubjectivity arises, about which I am of more than one mind. While I do see that we—the patient and I—are influencing each other I do not see it as an even playing field; we have an asymmetrical relationship. Thus, when I am pushed by the transference and my countertransference responses (both the ones that bring my transference to the fore and the ones seemingly induced by the patient's), it is still my office, my schedule, my time constraints, my willingness to deviate from my prescribed path, and my role as the helper not the helpee, that has a powerful, although clearly not total, grip over what I do as well as think. What I would like to focus on, then, is the initial issue that I raise in this paper: How far can the frame be stretched and continue to be psychoanalytic, or to put it another way, how does this stretching of the frame translate into psychoanalysis and is there a limit to that stretching? Further, does the stretching actually serve the patient's therapeutic needs, irrespective of whether one labels the activity as therapeutic or analytic?

I have spoken of variations in frequency; on the couch or not; telephone communication. Also, I spoke of shifting my office protocol, changing my style of speaking, dosage of silent listening, relative activity and the actual content of my interventions. These raise difficult questions, open to opinions, both positive and negative. But here is the issue: they have all been in service of the work—to try to stay with a difficult patient in difficult times. Such matters could easily evolve into sadomasochistic power struggles, and if the attachment is strong enough, into narcissistic injuries that lead to analytic impasse. Slow and steady makes the most progress: one keeps listening and the opportunities for interpretation and growth present themselves, if one is patient. I remember Fred Pine once quoting the idea: "Strike when the iron is cold." So, while I definitely do not advocate for "anything goes," I do feel that one's on the spot intuitive judgment must be trusted. That in stretching the frame I can provide a holding environment, I can provide containment that may—I say, may—allow the patient to work through what at the time does not seem available to words. That to me seems to be the essence of psychoanalysis: to help provide the person with a safe place to learn how to reflect on themselves, on their conflicts and their past and to come to understand that which has been enacted, repeated, and traumatic but not consciously verbalized, in order to help enhance internalization, mentalization, and integration. I also think that another result can be greater affect regulation, object constancy, and individuation. Even with the more deeply disturbed, we may eventually get sufficient consolidation to begin to tackle preoedipal and oedipal rivalries—who knows how far the work can go! Is that enough to qualify as psychoanalysis? I think so.

Turning to the theoretical thread of my analytic framing of the work, I hope I have shown in the brief vignettes that the way I work as a Freudian analyst has added many branches to my central tree of theory. I feel that my additional development beyond my initial grounding in Freudian thought has supported my identity as a Contemporary Freudian, even though I have taken concepts out of their full contexts from other psychoanalytic points of view. You may not have heard in what I have presented every newer theoretical addition to my lexicon, but much will seem evident. And while not specifically identified, echoes of influence would also include Kohut's self-object, Mahler's separation-individuation process, Bach's explanations of narcissism, and Wurmser's (and others') understanding of masochism. Further of importance are Klein who brought mother to the fore and helped me to people Freud's inner life with internal objects and part objects and the developmental oscillation between paranoid and depressive states of mind, plus Winnicott, for his emphasis on transitional phenomena and holding environment and Bion's containment and focus on thinking.

In sum, my work with patients who have strong narcissistic and masochistic features demonstrates that the conflicts can only be addressed successfully once the narcissistic and object relational pathology has been worked through sufficiently. My Freudian frame is laced, with threads from those current theorists who have specialized in very early narcissistic and relational approaches, and I close with the repetition of my wish to continue to be open to new additions to my Freudian foundation.

Thank you for listening.

REFERENCES

Loewald, H.W. (1989). *Papers on Psychoanalysis.* New Haven: Yale Univ. Press.

Smith, H.F. (2001) Obstacles to integration: Another look at why we talk past each other. *Psychoanal. Psychol.*, 18:485–1514.

———— (2003). Editor's introduction Round Table: Discussion by editors of major psychoanalytic journals on their perspectives of current and future trends in psychoanalysis. *Psychoanalytic Quarterly* 72:1–12

Wurmser, L. (2007). *Torment Me But Don't Abandon Me.* Lanham, MD: Rowman + Littlefield Publisher.

CHAPTER 21

Battling the Life and Death Forces of Sadomasochism[8]

(2010). *Int. J. Psychoanal.*, 91(4):969-972.
With Ellen Sinkman.

Harriet Basseches, Chairperson, introduced the subject by stating that some sadomasochism is found in every case. It is a matter of differing degrees. She noted that it may be natural to find pleasure in pain, both one's own and others' pain, although it may be a difference in kind when the severity of the sadomasochism functions out of the bounds of human expectations and becomes perverse.

Basseches recounted Freud's (1917) implication that a child's built-in potential for sadomasochism derives from both sexual and aggressive strivings. Shengold (1989) argues for the centrality of Freud's (1919) anal stage of development in organizing much of character and functioning. Klein (1957) sees the infant as struggling from the outset between love and hate toward the internalized essence of the caregiver. These theoreticians note the possibility of pathological, sadomasochistically tinged outcomes.

---

8 Panel held at the 46th Congress of the International Psychoanalytical Association, Chicago, Illinois, USA, 1 August 2009. Panelists: Nancy Goodman, Paula Ellman, Aiban Hagelin, Madeleine Bachner, Shmuel Erlich. The title of the panel was based on the publication of a book edited by Harriet Basseches, Paula Ellman, and Nancy Goodman entitled, ***Battling the Life and Death Forces of Sadomasochism: Clinical Perspectives***, 2013, Karnac.

Other authors have focused on sadomasochistic behavior as defensive and reparative (Bach, 1994), and on the primitive superego underlying sadomasochists' thinking (Wurmser, 2007). Basseches introduced panelists Nancy Goodman and Paula Ellman, who presented patients showing murderous transferential feelings and sadomasochistic features, as well as eliciting certain transference-countertransference dynamics. Three discussants commented on the cases.

Nancy Goodman used the metaphor of the Leviathan, a sea-monster, in her presentation, *Living with the Leviathan*, to convey forces of sadomasochism in her analysis of Mr. B. The Leviathan expressed active and passive forms, as well as enactments, of sadomasochism within Mr. B's psyche, her own psyche, and interactions of their minds. The giant squid had tentacles, a sucking and chewing mouth, a magical anal sphincter, and special visual capacity. Because confronting any difference between himself and another person ignited terror of destruction, Mr. B used disavowal to view the world. Disavowal helped him perversely to know and not know, and to use relationships as fetishes.

The divorced scientist entered treatment after a relationship with a woman ended, and he felt hopeless and invisible. Goodman was deeply concerned about his despair and sense of emptiness. She felt that Mr. B enacted deadness when he fell asleep or experienced what he called 'floating' on the couch. His silence evoked her silence as she imagined what his silence communicated. Important childhood memories were: (1) being kept in his highchair until he had eaten what his mother wished, and (2) receiving an enema every three days that he did not have a bowel movement. As an adult, he was reluctant to spend time and money.

These stories helped Goodman to understand her strong reactions including alternately wanting to force life into him and merging into his sleepiness. She felt that he wanted to deaden her in order to make her a safe partner. Issues of who would control and who would submit were active dynamics.

After three years of analysis, Mr. B began dating, but continually found imperfections in women. He also described images of an idyllic village; any imperfection in this scene propelled him to retreat in desperate depression.

Goodman felt powerless and teased by Mr. B's not exploring such potentially symbolic material. When she pointed out his attacking character assassinations, he delighted in his power to devalue her and make her feel unexciting. She used a dream of Mr. B's to elucidate his relating to her either as a not fully separate fetishized attachment or as a disavowed other. Being denied acknowledgement that she existed and feeling tortured by the pain he transmitted to her, she wanted to attack him. Goodman ultimately understood that her assessments of unanalyzeability were actually disavowals of sadism.

Mr. B began to tolerate one woman enough to live with her. In analysis, he conveyed some experiences verbally, not merely creating torture in his analyst. Then he abruptly announced that he was leaving treatment. Agreeing to working for a few more months, he and Goodman noted some ability to recognize her as separate and to wish to feel her. Nevertheless, fury about feeling forced, disinterested, and evacuated ensued. With a degree of mutual listening, they agreed to terminate.

Paula Ellman, the second panelist, gave a presentation entitled *Sadomasochism in work and play.* Her patient Diane was a lesbian academic who began psychoanalysis because of unhappiness with her female partner. A perfectionist who had always driven herself to excel athletically and academically, she suffered for years from crippling foot pain. Diane had had few satisfying relationships with women or men. She blamed herself and others for these difficulties and for sadomasochistic conflicts in her sexual life.

She had felt guilty about her homosexuality since 'coming out' in her 20's. She liked the idea of being in control. She felt pleasure in thinking of a penis penetrating her but disgust in thinking of submitting to a man's sexual urges. With women partners, she harshly criticized herself for never allowing herself pleasure but felt self-indulgent when sexually aroused. She described unbearable submission to her partner and arousal in that pain.

The sixth of seven siblings, Diane came from a strict Catholic family. Her oldest brother was revered by the parents although Diane's achievements surpassed those of the entire family. There were strict proscriptions against masturbation by her mother, who nonetheless accepted the father's masturbatory exhibitionism: genital scratching. Diane felt painfully rejected by her parents' contempt for her lesbianism.

Diane challenged Ellman's competence and ethics, leading Ellman to struggle with her own rage. Ellman believed that, when Diane became aware of the presence of another's need, she felt that there was no room for her own. She could not tolerate the frustrating difference between what she wanted and the satisfaction of that need. Ungratified urges caused her harshly to condemn and attempt to destroy the other (before the self), and to fall back on her isolation. Her struggles were rooted in her sadomasochism.

Clinical material included expressions of Diane's anger at masculinity, compulsive drivenness, self-condemnation, and terror of annihilation of herself and others. Her sadomasochism was closely associated with her ravenous hunger, which was partly manifested in fervor about oral sex. Ellman countertransferentially felt tortured, powerless to penetrate Diane with knowledge, desirous of forcing Diane to submit, and depriving. Ellman quoted Frosch (1995) when she noted that the sadomasochistic construction is a version of missing psychic structure that allowed the person to maintain differentiation between self and object (thought and action), when the structuralization necessary for differentiation has been compromised.

Aiban Hagelin, the first discussant, raised several issues. Has Diane's identification with her father, including his genital scratching, been worked through? Hagelin suggested that 'psoriasis' may give sadomasochistic pleasure with body parts which represent the father's penis. Does Ellman consider homosexuality a preference or an impulsive neurosis? Was Diane repressing heterosexuality while stating she is gay? Hagelin wondered whether Goodman's patient Mr. B is as monstrous as Goodman feels. He suggested applying empirical research methods, such as Luborsky and Crits-Cristoph's CCRT (1997), to analyze and measure the transference. Any sadomasochism would be manifested using this research tool.

The second discussant, Madeleine Bachner, began with Ellman's case. Bachner regards sadomasochism as linked to sexual arousal. The case of Diane illustrated sadomasochism in the libidinization of pain. Bachner would have liked to know more about the transference-countertransference dilemma and about the homoerotic transference. Bachner agreed with Frosch's quotation and was interested in how Ellman used such thinking about masochism as a version of missing structure. Perhaps it avoids disintegration and confusion.

Bachner asserted that Goodman enabled Bachner to empathize with the torment which Goodman felt. Goodman described very well the claustrophobic agoraphobic dilemma of borderline patients and their creation of gaps in order to break loose. Bachner believed that the paper illustrated a person wanting closeness but finding deficits, rather than a person who relates sadomasochistically. Bion's (1993) concepts of attacks on linking and of container-contained were of great relevance.

Shmuel Erlich, the third discussant, posed several questions. Should we always regard pain and rage as sadomasochism? Are there irreducible indicators of sadomasochism? What are the links between sadomasochism and the differentiation of self from other?

Erlich asserted that Mr. B suffered from a deep sense of not existing, not from a sadomasochistic disturbance. The death drive is experienced as inner deadness. This state is so difficult for him to communicate in words that he communicates by inflicting it on the analyst. Goodman demonstrated suffering with that deadness. Only analysis provides help: not by interpretation, but by maintaining an analytic setting where symbolization gradually appears. Erlich said that Mr. B, reluctant to expose his deadness to his analyst, hid behind aggressive attacks. On the contrary, Ellman's patient openly inflicted her erotized sadomasochistic experience on her analyst.

In discussion with the audience, additional issues emerged, such as defining sadomasochism. Is it libidinization of pain? Is it deadness? Arlene Richards included moral sadomasochism wherein patients experience pleasure through denigrating the analyst and others. Another audience member asked if the patients' hatred was aimed at getting rid of sexual excitement. Liz Fritsch wondered how to avoid enactments. Leon Wurmser remarked that sadomasochism is de-humanized sexuality and sexualized humanization.

REFERENCES

Bach, S (1994). *The language of perversion and the language of love*. Northvale, NJ: Aronson.

Bion, W. (1993). *Second thoughts: Selected papers on psychoanalysis*. London: Karnac.

Freud, S. (1917). On transformations of instinct as exemplified in anal erotism. *Standard Edition* 17, *125-33*.

——— (1919). A child is being beaten: A contribution to the study of the origin of sexual perversions. *Standard Edition* 17, *175-204*.

Frosch, A. (1995). The preconceptual organization of motion. *J. Amer. Psychoanal. Assn. 43:423–47.*

Klein, M. (1957). *Envy and gratitude.* NY: Basic Books.

Luborsky, L., & Crits-Christoph, P. (1997). *Understanding transference: The core conflictual relationship theme method.* Washington, DC: APA.

Shengold, L. (1989). *Soul murder.* New Haven, CT: Yale UP.

Wurmser, L (2007). *Torment me, but don't abandon me.* Lanham, MD: Rowman & Littlefield.

CHAPTER 22

The Challenge of Femininity Conflicts about the Feminine and the Masculine in Men and Women

Presented on Panel: The Challenge of Femininity.
July 28, 2019, IPA London Congress.

Abstract: Conflictual as well as ego syntonic feelings associated with the feminine and the masculine in both men and women occur side by side with their opposites regularly in psychoanalytic work. Clinical material will be offered to highlight these emerging analysands' self-states, supported by work in the transference. Significant underlying issues will be discussed with clinical material.

Before I speak about the conflicts over the feminine and the masculine, I want to clarify what I refer to when I say, "the feminine," or for that matter, "the masculine." There is a complicated series of terms related to "the feminine" and "the masculine" which convey both subtle, distinct meanings but also overlapping or converging meanings. For example, a person's sex is a biological concept, which carries anatomical, physiological/hormonal freight as well as genetic significance. In contrast, a person's gender is thought of as a social and cultural concept about a person's identification of himself as male or female and is closely connected to the person's sense of self. Gender can also be attributed to a person by others, starting with parental designations. A fourth concept which could certainly have relevance to the topic chosen here would be object choice, either heterosexual or homosexual. However, this topic will only be dealt with as it emerged in the treatments to be discussed as a source of conflict over "the feminine" and "the masculine" and will not otherwise be part of the discussion.

The focus here will be on the psyche. Of course, the psyche refers to the aspects of a person's mind where all these concepts are organized and processed. While it would not be amiss to include in the discussion biology and in particular the environmental influences both personal and societal, the magnitude and range of the subject invites a limit in focus.

Freud (e.g., 1925, 1927, 1931), when he spoke of castration and penis envy, seemed to be acknowledging the biological phenomena of the male having a penis that metaphorically could be lost via castration and the female lacking such an appendage, as well as the female having a clitoris and vagina. Yet, he was clearly not only referring to the biological, when he commented that "[t]he biological, social and psychological meanings of 'masculine' and 'feminine' are hopelessly mixed" (1914, p.55). Rather he was focusing on what goes on in the minds of the male and female child in their fantasies when he turned to "the feminine" (and "the masculine") (Freud, e.g., 1914, 1915, 1928, 1931, 1937). There, he seemed to consider these as attitudes that he characterized as "passive receptive," for the feminine, on the one hand, and "active, aggressive," for the masculine.[9] It was associated with these attitudes that his theory of bisexuality allowed for both the male and the female to have feminine and masculine states of mind. He further thought, on the basis of his understanding of female development, that the female child's discovery of the lack of an external appendage of the size of the penis centrally led her to feeling intense penis envy and ultimately to a feeling of inferiority. Moreover, Freud's hypothesis that fear of castration in the male child propels him to make a shift from early identification with

---

9 The antithesis active-passive coalesces later with the antithesis masculine—feminine.

the mother to the father—coupled with the development of his superego following the resolution of his oedipal complex—seemed to be viewed by Freud as a satisfactory developmental process; whereas he cast the female child's developmental and oedipal progression as leaving her with a feeling of inferiority, and with a weaker superego (1937).

There have been many criticisms of Freud's understanding of female development and psychology, and many revisions of his theory to accommodate other analysts' conceptualization. For example, the importance of the female child's anal stage development as a source for her aggression and feelings toward her mother (Oliner, 1982); the evidence that she knows early in her development about her own anatomy of vagina and clitoris helps in adding the concept of an inner genital phase—made up of prephallic and preoedipal factors—as described by Kestenberg (1982); and that penis envy, which, until this has taken place, has no psychological meaning" 2015, p. 134. does not stand alone as the central and sole source for the female child's passage of growth (Lachmann, 1982) are elements of the many changes in psychoanalytic thinking about feminine development that have moved well beyond Freud. My own analytic group reported on our research that supports later theoretical positions with regard to female development (Basseches, et al, 1996; Fritsch, et al, 2001).

Nevertheless, there is a point on this subject that Freud has made that bares further thought, and that is his contention of 'repudiation of femininity' (1937, p. 250) in both sexes. His claim is that this repudiation in the male and female take different paths. He states "...in the female, [the path is via] an envy for the penis—a positive striving to possess a male genital—and, in the male, [it emerges related to] a struggle against his passive or feminine attitude to another male. (1937, p. 250) Freud's emphasis on the meaning of feminine and masculine as primarily to do with "passive receptive vs active aggressive" may not encompass the entire meaning of the terms feminine and masculine, but I hope to share some clinical material to support the idea that there are conflicts for both sexes with regard to what one might think of as relevant to this premise. I believe my psychoanalytic data suggests that the struggle is broader than Freud had suggested for both the male and the female. When thinking about male patients, it has seemed that there can be strong evidence of concern not only with a passive attitude to another male, as Freud proposed, but also regarding both passivity and aggression toward another male as well as toward a woman; so too, women have expressed concerns over both femininity AND their masculine strivings with regard toward others of both sexes. I would like now to turn to some clinical material.

To start, I have observed in almost every female patient whom I have treated in psychoanalysis or psychoanalytic psychotherapy body image concerns that take the form of feeling too fat[10]. What does this mean, being too fat? A social explanation at least in the U.S. would attribute such a concern to a societal expectation that feminine beauty requires thinness. But in analysis, I have found instances of ambivalence toward the look of pregnancy—a unique capacity of a woman. There, the equation is "being fat equals being pregnant." But why would a woman not wish to look pregnant, especially since having a baby, as Freud suggested (e.g., 1937), has often been a driving force for many women—a truth whether or not one subscribes to Freud's notion that the "wish for a penis is destined to be converted into a wish for a baby and for a husband." (1937, p. 251). Perhaps, this conflict when present speaks to a fear of loss of feminine sexual allure—an impregnated woman might be viewed as "off limits" for sex and sexual desire, as if the pregnant woman's body was unappealing or even ugly. I have also found examples of women who fear pregnancy and having a baby, even as they pursue efforts consciously expressing a desire to have a baby.

---

10 Obviously, there are well documented examples of people—both female and male—who are concerned with being too thin, but members of that population had not graced my practice.

A second meaning, perhaps a corollary to a wish not to look pregnant, however, is the wish to have such slimness of body that her female shape would recreate her prepubescent boyish figure. On occasion, this wish has been cloaked in a wish for a body like Twiggy, a female model who was very thin, flat chested and minimally curvy. In that image, the female would aspire to being a boyish-looking female. Sometimes such an adolescent girl might be called a Tomboy, thus capturing a masculine wish, but in the form of a boy—not a man. A possible explanation for such a wishful boyishness has shown itself as her unconscious or preconscious fear that the father or mother might have favored the boy child over her. For these women, this perception or belief in the favored status of the boy did seem to encapsulate some advantage the penis-barer was said to hold. The fantasy of out besting the boy could as well have the effect of protecting her from the danger of competing with the oedipal father figure or her fear of provoking him.

While I have not often had a similar experience of male patients being focused as verbally on body image, there have been some cases. One male patient, who I will describe more fully, was obsessed with his fear of being fat, which he was not. He claimed that during his childhood, his mother had relentlessly expressed worry about his being fat and eating too much, and his father was said to always be critical toward him so that he felt he could never do anything right—even though the father was also said to speak boastfully about him to others. While not stated explicitly, his mother's attitude seemed to be interpreted by him as his being unappealing looking in physique, by implication, not being boyish or manly looking. While wanting to disregard her constant message, he described finding himself as believing her, well beyond his childhood years. Toward her, he described having a very hostile but dependent attachment upon her. He oscillated in portrayal of his relation to his father, between a feeling of admiration for his father and muted competitiveness with him, although his experience with his father was as if the father was the one who was competitive with him. He expressed a general liking of his father in contrast to his consistent anger toward his mother that at least toward the father seemed compartmentalized separately from the resentment of his father's described criticalness (Freud, 1928).

This 41-year-old patient was a 6 foot-1 inch man with a slender build. We came to understand that the "fat" issue, while intertwined with other ideas to be discussed shortly, was shorthand for fear of being perceived as feminine or passive, both by other males, but almost more so by females. This man had several traumas that crowded his analysis. The first of these occurred when he was 2 and ½: his mother became very ill at the delivery of his newborn sister and remained in the hospital for several weeks following the birth. He attributed his later flatness of mood and bent toward intellectualization as formed from this traumatic experience which he labelled as abandonment and led to a lifelong fear of abandonment. His fear of abandonment was so strong that it emerged in the very early stages of the analysis, when a brief absence by the analyst led him to claim feeling abandoned by her. At the time, the analyst did not experience him as having a strong attachment to her. But back to the trauma, his report of the loss of his mother was minimally associated with the birth of the sister, yet his disinterest and negativity toward the sister seemed residual. It seemed too that his blissful feelings toward his mother abruptly and forever were disrupted and his feelings toward his sister could be described as contemptuous, dutiful, and otherwise neutral. Further, he claimed that as a child, he would rather not have any toys than to have to share them. In growing up, he felt dominated by a mother who he felt would not listen to him and was resentful because he believed she took his prizes as her own. His resentment based on this assessment remained with him into adulthood.

The second painful trauma began when he was about 8, when a 3-years-older, and much bigger boy, son of family friends, pulled down his pants. When he told his mother, she dismissed it as just playing. When he was 11, however, that same boy, with whom he was often left alone, overpowered him by twisting his arm behind his back until he gave up. The end result was inspection and eventual mutual masturbation, a sequence repeated for some years, but never reported to anyone, until he had treatment in college. The mutual masturbation eventually was accompanied by tutoring on sexual encounters with girls. The abusing boy and his family moved away in my patient's teen years, which seemed to free him to pursue girls.

Fear of the feminine in himself took many forms. Besides his concerns about "fat," he harbored resentments toward his wife for dragging him on trips, which he eventually acquiesced to and even enjoyed, much as had been his description of his eventual dealings with the childhood abuser. Toward his wife he felt these were times when he was submissive. He replicated those feelings toward his analyst over a variety of frame issues. He described an insight which began with his thinking that his analyst distanced herself from him, but then realized that he was the one creating the distancing. When he would reassure himself that he had autonomy, for example, by keeping his distance in the treatment, then he would describe feeling manly and exhilarated.

Nonetheless, he suppressed his anger and tried to avoid conflict with his analyst, as he had done with his parents, and later with his wife, and did so in career moves with superiors AND subordinates. He had a mantra of it being "ok" to be second but not to win, which he attributed to his wish to defeat his mother by not getting prizes, but nevertheless experienced as disappointing misses from academic and career successes that could have been his. He would begin to compete and then fade back —similarly in a sport that he loved. He would describe in business his avoidance of conflict, even to the point of changing professions from an aggressive field to a creative food industry business.

The reason he came for treatment was primarily for sexual difficulties with his wife, having occasional impotence following successful foreplay. The difficulties seemed connected to his resentments for pleasuring his wife which again appeared to him as if she would take his prize, and was a submission; he was often able to achieve orgasm if he fantasized that he was a big muscular strong man. He denied homoerotic feelings expressing the idea of kissing a man as disgusting and fantasized wanting to kill the abuser from his childhood.

Another male patient, also in his 40's, came to treatment toward the end of divorce proceedings. He described a relationship with the wife that was sadomasochistic in tone, and in which she appeared to primarily play the role of the sadist and he the masochist or victim. The divorce, however, followed his having affairs, which could be viewed as retaliatory and sadistic. He, like the previously described patient, moved from feeling stoic and self-congratulatory that he could "take it," referring to the vitriol from the angry wife. He felt that her angry diatribes often cast him as unmanly, which shamed him. Later in the analytic work, his shame feelings shifted to his passivity and then to his deviousness regarding the affairs. In his professional life—in a very aggressive field—he both embraced competition but also disliked conflict; he sometimes ended up feeling shamed in the ways he avoided conflict. In contrast, he was unconflicted and very aggressive when playing sports. In the treatment, he was, on the one hand, very engaged and receptive to thinking analytically, and on the other hand, felt it was a submission, which eventually led him to conclude the treatment prematurely. Leaving the analysis, he returned some years later for once-weekly treatment.

I view these two men as demonstrating a struggle against passivity, with both men and women, but also fearful and avoidant of their aggression.

I turn to several woman who have been in treatment, also as exemplars. Here, I describe a 50-year-old woman who was the oldest of eight children and struggled with her wish to be boss, which could be thought of as a masculine wish, an attitude oscillating with a guilty and ashamed masochistic stance. As oldest, she had felt separate and superior to her siblings because she was often given responsibility over them. At the same time, she felt that the boys were always the favorites and were entitled to become doctors like her father, something she believed was off limits for her even though she also felt she was her father's favorite. First becoming a teacher, she eventually became a lawyer, but in her chosen profession never allowed herself the successes that would have appeared accessible. Later, as a contract attorney, she worried repeatedly as to whether she was too aggressive. She experienced her male siblings as advantaged over her, and was angry and hurt by her female siblings as well as her daughters for not following her lead as she thought she had done with her own mother, a mother whom she also felt favored the boys. Her marriage partner was mother-approved and was treated at times with the disapproval and criticalness with which she graced her brothers and blamed him for the inhibitions in their sex life. As an adult, when the parents went into a retirement facility, she stole her mother's necklace and then after discussion with her priest, returned it.

I have tried to show that this was a woman haunted by penis envy and strong masculine strivings, who at the same time, wanted to be a "good girl." Yet she also felt she could only have the perks of the feminine through resentful compliance and, in a kind of despair, through theft. While often wanting to lead, she was quick to feel shamed and inferior. As with the priest and wanting to be a good girl, her superego seemed childlike and naive.

This next example focuses on a woman whose conscious sense was that she did not want to become pregnant or have a child. For this woman, tragedy had befallen her when she was four years old following the arrival of her sibling. Shortly after her brother was born, her mother was diagnosed with cancer and died relatively quickly. The patient grew up close to her father, but remained in grief for the loss of her mother. As a grown-up, she sought treatment for adjustment disorder having come to a new area to live and feeling isolated and alone, although accompanied by a devoted husband. She was guarded but at the same time psychologically very receptive. The receptivity was tinged, however, with judging herself and she suffered readily from feelings of shame. After some years of treatment, the question of becoming pregnant emerged, she having been married for several years. She was very frightened about this, recalling her mother's death following a pregnancy. But more significant, she claimed, greater than her fears for her own health was her fear that she would not, could not, love this potential child. She eventually did become pregnant, barely could utter the news and discussed it with no one, wore non-maternity clothes well beyond what might be expected. She tried to control everything she could think of, including having a caesarian on a date specified. She did eventually look pregnant, i.e., "fat," but maintained an attitude almost of indifference. The delivery went well, and happily she was able to reassure herself that she could love the child, whom she gave the name of her lost mother. Eventually, there was to be a second child, and again she worried if she could make space for this child in her life, especially given her extreme devotion to the first child. This time, similarly, she planned everything, was very discrete about her condition, and this time, she stopped treatment just immediately previous to the scheduled caesarian arrival of the second child.

I never heard from her again after she said "goodbye" at that final session. The transference seemed to center on a longing for closeness and being mothered balanced by an expressed denial of any wish for such intimacy. I did not mention that this woman was unusually short, lending a child-like aura about her, even though she was a highly skilled professional in a psychological field. With great determination and will she struggled over that part of her which did not want to grow up and succeed at the maternal function that was only the entitlement, in her mind, of her own mother.

I will give one more example of a woman's attitude to her femininity, even though I could continue to tell of others. This was a talented young Asian woman who was in her 20's. She had a vibrant sexual life in this country, not the country of her origin. She left her own home country, where she described herself as submissive and to some extent disadvantaged and bullied by an older male sibling. In the United States, however, she behaved in a forward and aggressive manner both sexually, and in her choice of language as well. She explained that she would never have allowed herself to act and speak in the way she allowed herself to behave in the U.S. in her home country and home language. She had a dream that she was in a circular gathering of women, who were each sitting on the ground with legs crossed. Each woman showed off to the others her own giant erect penis that stood between her legs. The dream expression seemed to capture her wishful belief that in the United States she could be among women with penises, especially her analyst. But her anxiety suggested that forbidden wishes, while gratifying when safe to express, also led to great unease and guilt.

I have given examples from my practice of both men and woman whom I perceive as struggling with their passive feminine yearnings. To enjoy the pleasures of passivity and its companion of submissiveness seem reproachable and shaming. Yet the dilemma seems compounded by problems over aggression. To fight or dominate seems to create another set of conflicts, again in both men and woman and toward both men and women. I have highlighted Freud's contention of the repudiation of the feminine and I do not want to underestimate the importance of that, especially with regard to a lack that the members of each sex may feel. Nonetheless my sense of the difficulties over aggression makes me think that there is more. If one thinks of bisexuality as a longing for both the feminine and the masculine, then it is not a great leap to picture envy for what the other is perceived to have that one believes oneself lacks along with a fear of having too muchness—too much of what one fears is one's own endowment.

Thus, I have tried to make a case that supports Freud's contention that repudiation of the feminine is present in both men and women, suggesting that there is a feeling of lack or inferiority to be found in members of both sexes similarly (Chervet, panel paper and personal conversation). Despite that conclusion, however, it appears that the active aggressive masculine strivings present other conflicts for both sexes, as well, leaving the human condition in a state of imperfect reality.

REFERENCES

Basseches, H.l., Ellman, P., Elmendorf, S., Fritsch, E., Goodman, N., Helm, F.l., Rockwell, S. (1996). Hearing what cannot be seen: A psychoanalytic research group's inquiry into female sexuality. *Journal of the American Psychoanalytic Association* 44:511–528.

Chervet, B. (2019). Presentation on Panel: The Challenge of Femininity, paper entitled: "Why everybody is not bisexual?". London, IPA Congress, July 28.

Freud, S. (1914). On the History of the Psycho-Analytic Movement. *S.E.* 14:7–66.

——— (1915). Instincts and Their Vicissitudes. *S.E.* 14:117-140.

Freud, S. (1920). The psychogenesis of a Case of Homosexuality in a Woman. *S.E.* 18: 147–172.

——— (1924). The Economic Problem of Masochism. *S.E.* 19:159–170.

——— (1924) The Dissolution of the Oedipus Complex. *S.E.* 19:173–179,

——— (1925). Some Psychical Consequences of the Anatomical Distinction between the Sexes. *S.E.* 19:248–258.

——— (1926). The Question of Lay Analysis. *S.E.* 20:212.

——— (1927). Fetishism. *S.E.* 21:152–157.

——— (1928). Dostoevsky and Parricide. *S.E.* 21:177–196.

——— (1931). Female Sexuality. *S.E.* 21:225–243.

——— (1937). Analysis Terminable and Interminable. *S.E.* 23: 216--253.

Fritsch, E., P. Ellman, H. Basseches, S. Elmendorf, N. Godman, F. Helm, S. Rockwell (2001). *The Self, An Exploration of Early Female Development,* D. Mendell, Ed. New Jersey: Jason Aronson, Inc.

Lachmann, F. M. (1982). Narcissistic Development. Chapter 8 in *Body and Self*, D. Mendell, Ed., N.J.: Jason Aronson, Inc.

Oliner, M. M. (1982). The Anal Phase. Chapter 2 in *Body and Self*, D. Mendell, Ed., NJ: Jason Aronson, Inc.

CHAPTER 23

Panel: The Challenge of Developing New IPA Psychoanalytic Groups Harriet Basseches, Co-Chair for North America

I want to begin by saying how wonderful it has been to be a member of this committee under Claudio Eizirik's leadership. I am constantly learning from him, from the thoughtful other co-chairs and members of the committee and continually from Jo Beavis and her staff, who provide the glue that makes our work possible. Thank you all.

The ING covers the development of new IPA psychoanalytic group in three major regions of the world: Europe, South America, and North America. As co-chair for North America I am responsible for helping new groups that want to become part of the IPA family of component societies. These include primarily any new groups forming in the United States and Canada, and has included Mexico. At the present time, there is one group in progress at the Study Group level in Vermont, the Vermont Psychoanalytic Study Group (VPSG).

As you may know, there has been a clear set of procedures and progressions which have been carefully calibrated over time and are constantly evaluated when a need for change occurs. There also are organizational issues that emerge when new groups begin to form, and as they develop, that present challenges to the successful and creative success of groups. I will speak more about that in a moment.

First, though, I will discuss an example of the adaptation the ING is constantly invited to face. While the program is well developed in the three regions mentioned above, groups from a fourth region, Asia, have been expressing increasing interest in creating new IPA Psychoanalytic Groups. There are, of course, component societies existing in Asia, including Japan, India, and Australia, which have been a part of the IPA for a long time. Beyond these groups, however, there now is a lot of interest in psychoanalysis throughout Asia. In the early stages, those new interested groups have been assigned to the already existing regions to be carried until the Asian region is large enough and strong enough to be maintained as a fourth region on its own.

Pending that condition, in addition to my responsibilities in North America, I am covering groups in Asia, as follows: South Korea Study Group, Taiwan Study Group, and a brand-new Chinese Study group soon to be formed. The Taiwan and Korean Groups also have an Allied Centre, which is made up of people interested in psychoanalysis, but as an interest group, not a training center.

Each of the referenced study groups is assigned a Sponsoring Committee, that assists in all aspects of the formation of an Institute, helping the group to cohere as a group and meet the requirements to be a training center with the tripartite structure we are all familiar with of personal analysis, supervision, and educational seminars. Each Sponsoring Committee works with their group over a long period of time, in person twice a year, and then at regular short intervals in between. The Sponsoring Committees are also available to field problems that may arise and in general function as supportive guide. With that guidance, each new group progresses through its development from a study group to a provisional society—at which time it works with an ING Liaison Committee which provides a less directive support and on to become a component society of the IPA, having met the requirements of status first to form a study group, then to advance to a provisional society and finally to achieve full component society status, being voted into the IPA by the IPA Board and membership.

Each new group has its own challenges, based on the unique characteristics of its local circumstances. Such initial issues as having sufficient number of IPA members some of whom must function as Training and Supervising analysts, being able to convene together easily in an accessible location, having basic financial resources to operate, and a pool of potential candidates to train are all hurdles to be faced.

Moreover, there are cultural, historical and political aspects of such groups that may or may not be helpful to forming a psychoanalytic entity. Included in this latter perspective are historical and legal traditions within the local mental health establishment which support or discourage participation by one or another professional specialty. These traditions often run counter to psychoanalytic expectations of who could or could not be a psychoanalyst, and force potential new groups to struggle with whether to join the IPA's psychoanalytic approach or to remain nestled in their previously held boundaries.

There have emerged in addition a cluster of issues that seem almost to transcend the particular individual circumstances that each organization has. These issues seem to be found in many organizations. The first of these issues could be labelled rivalry. Rivalry may occur between two leaders of an organization, a rivalry that disrupts and sometimes defeats group formation by both parties leaving the situation; or such a rivalry may end up by one leader successfully defeating the other and thus emerging as the dominant leader. If both leave, the wounded group may still emerge with a lesser leader stepping in. Then it becomes a matter of whether the surviving group members can be generative enough to pass on to new generations their psychoanalytic organizational seed. While at first it may be a weaker entity, with time it can emerge as a stronger union absent the powerful, charismatic leader. The question that gets worked through, especially by the later generations, is whether the original traumatic rivalry stays buried in the fabric of relationships later to emerge as transgenerational trauma, or instead the later group can use awareness of that danger to be alert to and avoid the temptations and thus to unite.

While I do not know to what extent we can generalize more broadly to group formation, one of the most successful new groups has been led primarily (although not exclusively) by women, to broach a subject close to the theme of this conference. In this particular case, it happened that men provided guidance (as Sponsoring Committee) and a situation where a man was the original leader, but, like Moses, did not go on to the promised land of becoming part of the study group.

I mentioned a moment ago the charismatic leader. When the founder is such a leader, he brings enthusiasm and intensity to his role that draws a strong organizational group around him. It is then a meaningful challenge for such a person to not only provide the strong foundation for the group, but then, in the spirit of generativity, to help the next generations, to be able to continue the development of the organization. To let go of his centrality and transfer his leadership to others does not diminish but rather enhances his stature and respect. It seems to me the Moses metaphor mentioned above, though a lot to ask of someone who has achieved so much, creates an organizational triumph by letting go to build the greater legacy of a cohesive and forward-looking institution that can survive.

One point that I have mentioned only indirectly is the impact on groups of IPA sponsoring committees and later liaison committees. I believe that the role can be pivotal in the way that group foundation can be enhanced by their interventions or undermined. We in the ING need to pay close attention to the chemistry of those who function in these outside group supportive roles to be sure that it is actually a collaborative and supportive role and not an authoritarian one.

I close with the thought that the challenges of new group formation give all of us who are blessed with the opportunity to work on these issues our own sensitivity to the vitalness of keeping an eye on generativity.

CHAPTER 24

Infantile Sexuality and Trauma: Influence on Adult Sexuality

(2021), Presented on Panel entitled: In-between infantile
and traumatic quality
July 2021, IPA Vancouver Congress.

I am going to speak about a highly intelligent, self-reflective man named Alex. The patient's story could fit into many theoretical frameworks. I choose—based on the patient's associations what might be viewed as an old-fashioned psychoanalytic approach relying on Sigmund Freud's infantile psychosexual development (1905), Margaret Mahler's separation-individuation (1979), and Moses Laufer and M. Egle Laufer's central masturbation fantasy (1976;1984). I will hope to demonstrate the important roles played in the patient's life by the way these maturational and psychological developments appeared to proceed, as well as describing the impact of certain events which the patient experienced traumatically in both early childhood and adolescence that created the setting for his adult sexual feelings and behavior. I will also further describe those adult sexual feelings and behaviors. For now, however, I will only mention the symptom that led him to decide to enter psychoanalysis: difficulty and sometimes inability to ejaculate during intercourse with his wife.

Here is a brief picture of the patient's early childhood. He claims no memories of life earlier than when he was over 2 years old, but he, as an only child, seemed to feel closely connected to his mother. Nevertheless, when he was 2 and a half, a pivotal event seemed to change that. The adult patient,

Alex, recalled and often returned during the early years of his analysis, to this recollection or screen memory (Freud, 1922).

The description begins with his being awakened at night by his father, dressed, driven to Uncle Larry's, who then drove him to Grandma's home, where Grandma gave him her wonderful chicken soup, and where he stayed for the next several days. Then he was returned home, but he did not see his mother for many, many weeks. After some time, his baby sister, Sylvia, arrived home and at the same time came a lady whom he disliked intensely, a nurse who, he said, came to take care of Sylvia (and presumably, him). Many weeks later, his mother returned from the hospital. We speculated that when she did come home, she may still have been weak and not fully available to resume her motherly role for him and now also a newborn.

Alex marked this as the beginning of a fraught relationship with his mother, which involved both feeling very attached but angry and hostile. He described her as dominating, unable to listen to him, calling him fat all the way into his adolescence, not liking him, and in his view, wanting to get rid of him.

This set of beliefs held sway for Alex to the end of his mother's life, when she died of heart failure during the early years of his own marriage, and beyond. He attributed a long-held fear of abandonment to that 2-1/2-year- old's experience of loss of his mother. As an example of the continued presence of the abandonment theme, when the analyst reported to her new analysand that she would be observing national holidays by being out of the office on those occasions, he made no comment; however, when shortly thereafter, she actually reminded him of an up-coming national holiday absence, he reported feeling abandoned. That theme persisted long into the analysis, something we explored for associations many times; and later the theme seemed to weaken and eventually not be mentioned again until the termination phase of the work.

The recollection/screen memory of that 2-1/2-year-old episode would suggest that Alex might be destined to have severe sibling rivalry toward Sylvia, and he certainly described a somewhat belittling, superior, and patronizing attitude toward her as they grew up; but he also seemed to have a "big brother" supportive role as well.

I will mention two early life experiences with his sister. In one, when he might have been close to 5 years old, his parents were away, leaving the children with the nurse mentioned above. In a defiant act, he took his sister by the hand and walked to what he thinks was across at least 1 street, possibly 2, to a school playground. He reported that the caretaker came charging out, found them, and angrily brought them back. While he thought she was in a rage; I thought, also frightened. He, himself, reported the story as a triumph.

The second incident that he described in an offhand manner hints at but does not label sexual excitement: He, at about that same age, would bump unclothed bottoms with his sister following having been given a bath together. It is unclear when that activity began, how long it continued, nor any emotional feelings that he likely had toward either the bathing or the bottom bumping. Also unclear is who between them was the initiator.

That last thought has relevance in connection to his adult sexual activity as to whether he was the passive participant or the director of that behavior as a small child. In his adult life and in his psychoanalysis, he often complained of feeling "dragged along" by his wife's proposing an activity including sex. Further, he noticed that his first reaction to such initiations was with a "no" reaction, as in "I do not want to do that" or "I can't do that for a particular reason."

Nevertheless, he described that he usually "came around" to saying "yes," ending up expressing satisfaction with the activity, although during such times, noticed susceptibility to moments of resentment or irritability.

Another event that may have occurred when he was perhaps 6, was that the 3 years-older-son, John, of friends of his parents, when they were alone, pulled down his pants. When he told his mother about this unwelcome act, she brushed it off as "just playing." It is this same boy about whom he bitterly described a traumatic attack on him when he was 11 in which the older boy twisted his arm behind his back such that he felt great pain and mistakenly thought his arm might be broken. Afterward, the older child, John, pulled down Alex's pants and touched his penis.

In contrast to the patient's usual reporting of events without emotion, in this case, he expressed feelings of helplessness and that he had felt he had to submit for what he believed was his literal survival—in Freudian terms, possibly displaced castration anxiety (Freud, 1905, 1938). The event was the first of many repetitions of the sexual aspect minus the attack. What began as John's bullying changed after Alex reached puberty and could ejaculate. The relationship eventuated into a kind of friendship which continued with mutual masturbation until the patient was 15 when John went to college and his family moved elsewhere. Despite having readily told his mother about the earliest event, he never told either parent of the attack or the later activity. In fact, he never spoke of it to anyone until he went for therapy when he was anxious and depressed in his second year of college.

At first telling in analysis, he only expressed enraged feelings toward John and not the positive later friendship. Initiated at least originally by the older boy, the secretive part of the relationship focused mostly on the mutual masturbation; the public part consisted of craft activities, outdoor nature activities like fishing, plus an interest in fish procreating in a fish tank. These interests may have emerged from a combination of the older boy, John's, initiation and that of John's father who spent time doing projects with the boys. In adolescence, as the relationship with John continued, Alex's central masturbation fantasy (Laufer, 1976; Laufer & Laufer, 1984) crystalized into one person dominating another. It was unclear whether he rotated positions between being the dominant one or the one dominated.

Before moving from elements that seem to reflect derivatives of early infantile and adolescent states, I relate one more story associated with his belief that his mother wanted to get rid of him. On his birthday when he turned 5, on that very day, he proclaimed that she "dragged" him to school to begin Kindergarten—even though it was the spring, and the term was almost over—an act which he interpreted as her wanting to get rid of him.

While I have already inferred his generally hostile, but dependent attachment to his mother, I would like to give another example. When he was in 5th grade he won the science prize, which was a big deal. At home, he heard his mother boasting about it to her friend over the phone. He interpreted her boasting as "taking away his prize" and thereafter he claimed never to allow himself to do well enough to "come in first"; only second place would he allow. He cited a story, "The Long-Distance Runner"—in which a young man chose to stop short of winning a race for revenge toward a cruel authority figure.

In contrast to his attitude toward his mother, he seemed to feel more positive toward his father—nevertheless describing him as "present but emotionally distant" and critical. An example of the criticalness was described as walking with his father who told him he did not walk right, a criticism without clarity as to correction for the perceived problem. There were many such examples of criticism from both parents which appeared in support of Alex's sense of being unloved and/or to not like him in the way he needed. These ideas certainly suggest a difficulty resolving his oedipal strivings satisfactorily. On the other side of the ledger, however, he acknowledged that his mother seemed to provide him many cultural opportunities and seemed from his point of view attentive to the point of intrusiveness—particularly in his adolescence, and his father, in addition to being "present," paid for many opportunities for him including full payment for college expenses: Nevertheless, a muddied oedipal resolution.

He may have found some balance to his ambivalence toward the parents in the form of substitutes. In addition to his Grandma, I did mention his dislike of the early substitute nurse person, but this may have been counterbalanced somewhat by the Grandma. Also, he described becoming very attached to a couple who were friends of his parents. He described especially the woman of the couple as being a great listener (in contrast to his mother), and he continued the relationships well beyond the death of his parents. It is possible that he was able to work out his oedipal feelings to some extent with those sources. Also, I might have predicted a great deal more negativity toward me, the analyst; whereas he treated me with great warmth, respect, and interest, and described me also as a good listener, as if perhaps he saw me also as a better maternal substitute.

ADULT BEHAVIOR AND SEXUAL INTERESTS AND ACTIVITY

There are many interests that this patient described as an adult, but I will try to select only a few that I feel directly connect with his development. The first I will mention is cooking. He was a self-described excellent chef, cooked for himself and others especially during college and in his marriage. Further, he switched from an apparently successful career as a Ph.D. economist to become a professional chef, also a success although less remunerative. I can see this great interest both as tribute to his oral pleasures, his identification with his mother, and his replacement of her as the superior accomplisher. Of course, there are many male chefs, and cooking is emphasizing the positive elements of the oral phase. It does, however, raise the gender issue, as his mother was chef for the family. Parenthetically, you may recall, he began school at just 5, where he was the smallest and youngest. This haunted his early schooling, including in athletics. His feeling weak and small, being called fat by his mother (although so far as I could see, this was totally inaccurate) and, most importantly, the traumatic entrance into his life of his female sibling, ALL of these issues could have made him fear he was too feminine or, alternatively, wish to be feminine. But at least consciously that conflict was never reported as a concern. His sense of his maleness, albeit less physically powerful in his mind than he wished, was never at issue.

Following on his strong oral interests, the centrality of his anal phase development showed: In his wish to be independent, while also choosing to follow, his propensity to say "no," his obsessional tendency which has not been discussed but includes orderliness and being in control, ALL suggested the importance of anal phase development. Add to these the trauma of losing his mother for too long and the arrival of his sister, Sylvia, together creating a serious disruption in his previously on track separation-individuation process. As growth and time proceeded, whatever degree of oedipal solution was accomplished by the time of approaching preadolescence, the traumatic establishment of homosexual sexual activity with the boy, John, would have clearly further unsettled Alex's sexual choices.

It is worth noting that at some point during the relationship with John, the two boys would discuss "girls"; moreover, immediately following John's departure, Alex began to pay more active attention to girls. With no further sexual contact with boys, he established pal relations with several boys. In high school he had two different girlfriends, and with one, "fooled around" sexually. In college he felt anxious being alone with males in his dorm but had successful buddy relationships with both boys and girls. His first college girlfriend with whom he had his first intercourse was considerably older than he was. In his second year of college, she left town promising to return but didn't—possibly evoking separation anxiety that led Alex to therapy. After that, he seemed to have sex for sex only with women but with no commitment. Late in college, he again became serious with a young woman, but seemed unaware of any impact on his relationship with her when he went off for the summer with a male college chum on a travel adventure. When he returned, she gave him the cold shoulder. Understandably, her attitude made him very hurt and angry, and he did not see her behavior as provoked in any way by his own.

He met in graduate school the woman who became his wife. At the time of the psychoanalysis, they had been married for many years. They had some marital difficulties: first, when she wanted to have a baby something he did not want; he then believed that she claimed she would leave him if he did not concur—submit, in his view—which he resentfully did for fear of being left. Later, when the second son was around the age of 11—note the age—she became very active in her own career. He was furious with her and felt she abandoned both himself and the son. As Alex recalled, the sex between them in the early years, even after the birth of son number one, was very good. However, with this later set of events and following his anger and distress at her absences, the sexual difficulties to which I referred early in the paper began.

It is not clear whether his interest in homosexual pornography also began then, but he would masturbate admiring particularly well-muscled but not body-builder types of men who were very lean. The idea of having sex with a man repulsed him, but he wished he looked like such men. He also would masturbate thinking of an attractive girl whom he would dominate and overpower.

We worked on how angry he was at his wife still, and the primary symptom seemed to begin to ease. However, while pleased that the difficulty had eased, he also expressed concern over the fantasies that accompanied his successful path to ejaculation. He explained that after a certain point during intercourse, he noticed his arousal would diminish and he would feel numb; he would begin to fantasize that he was having sex with a tall, well-muscled lean man; and, as the excitement returned, he felt it was as if he would merge with the other man—as if it was now he, himself, who was this powerful man, at which point, he orgasmed. It seemed as if he was trying with some actual success to solve his oedipal conflict and to integrate his sexual dilemma into an acceptable outcome, but that it was still troubling to him. Alex continued to work on his solutions to the end of the analysis.

By way of conclusion, I have tried to demonstrate the way in which Alex's advancement through his early psychosexual development, including his separation and individuation interwove with experiences he had both with his primary parental figures and his younger sister; how the development and experiences coupled with his traumatic introduction to homosexual sexual activity with John, the older boy, profoundly influenced his adult sexual conflicts. In his mind, he was painfully caught between opposite outcomes and worked with great dedication in analysis to reconcile and resolve his conflict. To me, this exemplifies the impressive strength of the human spirit and the usefulness of the psychoanalytic process.

Thank you.

REFERENCES

Freud, S. (1905). Three Essays on Sexuality. *S.E.*, 7:135–243.

——— (1914). On Narcissism. *S.E.*, 14:73–102.

——— (1938). Splitting of the Ego in the Process of Defense. *S.E.*, 23: 275–78.

Kernberg, O. (1976/1984). *Object-Relations Theory and Clinical Psychoanalysis.* New York: Jason Aronson.

Laplanche, J. & Pontalis, J-B. (1973). *The Language of Psycho-Analysis.* New York: W.W. Norton.

Laufer, M. (1976). The Central Masturbation Fantasy, The Final Sexual Organization, and Adolescence. *Psychoanalytic Study of the Child* 31: 297–316.

Laufer, M. & E. (1984). *Adolescence and Developmental Breakdown.* New Haven: Yale University Press.

Mahler, M. S. (1979). *The Selected Papers of Margaret S. Mahler, Volume Two: Separation-Individuation.* NY: Jason Aronson.

Presentation on Panel:
When do the cure, our organizations and psychoanalysis become anchors?

IPA Lisbon Congress, August 1, 2025.

I have two separate goals in presenting this paper today: one is to talk about a clinical matter and the other to speak about several observations I have made of my psychoanalytic experiences regarding institutional practices of groups, particularly psychoanalytic groups, with which I have had contact over the span of my many years in the field. You may wonder why I have picked such diverse aspects of my work in the same paper, and I will try to explain. I have just completed a book of essays that covers a subset of papers I have written over the past more than 45 years. In the process of collecting essays for the book, I found that many of my papers fell into one of the two categories I mentioned previously: clinical reflections and observations of institutional practices of psychoanalytic groups. Thus, my assessment of the matters that concerned me over all those years led me to develop the book along those two lines, and now too, influence the topics of the paper I present today. Regarding the category of clinical reflections, it includes one particular clinical case because of my countertransference, which troubled me. When my patient, who is the subject of this discussion revisited a childhood trauma during therapy sessions, the retelling had a profound impact on my patient's transference and also on my countertransference. My internal reactions took me by surprise and made me feel vulnerable. I think part of the reason I felt vulnerable was because I, in a late stage of my psychoanalytic practice, began to discover feelings triggered because they were related to my own past traumas of loss. I discovered that both patient and analyst experienced similarities in certain core feelings.

Before discussing this further I go back to the thought I spoke of earlier—focusing on a situation when the patient's distress enters the transference and the countertransference, which trigger the analyst's own distress in this case of a series of personal loses. I must take a moment here to say that this may be my last attendance at one of these marvelous IPA Congresses. I am full of sadness and ambivalence-side-by-side with the pleasure of being with so many colleagues and friends. It is also a time when I am facing the challenging question of considering when the time is right to retire from practice? As for this very probably being my last IPA Congress, my daughter pointed out to me that I had said that also during the last Congress, so in fact, I cannot be sure that I will hold to the plan. Nevertheless, the feelings of loss and endings is present in my mind.

I mention the issue up front, well before I speak about the interaction of my personal events with my practical clinical work. There are several ways that these late stage decisions have affected both my life and my practice. Among the personal events that have interacted with my practical clinical work is first, the loss of my beloved husband of 63 years. Once he died, I experienced the ending of love and simultaneously, the loss of a significant way of life. Then my children started encouraging me to move from Washington, DC, where I have resided my entire adult life to move closer to one of them. Three years later, I finally determined to move from Washington, DC to a town close to Philadelphia, Pennsylvania where one of my children lives. This has not only entailed picking a place to live, uprooting me from my comfortable apartment and lifestyle, but also closing my office. Thus, after more than 45 years, I began seeing only virtually the small cadre of patients with whom I still work. I had worked virtually for a few months at the height of the pandemic but that was understood as a temporary precaution. As soon as I deemed it safe to go back, I quickly returned to working in my office. In the year before my husband became ill, my husband and I had also planned for me to reduce or close my practice in order to spend more time with him, since he had already retired. But as he became sick, then sicker, and as death was imminent, I changed that plan to keep my practice going, something that was a comfort in those most painful months after I lost him. But this time, as I was contemplating the move to Philadelphia, my patients and I understood that virtual interactions would be the only form of therapeutic communication I could offer after I had moved away from the area. This change was not only disruptive and a loss to my patients but especially so for me. I was uprooted, to move into a more institutional setting with all new connections and the requirement to adjust to a wholly unfamiliar locale.

With that background into my recent personal situation, I will turn now to the case. The example I am going to discuss for clinical reflection is complicated to describe. This is a case of a repeated disturbing family dynamic that, coursed through at least 3 generations of a family, and possibly more, in which each new instance repeats and intensifies the pain. One might use the terms, "family trauma," as a way to refer to the phenomenon. Before I describe the traumatic events and feelings, I do want to say a few words about what I mean by "trauma" without digressing deeply into a question of the meaning of the concept of trauma for the field of psychoanalysis. In this instance, I am using "trauma" to refer to instances that profoundly affect and negatively impact on the life and feelings of the child over which the child has no control, usually the result of behaviors of parental figures. These events are external, social events presented as facts, not feelings and thoughts. Thus, the description to follow is at the level of enactment and still missing underlying motivations.

The first iteration of this particular disturbing set of events occurs well before my patient was born. I only know bare bones information about this early disruption, experienced by the father of my patient when he was a little boy. My patient's grandfather, the father of that generation of the family leaves his wife, the mother, and their young son. I do not know the son's age at the time of the family loss, but I understand he is young. That father leaves to have an affair and eventually to marry this second woman. That son, my patient's father, grows up to marry and have a son of his own,–who will later become my patient. Nevertheless, repeating the behavior of the grandfather, this beloved father leaves his first wife and his son, the grandson. Like the grandfather before him, this father also leaves the original family unit of first wife and son to be with and eventually marry another woman other than the mother of my patient. The grandson, my patient, was approaching adolescence at the time of this family decomposition, lying about his age and getting a job after school, which demonstrates to him how he "does not need" the father. His contact with his own father with whom he had felt very close was irregular thence forward. In fact, at one point, he lost all contact with his father and had to hunt to find him again. This total loss of contact occurred after a period in which the father and his second wife had disallowed the son, my later patient, from their home. Parenthetically, I do not know if some aspect of actually or symbolically disowning the son also occurred in the first iteration, in the generation with the grandfather. My patient who had in the meantime married and had the first of three children is deeply hurt when the father only comes to meet his new grandchild at a motel but not with an invitation to their home.

Without then having conscious awareness of the repetition, after about ten or eleven years and difficulties in the marriage, my patient, the grandson, has an affair, leaves the marriage and eventually marries the "other" woman, as his grandfather and father had done before him. He enters treatment with me not long after leaving his wife and children with the expressed wish of wanting to explore his having left his wife with whom he seemed to have struggled in a masochistic way. At that time, however, he did not express awareness of the repetition in action.

Fast forward some years. My patient's new wife and he are trying to conceive a child. During this period, the second wife decides she cannot tolerate having his son from his first marriage, the great-grandson, in the house. At this point while listening to my patient as he discusses how he navigates the disruption in his own family unit, my countertransference begins to disturb me. I find myself hoping that he will not do to his son what was done to him and that he will tell his wife that he cannot follow through on her wish. I become aware that I believe I must not verbalize my own views on the matter because I am an analyst, not a counsellor, that is, not an advisor. In fact, had I followed my wish and helped him change the direction, would I not have entered into the family drama itself? Even so, I try to support him by acknowledging how painful this situation is while he is struggling with the issues. I start having a fantasy that through therapy I must somehow be a savior and must help this patient and this family. I imagine that by helping my patient to see the replications (parenthetically, of which I could relate more instances of parallels from the past), I can help him to avoid repeating the traumas of family decomposition and rejection of the son that have burdened the family for three generations. I learn that even with my efforts and support, and even though he professes that rejecting his son has broken his heart, my patient nevertheless decided to support and facilitate the wife's position and to reject his own son from their home, although he tells his son that the two of them will always continue meeting together at other locations than the home. The great-grandson reportedly expresses to his father, my patient, his feelings of rejection and expresses being heart broken. My patient reports that his second wife feels— perhaps correctly—that the son would like her not to exist, and that she feels similar wishes toward the son—that he not exist. And the father, my patient, in this repeating family nightmare is just heartsick in every direction as well as angry at all the participants. Nevertheless, he is seemingly doomed to continue the family pattern leading to an impasse because he is still incapable at this time of fully seeing, understanding and working through to ending the cycle of marital dissatisfaction, infidelity, expulsion of the son from the intimate family unit and loss.

The reason I picked this situation to speak about is that it shares some similarities with an aspect of my own childhood distress, a factor in me that has haunted me throughout my life. Later, contemplating my own childhood distress which while dissimilar in story line but similar in feelings of loss may have linked in my mind to my current issues of loss to the extent that I did not successfully help the patient find other solutions through analysis that could have prevented this sad—tragic— repetition. My patient's paternal family member's behavior turned into an ever repeating and devastating family pattern leading up to the impasse my patient experienced in the present day. My patient did experience an insight in the form of understanding why he chose as he did in the last decisions he had made, which was to follow his second wife's expressed needs shutting out the son. He realized that he feared that he would risk losing his wife— if he insisted on some continued effort at finding another and different resolution to partial estrangement from his son. He was concerned that the loss of his second wife would be a loss too close emotionally to the original traumatic loss of the father (and though not described here, had been preceded by an even earlier loss that made the entire situation even more painful). Also clearly relevant, as regards the transference relationship in his ongoing psychoanalytic therapy was the conscious but unfocused awareness that sometime – not yet determined-- the analyst would elect to "end the treatment," having moved to virtual communication, in itself a loss. As a result, the potential loss of the analyst served as yet another hypothetical loss, waiting in the wings to add potency and increased suffering into the mixture of losses. This loss, like the disappearance of his father, was a circumstance over which he had limited control. The only control he believed he had in this therapeutic relationship would be for him to take charge of the ending, something he was not ready to do.

While not wishing to make this discussion about an analysis of my issues, I can certainly point to my past and recent losses and my own protective stance toward further loss that led me to feel the bind of self doubt regarding how to help and support my patient as well as the boundary issues. Moreover, as I have had to confront my own aging and the disruptions that my recent move has engendered, as well as the amplification of any coincident limitations from both aging and moving, I have become aware that I have been conducting an ongoing assessment of my analytic capacities. This practice of reflecting on my analytic capacities is making me conscious of my own fear of losing my ability to fully use my analytic tools. In my mind, far from making me feel confident that I had identified a reliable and effective strategy to help my patient, I am instead experiencing feelings of shame that I was not doing my job to the best of my ability. Plus as a component of my countertransferance, I feel an identification with this patient in his grief. I do have the hope that with the new awareness of his fear of losing his chosen partner, he will make progress toward further self-reflection and find solutions that are less destructive for him and his family. Additionally, with the gradual, but not yet achieved awareness of his grief at the idea of the eventual loss of his analyst I also hope that he will in the near future become cognizant of the tools within himself needed to change the course of the unhealthy repeated history of family disintegration. In closing this section of the paper, I welcome your thoughts and ideas.

I turn now from this very personal rendition of clinical work to others of my experiences with psychoanalytic groups. In a review of these encounters, I have reflected on the fact that psychoanalysts (however versed in theories of the mind), still remain at the core, subject to the same forces as any other groups made up of human beings. In this closing section of the paper, I would like to share a few of these observations of psychoanalytic groups. As now a senior member of this community, I feel that sharing my observations may be relevant from a historical perspective.

The first observation came after a Committee representing a cluster of Independent Institutes in the US similar in training standards to the American Psychoanalytic Association invited me; to represent them. At the time, I was a candidate at the New York Freudian Society who lived in Washington, DC where COPA, the United States Accrediting Body, presides. I joined the American Psychoanalytic representative to argue before COPA, to stop another psychoanalytic group of less well-trained people from gaining dominance in the field. This other group, The Association for the Advancement of Psychoanalysis and its appointed Board for Accreditation (NAAP/ABAP) sought to become the single certifying body over all of psychoanalytic training in the United States. This possibility stood as an existential threat to the integrity and lifeblood of our combined group of disputers. Although we prevailed over their efforts at the time, this experience underscored to me that our psychoanalytic "tent" did not welcome these others into our fold. This position has always seemed to be especially ironic given how psychoanalytic enterprises are so often treated by the general culture with skepticism. We might then have benefited from expanding the reach of psychoanalytic thinking—albeit a less rigorous version—to a broader public acceptance as had been the case when Freud first introduced his ideas in his early writing.

I learned another lesson when I became active within the NYFS, no longer a candidate. At first, I was welcomed—as a member of a newly trained group of psychologists and social workers from Washington, DC, who at the time had been denied access to training within the American Psychoanalytic—onto the Education Committee of the New York Freudian Institute, and later onto the Board. Later still, I was voted Vice

President and finally, President of the organization. As I took on increasing responsibility within the institute, a subset of the original group of the NYFS began to express hostility toward me that was quite different in tone from their welcoming attitudes at the start of my experience with them. I was taken by surprise and did not understand this change in attitude. One idea shared with me was that I was too inexperienced. In hindsight, however, I now believe that more than that I had unknowingly overstepped the unspoken position in which I was tolerated, as the "outsider" from Washington, DC. By rising through the ranks, I had gone above my "outsider" status to the point that some members of the original group felt their own status was threatened. While this was an uncomfortable place to be, it did not last. As the years went on and other members of my Washington, DC cohort completed their training and began the same path of increasing involvement, the NYFS shifted in its attitudes. NYFS members accepted this new cadre of members from Washington, DC, eventually integrating our group into the larger whole. Likewise, over time we moved from "other" to a position of inclusion and acceptance. Subsequently, the organization was renamed the Contemporary Freudian Society to acknowledge this change.

Another lesson in group dynamics centers on my observation of group leadership. Coming much later, following a stint on the International Psychoanalytical Association (IPA) Board, I joined the New Groups Committee as the Co-chair for North American Groups to the IPA. I noticed that many new groups would form around a charismatic leader. Consistent with my previous lesson about inclusion, I observed that the forward success of a new group often depended on the charismatic leader's capacity for inclusion and transition. In instances when the leader was controlling and not ready to relinquish power, I saw a limit to the development of the new group. Thus, the capacity of a leader to flexibly reach out to make way for other members of the group to assume leadership often made a sizable difference in the overall progress of the group they were championing.

Still another lesson about psychoanalytic groups came from observing the allegiance and adherence to schools of thought. I have cited Rangell's insistence on a unitary theory of psychoanalysis. He outlined the benefits of a "big tent" of ideas. In contrast, what seems to be more prevalent is the notion that each new set of ideas must replace and usurp the importance of the previous knowledge base. Psychoanalysts are not unique in looking to the new, but with our important role in helping the people with whom we work, I strongly support retaining the value to our field of keeping hold of the best of our knowledge base, while integrating what is strongest from the older theories alongside of the new.

As outlined previously, the observations explored in this paper are not unique to psychoanalytic groups, nor exhaustive to group process or group formation. At the same time, these are insights that I personally experienced and witnessed in psychoanalytic institutes over many years and share them here in the hope that these observations are of interest and useful. Thank you for listening.

BOOK REVIEWS

Before I Was I: Psychoanalysis and the Imagination by Enid Balint

edited by Juliet Mitchell and Michael Parsons New York Guilford Press, London: Free Association Books, 1993, viii + 248 pp., $29.95
(1994). *Psa. Books*, 5(4):518-521.

This collection of Enid Balint's papers takes us on an impressive journey through her development as a psychoanalytic thinker over some 40 years, a process that places her "within the independent tradition of British psychoanalysis" (p. 2). It is difficult to read this highly straightforward account without feeling an emotional response to the material, a tribute to Balint's gift for engaging the reader in an intimate way.

The two admiring editors guide the reader through the chapters of the book with helpful introductory summaries. Juliet Mitchell interviews Enid Balint in a closing chapter that seems to "tie up loose ends" by stating explicitly ideas that had been left implicit.

The design partitions the book into papers related to Balint's work in individual psychoanalysis; papers on group consultation work with physicians who are GP's; and two papers associated with her training of marriage therapists at the Institute of Marital Studies at the Tavistock Clinic. The editors stress that Balint, in all three endeavors, was functioning as a psychoanalyst and not as some other kind of practitioner or educator. Balint shows, in a wonderfully candid style of writing, the many ways that a psychoanalyst can benefit society beyond the boundaries of an individual psychoanalytic practice.

Opening with a chapter that explains psychoanalytic clinical work to the general public and to beginning analysts in such an accessible way that it could easily capture for Balint the designation of "ambassador" for our profession. In the next five chapters, spanning the 20-year period 1954-1973, she shares her early thinking on clinical topics. The titles are vivid and evocative: "On Being Empty of Oneself" and "The Mirror and the Receiver." Four chapters represent her more recent work, from 1987 to 1991. It is of special interest that six of the eighteen chapters, including three of the four chapters articulating her current thinking, have never previously been published.

Balint offers nuggets of wisdom with regard to clinical technique that anyone, but especially a new analyst or therapist, could benefit from heeding. The following will give the reader a sense of her message.

Balint alerts us to the distinction between observation and inference. "It is important to realize that the patient has not been observed trying to please the analyst. What has been observed is a polite remark. That she is trying to please the analyst is an inference" (p. 12).

Balint iterates, throughout, the stance of waiting, not making inferences too quickly and not making premature interpretations. "[A]n analyst should test and retest both his observations and the inferences from them…" (p. 12) and "[The analyst] is to observe with a free and curious mind and not to be distracted by theories and the easy solutions they may offer" (p. 17).

"When we are tired and not on our guard, we may find ourselves paying less attention to the association of ideas, which is hard work, and instead discover that we are listening to a description of events in the patient's life which we might like to respond to in a friendly way.…Is the analyst felt by a patient to be near him when he is friendly and sympathetic?…[T]he part of the patient which needs treatment, the part that is more ill, may then feel left out of the sympathetic, friendly relationship,…may feel out of contact and not reached, even ignored (for instance, the aggressive resentful part)" (p. 59). "[T]he mirror model enables the analyst to be neither distant nor close, but just there" (p. 59).

What about the essence of Balint's ideas just described as possibly controversial? As the title of the book suggests, these ideas focus on the earliest times in human life, before a person has an identity of an "I" or self. Balint's central concept is "imaginative perception." She proposes that the creative life, which implies being alive and not dead although breathing, is achieved through a process of imagination and perception.

> I use the phrase "imaginative perception" to describe what happens when the patient imagines what he perceives and thus creates his own partly imagined, partly perceived world....He must create his own [meanings, not passively accept someone else's], but, again, they arise in relationship to another person. (p. 103)

She moves a step beyond Winnicott's idea that there is no baby without a mother to the idea that there is no mother [also picture/ "analyst"/or object] without the baby [patient]. She also moves beyond Michael Balint's idea of the "basic fault," in which there is "A mismatch of infantile experience and maternal perception, [a] misrecognition rather than maternal absence [that] sets up a void [in the child], repeated as an experience in the patient's later life" (p. 37). Balint proposes that the way out of that state is to allow the patient the space to return to a still earlier state preceding the basic fault situation. She is concerned with helping the patient to construct an imaginative perception of himself through the availability of the nonintrusive but "their" analyst, so that the patient may become alive for himself. She proposes that the patient can eventually, slowly, and at first intermittently create an imaginative perception of the analyst and thus achieve a two-person psychology and object relation with the analyst.

In often poetic language, Balint describes her work with patients who come to her with different degrees of deadness based on whether they had had no satisfactory, minimal, or interrupted, relationship with a maternal figure. Even for those cases where the depth of the primitive state is less archaic because the person has had some amount of "good relationship," she still states that "[i]n every treatment…patients have periods of regression" (p. 129). And even in those cases when she has "deliberately not gone back" (p. 224), she speaks of her constructions of these later experiences in very early-experience object relational terms, referencing maternal "neglect" and "tuned-in-ness" as primary factors.

Although Balint often refers to Freud's ideas in her writing, her picture of the patient's infantile life seems barely to include psychosexual development and its attendant conflicts. For her, the internal dialogue over what is essential to psychic difficulties remains centered on the two-person psychology of the mother-child relationship and all that precedes that state of relationship, that is, one-person psychological states rendered in the transference, as of part objects and no objects.

Her ideas push the boundaries of object relations theory to an ultimate meaning, to a preobject relations theory. Moreover, it is her position that psychoanalytic treatment should be a reparenting process, following Ferenczi, and her clinical case presentations suggest that she has successfully demonstrated this technique to represent a curative psychoanalytic road.

Even with enormous respect for her courage both theoretically and clinically, I nevertheless am left unconvinced. Preverbal experience profoundly affects later intrapsychic life but there is a split in views between those, such as Balint, who believe that it is possible for preverbal experience in a relatively pure form to become known and communicated and those, and I include myself, for whom growth is a constantly reintegrating and recombining of experiences as higher levels of physical and emotional development occur. While there certainly are fixation points to which a person will return, these regressive movements are always colored by later developments.

I am not in disagreement with Balint's repeated warning about the dangers of paying too close attention to theory. She cautions that analysts must beware of letting theory rather than observations and intuitive understanding guide their sense of the work.

Enid Balint's book is well worth reading because her thinking is important and representative of a major branch of object relations theory. She writes with genuineness and lyricism, making the act of reading a pleasure. For those of us whose experience differs markedly from hers, her ideas provide an opportunity to think and rethink carefully; and for those who see the human condition as Balint does, she can provide a guiding light.

CHAPTER 27

Freud and Psychoanalysis

W. W. Meissner, S.J. Notre Dame, IN: University of Notre Dame Press, 2000, xv + 279 pp., $20.00 paperback.

This ambitious compendium takes the reader on a journey both historical and topical through Freud's development of psychoanalysis. Along the way it gives a glimpse of ideas from some of Freud's coworkers and certain extenders of his ideas, as well as noting others who have used Freudian thought as a segue to their own divergent paths toward psychoanalytic synthesis. The word compendium captures the thoroughness of this effort, in that it designates a work that gathers and succinctly presents all the details essential to the comprehensive knowledge of a subject. W. W. Meissner's new book does just that, for the current state of psychoanalytic theory.

The book is directed explicitly toward informing "the potential student of general psychiatry about this fundamental discipline within psychiatry" (p. 1). Despite that expressed focus, however, there is nothing in the remainder of the book that would discourage readers from disciplines other than psychiatry. In fact, it would seem that the book is meant to interest students not only of mental health but of philosophy and religion as well. In short, anyone interested in the field may benefit from this systematic account of Freud's psychoanalytic thought and selective presentation of later theorists.

The organization of the book requires mention. Any selection from as vast an oeuvre as Freud's is a challenging task and is inevitably subject to questions about sequencing, emphases, and omissions. Certain points of view will be highlighted, while others are passed over quickly or ignored altogether. This is especially true when the aim is to include not only Freud's work but that of others in a burgeoning field. In acknowledgment of that constraint, the book is thoughtfully arranged, each chapter opening with general statements of the material to be discussed, followed by detailed explication with appropriate subheads to guide the reader. The text initially moves between an historical and a topical focus, starting with Freud's 1895 Project. An extensive discussion of the Project is followed by a chapter on the beginnings of psychoanalysis—Freud's work with Breuer and their *Studies on Hysteria*. As Meissner reviews these beginnings, he carefully conveys Freud's psychoanalytic discoveries in sequence, building a picture of inner motivations, fantasy, the importance of childhood sexuality, and the centrality of psychic conflict. At the same time, Meissner underscores the parallel advances Freud made in developing the psychoanalytic method to study these unfolding discoveries.

Meissner next devotes a chapter to *The Interpretation of Dreams* and its role in laying out Freud's seminal ideas on dreams and his first pass at the structure of the mind. That, of course, leads to a chapter detailing the topographical model. Logically, Meissner then discusses the theory of instincts, which at that stage of Freud's thinking was focused on libido and the ego (or self-preservative) instincts.

Development and object relations come next and nicely introduce Freud's inclusion of the object in his theorizing about infant development. Framing the discussion by using Anna Freud's concept of developmental lines charting the infant's psychic development from infancy through adulthood (1965), Meissner juxtaposes parallel lines for instinctual phases (Freud), separation-individuation (Mahler), dependence to independence in object relations (Anna Freud), and psychosocial crises (Erik Erikson's eight life-cycle phases). Placing Erikson in such august company suggests Meissner's special regard for him.

The next chapter, "Narcissism and the Dual Instinct Theory," is crammed with important themes: the development of Freud's observations on narcissism; its connection with object relations, which leads Meissner to question whether narcissism should be accorded a separate developmental line, as in the work of Kohut; the shift from Freud's earlier conceptualization of aggression as part of the sexual and self-preservative instincts to its being put on a par with libido and regarded as not self-preservative; explication of the regulatory principles (pleasure and reality) that govern instincts; and, finally, Freud's "speculations" on life and death instincts. The following chapter addresses Freud's first theory of anxiety and his second, the theory of signal anxiety. With that second theory of anxiety in place, Meissner can go on in the next chapter to discuss Freud's structural theory and ego psychology. Meissner's fine presentation of the former gives Hartmann his due and includes a respectful bow to Rapaport; there is also a noticeable absence of any mention of Brenner and his further development of Freud's concept of compromise formation.

The chapter "Ongoing Developments" is a brief account of Melanie Klein, Fairbairn, Balint, and Winnicott (no mention of Bion). Meissner also returns to Kohut's self-psychology and makes a passing reference to Sullivan and the interpersonal view. He includes a discussion of the psychology of character, mentions Wilhelm Reich, and ends the chapter with a return to Erikson and further consideration of identity and identity formation.

Throughout the book, Meissner is consistent in noting aspects of Freud's thought, as they emerge in the discussion, that have been controversial. These include such concepts as psychic energy and the progression of female psychosexual development. Perhaps because he is trying to accomplish so much in a relatively short text, he merely acknowledges that questions have been raised, rather than spelling out alternative conceptions.

The last chapter, "Classical Psychoanalytic Treatment," is in some ways the best. Here Meissner's comfort with the material shines through in almost lyrical prose. He covers such topics as psychoanalytic psychopathology, diagnosis, and analyzability. He also speaks about phases of the analytic process through to termination; treatment techniques; the role of the analyst with reference to transference; and his view of the transference neurosis. Another concept that Meissner highlights, one he clearly values, is the role of the therapeutic alliance. With such a nice chapter to end on, the reader might well be encouraged to deepen his or her experience with psychoanalysis.

To conclude, Meissner's Freud and Psychoanalysis gives a thorough and balanced view of its topic and renders difficult and complex material accessible and even inviting to the neophyte.

REFERENCES

Freud, A. (1965). *Normality and Pathology in Childhood: Assessments of Development.* New York: International Universities Press.

CHAPTER 28

A Psychoanalytic Life
Tragic Knots in Psychoanalysis:
New Papers on Psychoanalysis

By Roy Schafer
New York: Karnac, 196 pp., $35.95, 2009.

Roy Schafer's book is a meaningful read for psychoanalytic therapists for a variety of reasons. Among the most important of these is the opportunity for the reader to look into one man's intellectual journey of development through his career and his continued study of psychoanalytic ideas. Whether or not you see ideas similarly to Schafer (who is very persuasive), it is a model of thoughtfulness that we all might wish to emulate. Another reason for the book's value is Schafer's clinical acumen: he makes the exchange between therapist and patient come to life in a deeply penetrating manner. Not the least of reasons, but especially worth mentioning, is the way he weaves his clinical insights into a complex tapestry that repeatedly demonstrates the necessity of maintaining an open mind to "this and that" and abandoning "either-or."

I have known about Roy Schafer since I "hatched" as an adult, if I consider "hatching" to be when, while doing my undergraduate senior thesis on color/form incongruity in ink blots (Siipola, 1959), I was first introduced to the psychological testing book Schafer worked on with David Rapaport and Merton Gill (1945–1946). Following college and before graduate school, I worked as a research assistant to Dr. David Shakow, well-known for his research on schizophrenia and his leadership in clinical psychology education. He had formed the first laboratory of psychology at the National Institute of Mental Health (NIMH). Psychoanalysis was in its heyday in the United States then, although psychologists were mostly relegated to marginal roles (in that climate) as researchers and not regulars inside the APsaA tent until years later. In and out of our office came the famous in the field and I saw the backs of the heads of many important people. Among them was David Rapaport, who was especially close to David Shakow. When I left NIMH to go to graduate school in clinical psychology, I was soon studying the Rapaport, Gill, and Schafer psychological testing book firsthand. Later, as a member of a local chapter of Division 39 (the WPSP), and still later, as a candidate and then member of the New York Freudian Society (NYFS)—now called the Contemporary Freudian Society—I had occasion to meet Roy Schafer and his wife, Rita Frankiel, a member of the NYFS, and through planning scientific meetings and other activities I became familiar with his developing thinking and writings.

In the last chapter (chapter 10) of his book, *Tragic Knots in Psychoanalysis*, Schafer describes "The Author's Odyssey" that lays out the path he followed in his psychoanalytic thinking. In the description detailing his progress, he presents his major conflict in theory development: that he admires the founding thinkers in the field ("his psychoanalytic parents") and persistently wants to question their formulations. As he himself explains, he has "profound respect for the traditional and a strong impulse to challenge it, improve it, and if necessary, change its focus" (p. 158). He sounds to me as if he has found the metaphoric solution to his Oedipal conflicts and, in the process, developed the most wonderful way of enjoying his identifications while becoming his mature self. In commentary about another of his books, *Bad Feelings* (2003), Schafer is described as creating "a highly successful synthesis and integration of Freudian, ego-psychological, and neo-Kleinian theory." While I agree with that idea, I would want to add that he provides a very personal integration that constantly brings the ideas closer to everyday discourse; he make the ideas digestible, real, and sensible—as in, down to earth and capable of resonating with the readers' own clinical experience. At the same time, the changes he proposes do not seem superficial. He has taken his mentors' ideas into contemporary debates and updated those ideas to remain relevant in the current psychoanalytic world.

Schafer orients his chapters around a concept that he calls "tragic knots." The idea is complicated, but what I think he is getting at is that life, as it can be understood and studied in psychoanalysis and literature, can be experienced through impossible or tragic choices. These are not necessarily tragic in a heroic and fixed way, rather in the sorrowful recognition that reality limits sometimes in very unhappy ways. He also suggests that such tragic knots often have elements out of one's control and perhaps without the possibility of considering the outcome. He illustrates this with the dilemma of Cordelia in Shakespeare's *King Lear*. Cordelia loves her father and is asked to compete with her sisters to express devotion to their father beyond realistic possibility, but her personal integrity foreswears her participating in such distortion, leading to tragedy for her *and* her father. With that template, Schafer more directly enters into the field of the analytic setting.

Throughout the pages there are so many pearls it is difficult to settle on what to describe. I think what I found most useful was the repeated mention of the complexity of feelings and thoughts; Schafer emphasizes not only multiple determination—that is, feelings and thoughts come from multiple sources—but also, how often its opposite or perhaps variants can be at odds with the main tenor of the communication—be it verbal or nonverbal—making meaning so much richer. Furthermore, he sees that these feelings and thoughts influence and are influenced by the interaction with each other in the analytic discussion and are constantly infused with matters from external and internal realities. These are the tragic knots of the analytic situation.

For Schafer, the conflict model continues to hold a meaningful place in his sense of the analytic dialogue, which he describes as a narrative: the patient's narrative that makes space for the analyst. To me, the conflict model comes quite close to the idea of tragic knots. At least initially, the patient's often unconscious fantasies, wishes, efforts, and defending positions comingle and interweave with the analyst's interpretations and unconsciously driven reactions as well as the analyst's fantasies, wishes, efforts, and defending positions: making tragic knots that call for understanding. Schafer considers such concepts as forgiveness and whether it can ever fully occur and how frustration, if unattended, can thwart the analyst's ability to function most effectively. Schafer emphasizes the hermeneutic focus of explanatory interpretation that establishes reasons, not causes. While I do not think I do justice to Schafer's beautifully reasoned positions, almost any paragraph captures a meaningful peek into the theoretical but especially the clinical experience. For example, in chapter 4, "Caring and Coercive Aspects of the Psychoanalytic Situation," Schafer points out that, The analysand's desire to collaborate in the work of analysis is often associated with a fantasy of submitting to coercion. The fantasy centers on surrendering to the analyst's will. Following instructions and abiding by limitations is, of course, adaptive on one level, but on another it can be experienced as subjugation. Consequently, collaboration can foster mixed or alternating feelings of self-satisfaction, fright, humiliation, excitement, relief, and the bliss of utter passivity. (p. 62)

That small paragraph gives you a taste of the insights Schafer offers. It is like being supervised by a wise mentor who can help the therapist to see the interaction from a whole new angle and therefore improve one's listening capacities. The book is full of such wisdom. Do take a look!

REFERENCES

Rapaport, D., Gill, M. M., & Schafer, R. (1945–1946). *Diagnostic Psychological Testing* (Vols. 1 & 2). Chicago, IL: Yearbook Publishers.

Schafer, R. (2003). *Bad Feelings*. New York, NY: Other Press.

——— (2009). *Tragic knots in psychoanalysis*. London, UK: Karnac Books Ltd.

Siipola, E., & Basseches, H. (1959). The relation of color form incongruity and maladjustment to reaction time. *Journal of Personality, 27,* 324–345.

CHAPTER 29

Thanks for HIB Distinguished Service Award

It is more than an honor to be given an award by my beloved Contemporary Freudian Society. Thank you from the bottom of my heart. It is especially meaningful to be honored beside Helen Gediman, my long-time esteemed colleague and former teacher.

I must start by congratulating the current graduates who have accomplished so much by completing this rigorous and challenging training. While you all are undoubtedly experienced and wise clinicians, you have also embarked on the most gratifying professional career and will likely have many meaningful moments of satisfaction working to help others to understand themselves better, solve emotional conflicts, and develop into promising aspects of themselves. Hurrah!

As some of you know, I was a member of the first class from Washington, DC—a wonderful group of colleagues all of whom have gone on to outstanding careers and most of whom have continued to practice for many years. As a member of that group, I had unusual opportunities both in developing and running an organization as we were learning our craft. Initially, it was a time in the history of psychoanalysis that psychologists and social workers and others had a very difficult time in getting training—the NYFS being one of the few training centers with high standards to welcome us—although I do not think they had any idea that it was to be a long-term commitment.

Shortly after I graduated, the NYFS chose me to speak on their behalf to protect the legitimacy and autonomy of the NYFS before COPA, the Council on Postsecondary Accreditation. The success of that mission functioned as a gateway for me, leading to enhanced opportunities for my active participation in institutional life and the beginning of a long and fruitful relationship for me within our organization. I had many rewarding chances to work for the NYFS and over the next years participating in positions of varying importance in the governance of the Institute and Society. The effect of all that was to help slowly but steadily lead to the integration of the DC program with our New York siblings.

The proof of that is in noting the many members of the DC contingent who have taken leadership roles since then in our organization. The strength and continued vitality of our organization across the bridge of distance has been under the newer name: Contemporary Freudian Society.

I want to close with a plug for not only being active in the workings of the CFS, but the opportunities for active involvement on committees of the IPA and also in CIPS. With that participation you will be supporting and strengthening psychoanalysis worldwide. It is very special to get to know colleagues from other regions and to work with them too. All I can say is how lucky I have been to have had such enriching opportunities.

I want to end with my overwhelming gratitude for this honor, so validating and meaningful. Thank you so much!

Closing Remarks by Harriet I. Basseches

At the beginning of my preparation for this book, I had not set out to turn the spotlight of my observations onto psychoanalytic institutional group processes, but this review of my career has made me aware that the TAP articles have captured a period in institutional psychoanalytic activity in the United States of historical significance that may not be so clearly annotated elsewhere.

At another level, however, the description of interactions in our field calls attention to the universality of psychoanalyst groups (however versed in theories of the mind its members may be), still remain at the core, subject to the same forces as any other group made up of human beings. In this closing section of the book, I would like to share these observations so that they are captured here.

The first observation comes after a Committee representing a cluster of Independent Institutes in the US similar in training standards to the American Psychoanalytic Association (**APsaA**) invited me, to represent them. At the time, I was first a candidate and later a recent graduate at the New York Freudian Society (**NYFS**) who lived in Washington, DC where **COPA**, the United States Accrediting Body presides. I joined the **APSaA** representative to argue before COPA, to stop another psychoanalytic group of less well-trained people from gaining dominance in the field. This other group, The Association for the Advancement of Psychoanalysis and its appointed Board for Accreditation (**NAAP/ABAP**) sought to become the single certifying body over all of psychoanalytic training in the United States. This possibility stood as an existential threat to the integrity and lifeblood of our combined group of disputers. Although we prevailed over their efforts at the time, this experience underscored to me that our psychoanalytic "tent" did not welcome these others into our fold, as we made no effort to offer them any form of inclusion. This position has always seemed to be especially ironic given how psychoanalytic enterprises are so often treated by the general culture with skepticism. We might then have benefited from expanding the reach of psychoanalytic thinking—albeit a less rigorous version—to a broader public acceptance as had been the case when Freud first introduced his ideas in his early writing.

I learned another lesson when I became increasingly active within the **NYFS.** At first, I was welcomed—as a member of a newly trained group of psychologists and social workers from Washington, DC, who at the time were not allowed training within **APSaA**—onto the Education Committee, and later onto the Board. Later still, I was voted Vice President and finally, President of the organization. As I took on increasing responsibility within the institute, a subset of the original established group of the **NYFS** began to express hostility toward me that was quite different in tone from their welcoming attitudes at the start of my experience with them. I was taken by surprise and did not understand this change in attitude. In hindsight, however, I now believe that I had unknowingly overstepped the unspoken position in which I was tolerated, as the "outsider" from Washington, DC. By rising through the ranks, I had gone above my "outsider" status to the point that some members of the original group felt their own status was threatened. While this was an uncomfortable place to be, it did not last. As the years went on and other members of my Washington, DC cohort completed their training and began the same path of increasing involvement, the **NYFS** naysayers shifted in their attitudes. NYFS members accepted this new cadre of members from Washington, DC, eventually integrating our group into the larger whole. Likewise, over time we moved from "other" to a position of inclusion and acceptance. Subsequently, the organization was renamed the Contemporary Freudian Society to acknowledge this change.

Another lesson in group dynamics centers on my observation of group leadership. Coming much later, following a stint on the **International Psychoanalytical Association** (**IPA**) Board, I joined the New Groups Committee as the Co-chair for North American Groups to the **IPA**. I noticed that many new groups would form around a charismatic leader. Consistent with my previous lesson about inclusion, I observed that the forward success of a new group often depended on the charismatic leader's capacity for inclusion and transition. In instances when the leader was controlling and not ready to relinquish power, I saw a limit to the development of the new group. Thus, the capacity of a leader to flexibly reach out to make way for other members of the group to assume leadership often made a sizable difference in the overall progress of the group they were championing.

Still another lesson about psychoanalytic groups came from observing the allegiance and adherence to schools of thought. I have cited Rangell's insistence on a unitary theory of psychoanalysis. He outlined the benefits of a "big tent" of ideas. In contrast, what seems to be more prevalent is the notion that each new set of ideas must replace and usurp the importance of the previous knowledge base. Psychoanalysts are not unique in looking to the new, but with our important role in helping the people with whom we work, I strongly support retaining the value to our field of keeping hold of the best of our knowledge base while integrating what is strongest in the older theories alongside of the new.

As outlined previously, the observations explored in this book are not unique to psychoanalytic groups, but rather to group formation and progress more generally. All the same, with the wisdom borne of many experiences in the field, I have witnessed these aspects in psychoanalytic institutes over many years and share them here in the hope that these observations are of interest and useful.

ADDENDUMS

At Century's End: A Unitary Theory of Psychoanalysis[11]

(1997). *J. Clin. Psychoanal.*, 6(4):465–484.
Leo Rangell, M.D.

Current wisdom has it that we live in a period of theoretical pluralism. By common consensus this has become the accepted ambience in the present psychoanalytic culture. In the official opening of the last International Congress in San Francisco, the Chairman, introducing the program for the week, stated both the fact and its motivation explicitly, "The main theme of this Congress was chosen to encourage pluralism as well as to stimulate the development of new ideas compared with the more classic ones" (Grinberg, 1995, p. 1).

In this paper I present an alternate view of psychoanalytic theory and understanding that exists parallel to this dominant view. The theory I present and represent is a unitary theory of psychoanalysis, which embraces all sufficient and necessary ingredients into one total, composite psychoanalytic theory. Besides this being my personal orientation, I have found a definitive voice expressed in private for this opposite view, which is inhibited from public expression in today's psychoanalytic culture. The mainstream, though still called that, is no longer main, but is now the minority within a minority.

---

11 Presented as the Plenary Address at the Annual Scientific Conference of the New York Freudian Society, "Into the Second Psychoanalytic Century: One Theory or Many? The Fit between Practice and Theory," November 23, 1996.

Psychoanalysis is still a small and beleaguered group, an island within a larger land. But its core beliefs within its own boundaries are fragmented and shattered. In that fact, in my opinion, lies the most important of our problems, not in the sociology or the external political swirls at whose feet the onus is usually placed. The science of psychoanalysis is not as secure in its basic moorings as we would wish, or as it once was.

There are many, probably most analysts, who feel otherwise. These analysts point to a rich diversity in our theory and science today, which they see as a creative advance. Psychoanalysis, in this view, has broken away from restricting boundaries, and is now becoming more realistic and useful. There are multiple theories, alternative explanations, many understandings. The current ambience holds that these are equal, interchangeable, a matter of preference or choice, based on one's experience or taste or scientific convictions.

This paper will explore these two opinions or attitudes. In the meantime, despite what is written and what one professes to accept about common ground, in operation a patient is sent for a different treatment to a classical analyst, a self psychologist, a Kleinian, or Lacanian. Groups (around theories) stay together, as they have done in Great Britain for decades, and as is currently the case where such divisions exist in this country. Even within societies or institutes that label themselves eclectic, each student and later analyst acquires a self-identity. If divergent theories do not result in qualitatively different treatments, either an inconsistency and failure of synthesis (an ego factor) or a subtle superego effect may be operative in the analyst.

Psychoanalysis has been from the beginning a unified, parsimonious, yet complete, coherent theory to explain and encompass a multitude of behavioral observations. Central to the longitudinal development of its theory is the retention of integrity, in two senses, only one the moral, the other in the sense of the trait that makes possible the retaining of new data won, and integrating them into a coherent whole. This use of "integrity" is thus from its stem in common with "integrate," to contain as well as discover. In distinguishing an academic theory of learning from a psychoanalytic one, Rapaport (1952, quoted in Gill and Klein, 1964) states, "The question raised is not how much and how rapidly something is learned, but rather how does something perceived turn into something retained" (p. 29). In addition to the integrative function of Hartmann (1939) and the synthetic function of Nunberg (1931), the differentiating function of the ego, most definitively described in modern times by Needles (1978), also plays its part. Openness to new ideas is central to the historical development of psychoanalysis. This is not a trait to be preempted by one school of thought over another. New ideas, following new data, are to be filtered through selective discrimination and tested for their validity.

This account of history will be an explicitly personal one. It is, however, a personal experiential memoir not of a private life but a public scientific one. While I introduce an element of history usually not included and even off-limits in a scientific exposition, I feel not only that this belongs but that such history cannot be complete without it. It took fifty years for comparable problems in Great Britain to be exposed and studied by King and Steiner (1991). It is now twenty-five or thirty years since the American version of similar problems began and burgeoned. It is not too soon to reflect on these.

My view will be from mid-century looking both ways. I entered the field in 1941, when, during a psychiatric residency at Columbia, I started psychoanalytic training at the New York Psychoanalytic Institute. That year, Otto Fenichel published the first draft of his classic textbook, which was to become my most admired psychoanalytic summary for the rest of my career and life. Fenichel (1945), who bisected the psychoanalytic century, summarized encyclopedically what was known up to that time. At the halfway mark, the literature of psychoanalysis was still encompassable. But in retrospect, Fenichel also prophesized the future. Many of the problems, principles, and pitfalls to come were presaged in his two classic books, on theory (1945) and technique (1941). Besides an early, lively debate with Theodor Reik on what was to be a perennial controversy over ideation vs. affect, Fenichel saw already the coming overemphasis on transference, comparing it to the earlier mistaken thought of many that psychoanalysis was only about sex. The intrusion of the irrational into the theory of psychoanalysis was spotted and forewarned, and anticipated much of future divisions. "The subject matter not the method of psychoanalysis is irrational," Fenichel (1941, p. 13) wrote. This has been a beacon to me for many years.

Fenichel has remained for me an inspirational model, not the man, whom I cannot say I knew, but his psychoanalytic way of thinking. While I will look from 1940, as he did, but in both directions, my aim will not be to be inclusive, or to be substantive about specific theories. Rather I will trace the vicissitudes of one problem, the retention of completeness of theory as theory advances versus derailing the direction of the main thrust by discarding discoveries made, amputating gains achieved, and stunting the growth of the total theory. There was less controversy in mid-course than now, although the seeds and the early forms of present pitfalls were laid down long before.

Freud started the path toward unification and integration. Symptoms (Breuer and Freud, 1893-1895) were seen to arise from the same base as dreams (Freud, 1900); both were tied to character traits. Slips (Freud, 1901) and jokes (Freud, 1905) came from the same source. Freud's self-analysis was in the same genre and from the same origins as those of his patients. Findings from all provided a bridge to the psychology of mankind. Diversity and unity were at once visible as concepts. The diversity was in the scope and multiplicity of what was explained, unity in the parsimony of the explanation.

The integrity of integration also led to Freud's ability to see obstacles to progress as data in themselves. It was by his refusal to yield or bend to opposition, from without in the form of external criticism, or from within in the form of inner discouragement, that he was able to discover the two pillars of the psychoanalytic method, resistance and transference. Anger or love for and submission to the analyst were also no cause to turn back or away, as they were for Breuer. They too were findings; they led to transference, displacement, reaction formation, and more.

These were the beginnings, the first plowing of the new field by the individual who discovered it. His next tasks were two, to advance the knowledge he had begun, and to navigate through the period of peer relationships, necessary and inevitable, based on these discoveries and new insights. The two experiences, as an individual researcher, and as a group participant, were not to have the same lines of development. Freud's relations and cooperative endeavors with his original early colleagues varied from his positive relations to the likes of Abraham, Jones, and Ferenczi, and early to Rank, to his difficulties, ensuing shortly, with such as Jung, Adler, and Stekel, and before the end, with Ferenczi and Rank as well. These relationships were not the same as those to Dora or Anna O. or, although indirect, to Little Hans. In the therapeutic dyad, relationships were defined, roles established; an observer, the first analyst, was in control. The peer groups were composed of participants on another basis. What the patient was not permitted to translate into action remained uncontrolled in psychoanalytic groups, from the first ones continuously thereafter. It was from the beginning not what each new analyst contributed but what each left out that led Freud to feel it necessary to guard the new science. This was to persist throughout subsequent history. Inside the new field as much as from outraged critics on the outside, it was necessary to protect and preserve the Oedipus complex, childhood sexuality, repression, the unconscious, sexual conflicts, and latent perversions in neuroses and the normal.

From 1890 to 1920, the first phase of his theory building, Freud, and his original close collaborators, constructed a good part of the edifice of early psychoanalytic theory. The observed phenomena of dreams, clinical data from patients' free associations, and insights from Freud's self-analysis, were understood as one unified stream. The explanatory theoretical system seen as the means of understanding the accumulated data, included early instinct theory; the dynamic, genetic, topographic, and economic points of view; repression as a defense against instincts; the first theory of anxiety as a direct physiological transformation; and a problematic and aborted attempt to penetrate psychological and somatic interrelationships (Freud, 1895).

Freud's second phase of theory building, from 1920 on, went far toward rounding out though not completing his metapsychology, converging upon psychic phenomena from multiple directions. Freud's theory of psychoanalysis grew by accretion, expansion, and modification where necessary. To borrow a phrase claimed in favor of alternative theories, Freud was always "open to new ideas." In "Beyond the Pleasure Principle" (1920) and "The Ego and the Id" (1923), the structural view, the most ambitious, complex, controversial concept, the most in need of internal elaboration and clarification, was added to the other metapsychologic paths of understanding, and was lain down for future generations of psychoanalysts to clarify and integrate. Equal to all his other insights, the theory of anxiety was amended into Freud's (1926) second theory, that of anxiety as a signal of danger. It is worth noting that his first concept of anxiety was not withdrawn but was put aside. Of the now two theories, Freud (1926) wrote, "non liquet." On the subject of unification, in two papers written three and four decades later, I (Rangell, 1955, 1968a) unified Freud's two historical theories of anxiety, from which I stated that now "liquet."

Freud died in 1939, and that same year, marking the beginning of the post Freud era of scientific advance, Heinz Hartmann (1939) wrote his classic work,

Ego Psychology and the Problem of Adaptation. At the memorial service for Hartmann in 1970, I stated (Rangell, 1971b) that in 1939 Freud handed the baton to Hartmann on the top of a mountain, which Hartmann went on to build twice as high. Hartmann was followed, or accompanied by Rapaport, whose work was monumental on thinking (Rapaport, 1951a), and on affects (Rapaport, 1953), the two major areas of ego functioning, and who extended the understanding of autonomy (Rapaport, 1951b, 1958), which Hartmann had started. Neither arrived at a completion of this subject, nor a rounding out of this beginning into a psychoanalytic theory of action (Rangell, 1989).

Disagreements and dissident movements were not episodic but continuous. Before Freud's death, beginning before his theory reached its final stage of the structural theory, another divergent stream, parallel but separatist from Freud, began to escalate in the United States, and overlapped with the previous group of original dissidents. I might call this the second stage of multiple theories. The theories of Sullivan, Horney, Fromm, their roots in the 1920s, matured in the 1930s and 1940s into the interpersonal school of Harry Stack Sullivan, and the William Alanson White and Horney Institutes. All stressed the environment over what they felt as an innate, biological Freudian base, and emphasized the external culture as contrasted to instinctual drives. Sexuality was downplayed as a source of conflict. Aggression was a sequel of frustration, not a drive.

This was actually an active and fertile period, although not organizationally or in a sense of integration and cohesiveness. Much was laid down that was to return repeatedly in different forms in future developments. Some were positive contributions that could be added to total theory, while others were to contribute to repeated obstructions and distractions. Clara Thompson (1950), in a lecture series to the Washington School of Psychiatry and the White Institute in New York, pointed out the similarities and overlaps as well as the differences among the multitude of theories. In my opinion, however, she did not pinpoint the crux of the difficulties which made for dissension. As in the prior group of separatist movements, it was not what each theory stressed, but what each left out, which made for controversy and isolation. Culture certainly plays its part, but why not the drives as well? The interpersonal is of course central, but is not also the intrapsychic? Environmental factors do not eliminate an innate base. And does this not include the biological? The Oedipus complex, experientially determined in both biologically and developmental terms, found little place in any of the new systems. Every viable element of the new theories was included in the Freudian system; the reverse was not true.

These theories as a whole could be seen as a transitional group, linking to alternative theories that had preceded them, and pointing to related ones to come. There was overlap as well as differences, as was always the case, between the various new views themselves and between those views and the more enduring central theory. Thompson pointed out that Horney's views on cultural conflict merged into Adler's on power and mastery, and linked Rank's and Fromm's with Jung. Sullivan's interpersonal school presaged future object relations theory, while his description of a self-system was a prelude to self psychology, however much Kohut himself strongly disavowed any connection of his views to Sullivan or to Alexander. Rank introduced "will," but in a different context and unintegrated with the total psychoanalytic theory of intrapsychic dynamics as I (Rangell, 1969a, b, 1971a, 1986), in later years, described the place of ego will in a structural sense in unconscious mental functioning. Fromm spoke of the "true self," linking to the "false self" described later by Winnicott (1965).

Horney (1937, 1950) considered values and the role of idealized objects, both of which were to be stressed in future writings by Kohut, Ferenczi, and Reich, and both of which stressed that analysts should admit mistakes, as Gill (1982, 1994), Stolorow, Brandchaft, and Atwood (1987), Renik (1993a) and others did in various contexts sixty years later. Carrying this theme forward, these current theorists stress that an analyst should be on an equal basis with the patient. Did Freudians consider themselves immune from fairness? Any analyst, then and now, takes this as a given, yet aims for the analytic attitude as well. The two are not incompatible, and both are intrinsic to the analytic process.

All of these movements were synchronous with the later emphasis on the here-and-now, the energized transference countertransference interactions, the stress on empathy, intersubjectivity, and the current social constructivist theory. Along with the hypertrophy of some elements and atrophy of others at that time and currently, both periods downplay or eliminate the role of reconstruction and insight, central nuclei of the psychoanalytic method and understanding.

Freud himself recognized and named this fallacious mechanism in the very earliest views antagonistic to his evolving theory. In his discussion of the Wolf Man, Freud (1918) named and described "the principle of *pars pro toto*. From a highly composite combination, one part of the operative factors is singled out and proclaimed as the truth … What is left over, however, and rejected as false, is precisely what is new in psycho-analysis and peculiar to it" (p. 53). This was applied at that time to Jung and Adler. "Thus, Jung picks out actuality and regression, and Adler, egoistic motives." In a letter to Jones in 1927, Freud (Freud and Jones, 1993) compares Klein's "heretical" theories to Jung's (while declaring that the part that she does proclaim as the whole is excellent). "It is remarkable that people find it most difficult to recognize over determinism and multiplicity of etiological factors. All our apostates always grasped part of the truth and wanted to declare it as the whole truth" (p. 635). Anna Freud (1965) similarly opposed reductive oversimplifications of theory, in proposing her total, balanced developmental profile as an empirical research method of clinical study. I have repeatedly pointed out (Rangell, 1982, 1988, 1990) the same mechanism operative in the succession of theories in the modern era. It is characteristic of the scientific dialogue on this issue, however, that while logical argument is not disputed, the fallacy continues to be reenacted. This is due, in my opinion, to affective motivations, charisma in leadership, and the role of the group process.

Fenichel died suddenly at the age of 48 in 1946. Los Angeles, after the deaths of Fenichel and Ernst Simmel, a co-pioneer, shortly after, was an atmosphere ripe for something to happen. Nineteen hundred fifty was the year of the split, into the Los Angeles and Southern California societies; three other splits had taken place shortly before: New York-Columbia, Baltimore-Washington, two societies in Philadelphia. The splits were over the contrasting theoretical views of Fenichel and Alexander, both of these leaders actually present, although at different times, in Los Angeles, while other adherents represented the same views in the other centers. Was it to be the analytic attitude and relentless analysis, or the analyst playing therapeutic roles, supplying what he concluded had been missing in the patient's early life? This was still the time when analysts who could not get along with each other separated. Factually and historically, splits are due to theories and people, divergent theories and human advocates associated with them who eventually prefer to live and work apart. Without both, there is no split. Divergences exist in all groups, psychoanalytic and others, and are compatible with coexistence. Ideas that differ, held by people who can get along, or, in a psychoanalytic group, people who do not like or socialize with each other but are not divided by a scientific schism, make accommodations, and comprise every analytic society in the world.

The American, during these years, continued to maintain dominance and to preserve the development of total (my word) "Freudian" theory, which stressed the psychic interior as the specific unique area of psychoanalysis, while including and not overlooking its interaction and reciprocity with all external experiential factors. Following the splits of the 1940s and 1950s, to the extent that it bridged the new divisions, the American was now the overseer of at least two points of view that needed to be amalgamated scientifically and administratively. The differences, however, were essentially over technique, not theory, over the analytic attitude, not metapsychology. Fenichel's idea, "There are many ways to treat neuroses, but there is only one way to understand them" (1945, p. 554) was generally believed and followed. This was in contrast with the rest of the world, in which, concentrating in Great Britain, and derivatively from there into Europe, South America, and as far away as Australia, the three well-known theoretical splits had already profoundly affected the analytic population, with the decision for three different and operatively separate training arrangements to live under one administrative umbrella. The International Psychoanalytical Association (IPA) represented this theoretical diversity. During these decades, the American, within the International, required and retained its autonomy, over scientific principles, training standards, and criteria for admission to training. It is essential, to fully appreciate the complexity that follows, to keep these issues separate. Democracy as to who should practice psychoanalysis does not automatically flow over into determining the science of psychoanalysis.

The mid to late 1960s saw the crest of the wave, and a curious turn downwards of the curve of development, with a questioning and in my opinion a gradual erosion of the central trunk of the "Freudian" theoretical tree. This was now not a theoretical quarrel from a cultural, outside position, but a dissatisfaction with the intrapsychic view of the psychic apparatus and its functioning, as these had been developing from Freud to his almost official successors, Anna Freud, Hartmann, and Rapaport. The course of psychoanalytic theory in the thirty years since then has undergone a qualitative change. Both the methods of observation and the theoretical reasoning about data have been affected.

To briefly cite a few of the incremental stages of the progression into the modern era, for an aerial view, as it were: In the mid-1960s, in Topeka, most of the second echelon of staff under Rapaport, in what has been considered by many as a palace revolution, rallied under George Klein (1973) to disagree with the metapsychology of Freud, so much furthered and developed by that same group under Rapaport. There were two, not one, psychoanalytic theories, they now believed, distinct from each other, one clinical, based on direct observations, the other abstract, speculative, and abstruse, unconnected or insufficiently linked to the clinical situation.

A next development, equally divisive of a unitary theory, was brewing in Los Angeles. From a series of relationships and actions—I date its apex as 1969, the year of my election as President of the International, to which it was not unrelated—there began a procession of Kleinian analysts to Los Angeles, later joined by Bion. It was the first concerted incursion of this theoretical view into the United States, fueled by and embedded in a contagious group excitement, which not only stamped the decade of the 1970s, but affected future training, the base for the 1980s and 1990s as well. The classical, the oedipal, became objects of antipathy, its adherents on the defensive, subject to depreciation, scorn, even calumny. While I am adding subjectivity to objectivity in theory formation, affective to cognitive factors, and the role of the interpersonal to the scientific method, this is not matched by an equal freedom to document the specific relevant background events and issues on this occasion. People have as much to do with the course of theory as the disembodied ideas that they represent and further. This has been the case from the beginning to the present day. Identifications, alliances, transferences, and the group process make the two merge imperceptibly. Richards (1995) pointed to the intrusion of politics and power into the course of psychoanalysis during the time of A. A. Brill at the very onset of psychoanalysis on the American scene.

There was a third determining sociopolitical event in this series that played an equal role in shaping the direction of theoretical life to come. Heinz Kohut became a Kohutian in July 1969, following the Rome Congress of the International that year. In oral history, we ask for the personal. In written, "scientific" accounts, we eschew it. To leave out the people, is to leave out half of history. Self psychology began around events at this Congress, built, to be sure, upon several good papers by Kohut written years before, on empathy (1959) and narcissism (1966), which had fitted well into total analytic theory. His first book, *The Analysis of the Self*, came out two years later (1971). In my Presidential Address in Paris in 1973, I (Rangell, 1974) referred to the new book as belonging within psychoanalysis. I was being hopeful, although I felt and feared differently. Anna Freud backed the first book. Of the second (Kohut, 1977), after Kohut had moved away from the main body to stake his own claim, she wrote ruefully, according to Young-Bruehl (1988, p. 440), referring to a letter from Anna Freud to Greenson, "that the work of Heinz Kohut, once a member of their circle, had become antipsychoanalytic." I did not go as far. "Differently—analytic, not anti-," I felt.

In Los Angeles, after Klein and Bion had run their course, the new factions found self psychology, as I had predicted; the two systems could not occupy the same space. The Kleinians for the most part became Kohutians en masse, the same leader (s), the same followers, for the same reasons of group psychology and cohesion. Any claim that theory follows a period of observations could be seen to have evaporated after each rapid conversion to explanatory systems of such different etiologic bases. From the 1970s into the 1980s, the atmosphere and the theoretical ambience of a psychoanalytic city changed tumultuously. Where two groups had split over the "classical" approach, they now shared interests energetically, vying to entertain the new theories and people in rapid succession. Klein, Bion, Fairbairn, therapeutic immersion, self psychology, intersubjectivity, united the two groups, where "old" analysis had divided them. In a paper on "Transference to Theory" (Rangell, 1982), I described how certain new, "eclectic" groups leapfrog over the oedipal, standing first for cultural, environmental, postoedipal conflicts, then leaping with equal vigor to the preoedipal, infancy, and postnatal, skipping over the oedipal, sexual, castration complex, in a child of between 3 and 6, where the bed for a neurosis develops, such as we see in analysis.

The era that followed, which I characterize as a derailment from course, was one of increasing dispersion in the direction of the eclecticism and pluralism that has become the psychoanalytic venue today. The divisions set in motion in the locales described, increased incrementally and spread geographically until they became the dominant position nationally. No event gave this mushrooming process as much currency, however, and an official stamp, as Wallerstein's (1988) Presidential Address at the Montreal International Congress in 1987, in which he posed the question "One Theory or Many?" and supplied his answer: many. Providing a conceptual umbrella, all theories had equal valence and validity, and none had the right by logic or performance to claim superordinacy over any other. While many regarded this as a political rather than scientific solution, the receptive audience jubilantly embraced this democratic principle, and proceeded to coalesce into a seemingly homogeneous view the varied existing divergent theories.

As gulfs remained and lines of demarcation continued to separate disparate divisions theoretically and clinically, the question as to how to contain the separate theories, some with parallel, separate mini organizations from local to international, was solved in various ways by different analysts. Many agreed with Wallerstein's conclusion on the basis of his view of common ground. Clinical theory, Wallerstein states, is what unites all theories, and makes them equal and interchangeable. It is abstract theories, which are speculative and unconfirmable that separate them. To this view, I would point out there is ample divisiveness within clinical theory itself. Defense and resistance, conflict and compromise, transference and countertransference, which Wallerstein offers as the common clinical ground that binds divergent theories together, are concepts as unevenly understood and as disparate as many more abstract aspects of theory. Conflict and compromise are not always foremost clinically; often defect and deficiency supersede these. Defense and resistance are not universally agreed upon, either as concept or technique. Even the much-vaunted transference and countertransference are not as common a bond between analysts as one would think. Not only are there differences with regard to the centrality or exclusivity of transference, but there are important differences in the definitional concept of what transference is. In a similar vein, countertransference, as is well known, divides analysts as much as it unites them. To most analysts it is a phenomenon that is always present and has to be recognized on all occasions. Beyond this, however, it is guarded against by some and embraced and utilized by others.

However, there is always common ground between alternative schools that unifies theory even as they are considered separate; this common ground is the use of Freudian theory. While Sandler (1983) stated that analysts commonly profess to be Freudian in public while in private finding other theories more useful, I (1984) have pointed out the opposite (granting that empirically both may hold), that analysts commonly speak publicly about major divergences, while privately finding long-standing Freudian concepts, of objectivity, uncovering of unconscious conflicts, interpretations, reconstructions, and the use of transference in the original sense as displacements from the past, more compatible with the practice of analysis.

Many analysts of all persuasions adhere to core prerequisites in the Freudian sense of psychoanalytic technique, to transference and resistance, and the aim of reconstructing and uncovering repressed unconscious conflicts. All theories that are psychoanalytic use Freudian theory, employing various combinations of its essence, the unconscious, intrapsychic, conflicts, final psychic outcomes from a variety of compromise formations. Other theoretical beliefs separate them, however, such as Klein from Kohut from Lacan, and all of them from Freud, lines of separation that in the present new ambience would be denied or overlooked. Fenichel's (1945) statement "there are many ways to treat neurosis, but there is only one way to understand them" (p. 554) becomes the opposite in the new view, that there are many understandings but one treatment. I feel the former better fits the operational facts.

Another formulation of Sandler's (1984), quoted by Wallerstein as an explanation about what unites and separates divergent theories, relates to the Sandlers' division of the past unconscious from the present unconscious. The main Freudian system, according to this view, points to the past unconscious, while more modern theories aim toward the more accessible present unconscious, this explaining differing practices between main and alternative theories. This explanation, in my opinion, creates a strained and inaccurate division, reminiscent of the separation between analysis by reconstruction and by the here-and-now. Just as analysis is by the here-and-now and reconstruction, between the present transference and the repressed past, so does analysis deal with the total, not partial unconscious, including its temporal aspects. Although the unconscious is timeless, different aspects present themselves or are available in any analytic hour. Analysis is from the surface down. There is no dividing line in the unconscious between old and new repressions, but a fluid path between them. Aspects of repressed contents, which can be from the present or past, are closer to the surface at different dramatic moments, related to the state of the defenses and resistances. No such division separates one theory from another. All psychoanalytic theories use all of the unconscious as aspects of it may become available to ego understanding and mastery.

Continuing to move beyond social harmony to the scientific issues, the question of one or more theories becomes complex. How many theories are to be equal to each other, two, four, any number? The two theories of George Klein, clinical and abstract, did not remain the division between theories for long. All theories, as reasoned so well by Waelder (1962), are both clinical and abstract. Many analysts, favoring closer attention to diagnostic categories, see three theories, and their derivative techniques, applied selectively to three different types of patients. Classical theory is for more benign, hysterical, neurotic patients; self theory for narcissistic patients; and object relations theory, following Kernberg (1975), for borderline and "the more disturbed" category of patients. The Fines (1990), in a research study of what analysts of different theories actually do in the conduct of their analyses, in which they found distinct clinical differences to exist, consider there to be four theories, after Freud, Klein, Kohut, and Kernberg. Pine (1990) also dealt with four, but four different theories from the Fines, drive, ego, self, and object theories. One analyst espouses "a cafeteria of paradigms," while another feels there is a theory for each patient, and another, a theory for each analyst.

The modern era has been one of chasing and trying to overtake the irrational. Rather than rational analysis of the irrational, primary process reasoning has become part of the analyzing instrument itself. Misperceptions, misunderstandings, misrepresentation, straw-men abound. In one institute, in which drive-defense theory is the target, analysis of resistance is regarded as criticism, interpretations as confrontations, both as accusations. The patient is a victim, not a benefactor of traditional analysis. "I don't like resistances," one discussant stated at a Panel (1983) on the subject.

Fallacies have been widely in operation and uncontested. In the fallacy of *pars pro toto*, which has by now been institutionalized, one part is emphasized and treated as the whole. Some analysts object to drive psychology, or differ from ego psychology, as though either one can stand alone, or favor transference to the exclusion of reconstruction. In the opposite fallacy, the whole is focused upon without acknowledgment of internal parts, regressing scientifically to preanalytic understanding. Or the genetic fallacy holds sway: what precedes, or the first of a sequence, must be the cause of what follows. It is well to keep in mind Anna Freud's (1976) statement that earlier is not necessarily deeper. Or one must choose between two poles of a dichotomous pair, such as intrapsychic versus interpersonal, or oedipal versus preoedipal, instead of both being operative and reciprocal. One point on a continuum is highlighted, rather than the total view of a developmental line. Accompanying and in support of the new views has been a turning away from Hartmann, Rapaport, and Freud, and I include Fenichel, from science and intellect in favor of subjectivity. Intellectualization as a defense is used as an argument against the use of intellect.

A polarized general division that has crystallized out of the diversity consists of "interactional" versus interpretative analysis. The former, a composite of the empathic, the self and object oriented, the intersubjective, and therapeutic immersion methods, all of them centering on relations and interactions, constitutes "modern," "liberal" theory and method, as contrasted with classical, "conservative" analysis, oriented toward objectivity and interpretation. Political terms, applied pejoratively, are freely used. Democracy and science are equal but separate, and not necessarily reciprocal. Popularity is not the criterion for validation. Science can explain democracy, but democracy does not always further science. Politicalization can in fact supersede and negate science. Is homosexuality, for example, outside the field of psychoanalysis? Are the varieties of sexual deviations, from sadomasochism to fetishism to transvestitism, or for that matter the nature of object-choice, heterosexual or unisexual, to be considered as exclusively determined by genetic constitution, and therefore outside the realm of dynamic exploration? Is it to be politics over science or are we to include in psychoanalysis the science of politics? While a celebration of diversity and mutual respect in ethnicity is appropriate in social affairs, it is less the mode of verification in science, where logic and parsimony have a rational place, from Einstein in the physical universe to Freud in the psychological, in a specific way fitting for each.

The trend in the direction of equality and democracy continues into extreme positions. The most recent is to assert the equal position of patient and analyst in the psychoanalytic situation by questioning the existence of special knowledge on the part of the psychoanalyst and of the "authority" of the analyst to make an interpretation. Analysis being a mutual project, patient and analyst are given the same "rights" and roles. In each instance, a normal aspect of analysis is carried to an extreme, then opposed. Authority needs to be separated from authoritarianism. The analyst has the authority, the special knowledge, and the responsibility to function as an analyst. Along the same line of extremism is the recommendation for enactment as a central feature of psychoanalytic technique. The ubiquitous appreciation of the role of nonverbal communications in analysis, becomes hypertrophied into acting in within the analytic exchange by both patient and analyst. Action comes to rival, if not replace, the centrality of verbal interchange between the two participants in the analytic dyad. Basic tenets are lost or overturned. Blum (1996) points out how the recent movement toward intersubjectivity changes the basic theoretical concepts of transference, countertransference, pathogenesis, and therapeutic action, among others. None of the exceptions I have taken to any of the alternative theories is to diminish or negate specific contributions by any of their authors. The contributions of Melanie Klein on early infantile mentation point to important and helpful directions. The emphasis on preservation of the self and the role of empathy added valid concepts, as did Alexander (1948) in pointing to the corrective aspects of the analytic relationship. Even Jung's veering to the spiritual was not without value and is echoed in mainstream psychology by the emphasis on the affective, creative, and unknown. In a paper on friendship, I (Rangell, 1963) found the contributions of Alfred Adler (1973) most helpful. Adler was also the first to lay down the seeds of ego psychology, before Freud came to this. His error was to discard what had been discovered before. It is what each theory omits, and the elevation of any of these individual contributions to a new system or theory, with which I differ.

Adding together all theories that omit, would result in leaving out many, even most essential elements. Minus 1 plus minus 1 equals minus 2. What is lost in the sum of interactional analyses are the instinctual drives, the oedipal conflicts, castration anxiety, the sexual etiology of neuroses, the neurotic anxiety behind sexual psychopathology. The combined effect of theories that omit is the ultimate disintegration of psychoanalytic theory. Integration, and its contained integrity, are removed, the latter in terms both of wholeness and in the moral sense of consistency, of disciplined versus undisciplined scientific principles. Theory is gradually denuded of its essentials, resulting in fragmentation and in the discontinuity of history.

While new theory should always have an open path, I do not believe there has been any new paradigm in the Kuhnian sense (Kuhn, 1970) that can constitute a total theory as was the case with the advent of psychoanalytic theory. Following Kuhn's reasoning, the possible applications of the normal science have by no means been exhausted, and no new theory comes closer to fulfilling that possibility than the continuously expanded theory of psychoanalysis. Only a seamless continuity between infancy, preoedipal and oedipal, and beyond, is empirically valid and rational. There is no theory of psychoanalysis to explain any human being, made up of drives alone, or ego alone, or superego only, or objects without a subject and its interior. I am not an "ego psychologist," as is conventionally but loosely stated, another of the common straw-men fallacies. I have said in many papers that I am an id-ego-superego-internal-external-psychoanalystpsychosynthesist.

With the spread of less uniform thinking, along with a burgeoning interest and increase in numbers, has come a sharp decline in the conviction of an intellectually coherent body of understanding and explanation. There is another way. In the ongoing debate over one theory or many, I (Rangell, 1988) favor one total composite psychoanalytic theory, which is unified and cumulative, total because it contains all nonexpendable elements, composite because it is a blend of the old and all valid new concepts and discoveries, and psychoanalytic as fulfilling the criteria for what is psychoanalysis. Every viable contribution made by alternative theories finds a home within this total composite theory. Fitting snugly under its embracing umbrella are drives and defense, id, ego, and superego, self and object, the intrapsychic and interpersonal, the internal and external world. This theory, aiming toward completeness with parsimony, comprises a unitary theory of psychoanalysis.

Such a unitary theory is not monolithic, as feared by some. Within it there are many concepts of multiplicity, such as the theory of overdetermination, Waelder's (1930) principle of multiple functions of the ego, and Freud's multiple metapsychologic points of view converging upon any single psychological phenomenon. Hanly (1994), in a discussion of Pine's (1990) four psychologies, also feels that classical theory provides the best approach to understanding the interconnections between drive, ego, objects, and narcissism, that its strength lies in its ability to hold the four psychologies in a productive tension without one viewpoint being given disproportionate weight at the expense of the others.

There is another set of observations I can add as data relevant to my central theme. This involves recent developments in the nature of reconciliation, offered solutions, corrections of excessive waves and pendular swings. Such a phenomenon is in progress and worth noting, as we reach the centennial of psychoanalysis, perhaps a reflection of a universal cycle in nature. A definite rapprochement, a unifying trend, is visible and in progress. While this in itself is reparative, what is not in evidence and does not accompany this forward movement, is the insight this too engenders, ironically the very goal of psychoanalysis, a rational gain that might prevent repetition rather than cyclicity.

With altered political arrangements, social experiences of members facilitate gradual ideational fusions, as bonds of friendship ease the way toward theoretical synchrony. The passing of charismatic leaders, or of inspirational models, liberate their adherents who had lived their lives affectively within a hierarchic order in the family of their theoretical school. Reactive readjustments to such events have affected new theoretical lineups throughout the history of psychoanalysis. As previously at Freud's death, the deaths of Melanie Klein and then of Anna Freud cannot be omitted from influences on future history. With roots in Britain, but now everywhere, "contemporary Freudians" and "modern Kleinians" are forging a bond not only affectively but scientifically.

Considerations of projective identification in depth by Freudian panels in the late 1980s did not arise upon an unchanged soil, but within an altered surround. In an international panel on common ground (1989), as a follow-up of the previous congress on "many theories," it was the Kleinian speaker (Feldman, 1990) who chose as his subject the Oedipus complex.

What is overlooked in these salutary developments are the rational terms of the comings together and their historical significance. These, I aver, are on the basis of the correctness and validity of composite theory. Generally, the newly unified colleagues agree now on inclusion rather than exclusion. The oedipal holds, as does the preoedipal, and infancy, and the constitutional givens (of Hartmann [1950], now of Stern [1985] and other infant researchers) even before initial experiences. As fantasy was added to seduction as etiology, tragic man does not replace but is added to guilty man, both of them parts of man's fate. Structure and hermeneutics, meanings and mechanism, coexist and are complementary. The self is included in total theory, along with drives and deficits. In total modern technique, empathy is accepted as accompanying the objective analytic attitude. What one does not see in this theoretical coalescence is a homage to projective identification, or clinical access to early infantile or neonatal fantasies during reconstruction in analysis. These selective reversals have not been sufficiently defined or articulated, while the new amalgamation is celebrated as though separate theories are coming together on equal terms and there never were any differences in the first place.

The years of separation, bad faith, even mutual calumny are not forgotten but repressed. In fact, those who held to the totality from the beginning, and point out to current theorists the directions of the changes, are reacted to as self-serving. The mechanism is reminiscent of the political label of "premature antifascists" applied in earlier years in the sociopolitical arena; they were right too soon. On a panel on psychic trauma, Anna Freud (1967) observed that people often give praise to traumatic occurrences, when reparation afterward advances to the degree of bettering conditions even more than they were before. It is like giving credit to an earthquake, when a city is rebuilt after it into a finer grandeur than it had before, rather than to the industrious people who did the rebuilding.

It is a unified, composite theory that is confirmed and strengthened by modern reparative developments, not the equivalence of separate systems. This unification is in my opinion the inevitable direction of the future, if logic and reason are to prevail, and confidence and a sense of intellectual conviction are to return. In the end, the parts and the nature of their togetherness that are the most coherent and valuable will endure.

Developing, holding and containing new psychoanalytic groups

by Cláudio Laks Eizirik

In this paper I will describe and discuss some aspects of the development of new psychoanalytic groups within the International Psychoanalytical Association (IPA), a work carried out by the International New Groups Committee (ING).

The IPA is an association including 12517 psychoanalysts as members and 5333 analysts in training and works with 83 constituent organizations. It was founded by Sigmund Freud in 1910. The Board of the IPA delegates the responsibility for the development of new IPA groups to its International New Groups Committee, whose members ordinarily consist of the Chair of ING and the ING Co-Chairs for each IPA region. The ING purpose is to stimulate the development of psychoanalysis by facilitating the development and progression of new groups, ensuring the proper development of a group´s capacity to work as a scientific society and to deliver high quality training programs.

This is a complex and delicate process, to which many IPA members have dedicated and continue to dedicate their tireless efforts and skills. Among these skills is their capacity to hold and to contain all sorts of anxieties, side by side with huge amounts of work and trust in the development of psychoanalysis.

I have had previous opportunities of dealing with and even making decisions concerning this extremely important activity, during my term as IPA President for four years, and my ongoing interest in psychoanalytic institutions and psychoanalytic training (Eizirik, 2011, 2018, 2019). However, it was only recently that I was able to engage directly and intensely on the development, holding and containing of new psychoanalytic groups, as ING Chair, in the last four years.

THE ING PROCESS AND THE ROLE OF SPONSORS

The ING currently works with 14 Sponsoring Committees, (assisting the development of our Study Groups); 9 Liaison Committees, (working with our Provisional Societies), the European Psychoanalytic Institute—EPI (formed jointly by the IPA and the EPF), the Latin American Psychoanalytic Institute—ILAP (formed jointly by the IPA and FEPAL) and the China Committee—working in China to train IPA candidates.

Together these bodies train over 400 candidates.

The ING also includes Allied Centers, which are groups of mental health workers interested in psychoanalysis and in having a non-training relationship with the IPA.

The ING Committee works through a continuous communication among its Chair, Co-Chairs, Sponsors, Liaisons and the London Head of ING office and her assistant, with whom the ING Chair holds weekly online meetings. There are in person regular meetings, as I will describe later, as well as meetings with Sponsors or Liaisons when a specific situation so requires. From now on, when I say "we" I mean this central team I have just described.

Broadly speaking, a future new group represents a new initiative. This could be in areas where an IPA society already exists or there is no IPA training or as the result of a split in an existing society (as I will discuss later).

When a group first contacts the ING to apply for Study Group status we assess the readiness of the group. An IPA Study Group must be composed of at least four IPA members. These members must maintain membership in their IPA Constituent Organization or be Direct Members of the IPA. They must live close enough to each other to enable the group to function as a cohesive unit, meet regularly and develop a strong training program. All four members must be actively involved in the group and its development. We also take into consideration potential ethical issues. From the documents that are sent by the group, and the exchange of letters with the applicants, we assess how the group was formed, how much experience they have, what their achievements have been and what kind of identification they have with psychoanalysis. It is important to study the history of each group, their previous engagements, if all IPA members in the area are included and if not why and so on. This initial assessment is both procedural and offers a preliminary prognosis of what can happen in the group´s future development.

Basseches (2019) considers that there are organizational issues that emerge when new groups begin to form, and develop, that present challenges to the successful and creative development of the group. Each new group has its own challenges, based on the unique characteristics of its local circumstances. Such initial issues: having sufficient number of IPA members (some of whom able to eventually function as Training and Supervising Analysts); being able to convene together easily in an accessible location; having basic financial resources to operate, and a pool of potential candidates to train are all hurdles to be faced.

Moreover, according to Basseches (2019) there are cultural, historical and political aspects of developing groups that may or may not be helpful to forming a psychoanalytic entity. Included in this latter perspective are historical and legal traditions within the local mental health establishment which support or discourage participation by one or another professional specialty. These traditions often run counter to IPA expectations of who could or could not be train to become a psychoanalyst, and force potential new groups to struggle with whether to join the IPA's psychoanalytic approach or to remain nestled in their previously held boundaries.

If we are satisfied with the information provided, a small committee is appointed to visit the group and assess its application in person. In this first visit, the site visiting committee is asked to observe the group dynamics, the quality of relationships among the members, in group and individual interviews, trying to evaluate the ethical values and foresee any possible problems. This process is extremely important and challenging at the same time. Sometimes it is compared with the initial assessment of patients for analysis or potential candidates for training, but in my view, this is an unfortunate comparison. Group dynamics, history, motivation, limitations and possibilities present a very complex situation, and one of the challenges we face is to select colleagues who are able to perform these functions well.

A sponsor or a liaison has to be a training analyst in his/her Society, with a lot of analytic and institutional experience, and a particular ability to connect with colleagues and to work with groups. Usually there are two sponsors working with a study group, but sometimes three, according to the size of the study group or its specific needs. In my experience, these couples of sponsors mostly develop a positive working relationship and very often a personal friendship. They work together for many years, and they face together several challenges, connected with their role, both objective and symbolic. Mostly, the sponsors are felt as inspirational objects, and even protective ones; they dedicate long hours of voluntary work to reading documents, reports, theoretical and clinical papers and mainly visiting the groups twice a year, for an intensive immersion in the group`s life, achievements and problems.

Sometimes, however, sponsors are unconsciously seen as agents of an external power, the IPA, trying to impose rules, procedures and requirements that the new group or part of its members feel as unacceptable. Then, at some point of their meetings with the sponsors, one or more members of a study group may recall the experience they previously had had in their countries with dictators, tyrants, and other dangerous people, associations that may show how the sponsors are being perceived at that moment. Sometimes, there is a splitting in the group´s mind, leading to viewing the sponsors as the benevolent parents and the ING chair and co-chairs as the persecutory ones.

All these situations are better dealt with when the sponsors have a strong connection between them and are able to discuss and deal with these challenges taking into account their institutional and psychoanalytic experience. In general, the understanding of unconscious fantasies producing group conflicts or the presence of the basic assumptions described by Bion (1961) are enough for the sponsors to deal with the group; in others, it is necessary to discuss them openly with the group in order to have a joint understanding and move forward with the group activities.

According to Flechner (2019), at the beginning, we can see a period of adaptation between the group and the sponsors, paranoid anxieties inside the groups are sometimes handled as feelings of strangeness that come from a sensation of surveillance from the IPA representatives, but over time the sponsors end up being accepted and considered as true collaborators. Sponsors accomplish their task with admirable dedication. Their commitment and interventions in each visit or virtual contact with the new groups allow them to carry forward their growth, maintaining the ethical parameters required by the IPA.

When a Study Group is approved by the Board, a Sponsoring Committee is appointed with the task of guiding and setting the basis for a future psychoanalytical society: the organizational structure, training, scientific life, ethical code and outreach activities. Sponsors play a crucial role in the development of a group at all of its stages, but perhaps more so during the initial one, when there is a strong need to obtain and develop a feeling of belonging to the IPA, the group`s own identity as separate from previous analytic or other groups, and a growing trust on the ability to work analytically.

Basseches (2009) stressed the impact on groups of IPA sponsoring committees. She believes that their role can be pivotal in the way that group foundation can be enhanced or undermined by their interventions and emphasizes that the ING needs to pay close attention to the chemistry of those who function in these outside group supportive roles to be sure that it is actually a collaborative and supportive role and not an authoritarian one.

The ING has a close relationship with all sponsors, through their reports, sent twice a year, after each visit, and also through a meeting in person each year. At each regional and IPA congresses, we hold a general meeting with all sponsors and liaisons from the relevant region, where we discuss some theoretical or practical issues related to their activity. In recent years, these joint meetings discussed relevant issues such as: "First generation officers (founders) of new analytic organizations and their relationships with the Sponsors, "Splits in psychoanalytic societies and new groups," "The first steps of a Study Group after a traumatic split," "The history of a Study group that developed successfully and the role of its Sponsors." In each of these meetings, both sponsors and liaisons and ING chair and co-chairs present initial papers, to introduce the discussion.

We also hold a private meeting with each Sponsoring and Liaison Committee, where they can speak more openly and discuss complex issues or concerns, including ethical ones. For example: how to deal with an aging training analyst, with clear signs of dementia, to whom some of his colleagues continue to refer patients and supervisees; how to face rivalries between two leading members that threaten to impair the development of the group; how to face strong demands from a study group members to become a provisional society before the time established in our procedures and the maturational work is completed; how to deal with fights for power that may involve ethical breaches at a study group, splits and conflicts among the generation of pioneers which can continue in the following generations. (Aisenstein, 2019; Eizirik, 2019).

These private meetings are a continuous source of learning for all participants, because the chair and co-chairs do not have prepared answers to each of these and many other questions, so what often happens is a candid exchange of previous experiences, to establish reasonable ways of facing difficult situations. It is a conversation among colleagues with institutional and psychoanalytic experience that is helpful to find new ways of thinking about and understanding individual and group dynamics.

When a group has accomplished all the tasks required and the sponsors and the ING feel they are ready to be accepted for Provisional Society status, and this decision is approved by the IPA Board, a Liaison Committee is appointed to visit the group once a year to guide them through the final stages of development until they are ready for Component Society status and complete autonomy. This last stage towards becoming a Component Society is also not without conflicts and struggles involving autonomy versus dependency, the wish to have freedom to develop its analytic life versus the fear of not being able to do so, need to be carefully worked through with the liaisons.

Since the beginning of the coronavirus pandemic, ING activities have been undertaken online. From the reports and the meetings we have had with sponsors and liaisons, following our usual procedure of monitoring, holding and containing, it is possible to say that the work continues, with the unavoidable losses of in person communication and meetings, but at the same time with the effectiveness that the circumstances allow. This new situation will have to be studied and evaluated as time goes by.

SPLITS IN PSYCHOANALYTIC SOCIETIES AND
THE BEGINNING OF STUDY GROUPS

In order to introduce some remarks about splits in psychoanalytic societies, I will describe the history of a fictional society (using observations about several ones). This fictional society was founded in the fifties, developed well until being recognized by the IPA in the early sixties, became one of the main societies of the country, and in the early nineties went through a split of part of its members, who joined with analysts who had arrived from another country to begin a new IPA study group in the same city.

This split was a traumatic event, that went beyond the walls of the existing Society and the new group, and produced several wounds that took many years to heal, or did not heal at all. Friendships ended, analyses were interrupted, confrontations were publicly exposed, and a strong competition was established, both into the psychoanalytic movement and at the external community. Apart from the fact that the newcomers from the other country brought some theoretical new emphases, analysts from both groups, the old and the new one, remained connected to the main authors and theories that prevailed since the beginning of the old society, and both groups followed the natural theoretical developments of our field. In short, there was no theoretical reason for the split.

As time went by, new generations of analysts were trained in both societies, relatives of members of one society went into analysis with members of the other, members of one society married members of the other, and then even the main characters of the drama of the split resumed their former relationship, of course somewhat cautiously. In this new scenario both societies organized joint activities, received hosts from other places and shared national boards of analytic institutions.

So, the first question is: why did this split happen?

In my view, the basic reasons can be found in Freud ´s Totem and Taboo(1913), Group Psychology and the Analysis of the Ego (1921), and in papers by Bion (1961), Jaques(1976), Kernberg (1998), among others. So, I will suggest one possible way of understanding the origins of that split.

It seemed that the relationship of the founding members was very good, under the leadership of the founding father, with strong ties and a feeling of joint work, with concrete results and a real pride in the group`s achievements. However, one of the brothers apparently was or at least did his best to look or to act as if he was the favorite son. Maybe this was the view of his colleagues, many of them unhappy with his analytic development. The original pact was broken and in a complex network of crossed transferences and countertransferences, involving the third generation (candidates in analysis with members of the second one) this supposed preferred son was slowly undermined in his ambitions and eventually decided to leave the society with all his candidates, and to join with the newcomers.

Looking from a psychoanalytical perspective, he was symbolically killed, and then there was no other possibility except to leave. One could also consider that this fight was also a way of attacking the founding father, who was still alive but too old and unable to manage this crisis, as he had done with past ones. What could be the origin of this crisis? The brother`s narcissistic needs? The envy of the other brothers of his national and international prestige? The feeling that the founding father loved him more than the others? The long-repressed rivalry, competition, jealousy, envy among the brotherhood and all those bad feelings that apparently did not exist under the disguise of a happy family? All of those?

Elliott Jaques (1976) distinguished two types of social organizations, requisite and paranoiagenic. Requisite organizations are structurally sound- that is, authority and accountability are matched, and it is possible to get the right number of people for the right task at the right time; they are organizations with a functional administrative structure. Such organizations, according to Jaques, enable people to relate to one another with confidence and to rule out suspicion and mistrust. Paranoiagenic organizations, notes Jaques, make it impossible for individuals to have normal relationships of confidence and trust. They force social interactions into a mold calling for forms of behavior which arouse suspicion, envy, hostile rivalry, and anxiety, and put brakes on social relationships, regardless of how much individual goodwill there might be.

In my view, we can observe, in our psychoanalytic organizations, the alternation or predominance of one of these two structures, and when the second one prevails, splits or endless crises will occur, but we can also observe these two kinds of functioning in the same institution, simultaneously or one after the other. In Kleinian language, we can describe these ways of functioning as schizo-paranoid and depressive, obviously.

In the aforementioned example it seems to me that the requisite organization of the first years was substituted by a paranoiagenic one and that this type of functioning remained between the two societies for a long period, until more recent developments, according to this fictional example.

The second question is whether this split could or should be prevented. In this point, I strongly agree with Aisenstein (2019), when she states that our first attempt should be to reconcile, but sometimes it is better to let each one, be it a couple or two groups, to follow his or her or their way. In this case, it would be impossible to reconcile, and the split stimulated each group to follow its own way. The paranoid atmosphere naturally led the old group to call the new one irresponsible, untrustworthy, psychopathic, and so on, while the new one called the old one conservative, reactionary, rigid, old fashioned and so on. But both groups devoted their effort to study, train candidates, publish, research and develop psychoanalysis. When they were able to meet and to talk, eventually, they could share mutual experiences, difficulties and achievements.

According to Aisenstein (2019) the reasons mentioned to explain splits are often theoretical and technical divergences, but she recalls the fine example of the British Society and the passionate Controversies between Anna Freud and Melanie Klein in London during the war.

She recalls that London was being bombarded while the psychoanalysts were fighting with words over psychoanalytic concepts…and today, the Kleinians, Anna Freudians, Independents and Middle Group coexist, not without tensions, but without being separated, within the British Society.

In other words, it seems to her that divergences, even profound ones, can be fruitful if dialogue is not cut off.

Aisenstein is convinced that the deep and implicit causes of certain splits are linked to the confrontation of characters and narcissisms that cannot tolerate each other.

She is, of course, in favour of attempts to bring about a conciliation between the parties in conflict, and the IPA often takes on this third-party role, sometimes very fruitfully.

On the other hand, she thinks that just as there are bad marriages in which two personalities of quality would benefit from separating, there are toxic confrontations.

Taking into account her long experience with new groups, she prefers to have in one place two good groups that are in rivalry but work well than just one group that is paralysed by conflicts and hatreds that impede creativity.

THE ROLE OF LEADERS IN THE DEVELOPMENT
OF NEW GROUPS

We are well aware of Freud`s insights on the role of leaders and their relationship with the group or the masses (Freud, 1921). Previously I mentioned several analytic thinkers who discussed this issue more recently.

What I will present here are recent reflections from two ING co-chairs, Harriet Basseches and Marilia Aisenstein, based on their past and current experience and then I will describe my own views on this relevant issue.

According to Basseches (2019) the first issue that deserves attention is rivalry. Rivalry may occur between two leaders of an organization, a rivalry that disrupts and sometimes defeats group formation by both parties leaving the situation; or such a rivalry may end up by one leader successfully defeating the other and thus emerging as the dominant leader. If both leave, the wounded group may still emerge with a lesser leader stepping in. Then it becomes a matter of whether the surviving group members can be generative enough to pass on to new generations their psychoanalytic organizational seed. While at first it may be a weaker entity, with time it can emerge as a stronger union in the absence of the powerful, charismatic leader. Here Basseches is referring to the concept of generativity, proposed by Erikson (1963), to denote a concern for establishing and guiding the next generation.

The question that gets worked through, especially by the later generations, is whether the original traumatic rivalry stays buried in the fabric of relationships later to emerge as transgenerational trauma, or whether the later group can use awareness of that danger to be alert to and avoid the temptations and thus to unite.

Basseches (2019) describes that one of the most successful new groups she monitored has been led primarily (although not exclusively) by women. In this particular case, it happened that men provided guidance (as Sponsoring Committee) and a situation where a man was the original leader, but, like Moses, did not go on to the promised land of becoming part of the study group.

Basseches reflects then on the charismatic leader. She thinks that when the founder is such a leader, he or she brings enthusiasm and intensity to his role that draws a strong organizational group around him. It is then a meaningful challenge for such a person to not only provide the strong foundation for the group, but then, in the spirit of generativity, to help the next generations, to be able to continue the development of the organization. To let go of his centrality and transfer his leadership to others does not diminish but rather enhances his stature and respect. It seems to her that the Moses metaphor mentioned above, though a lot to ask of someone who has achieved so much, creates an organizational triumph by letting go to build the greater legacy of a cohesive and forward-looking institution that can survive.

The issue of leadership was also explored by Aisenstein (2019). According to her, as the groups are totally disparate, their organizations different, their sizes variable, and their stories not comparable, we have to look for what she calls the "common denominators."

In her view, we underestimate the immense efforts made by "charismatic leaders." We underestimate this because we arrive as IPA members when the group is ready to be evaluated. We do not know about the years of prior work on the ground led by the "founding leaders." Often these people have sacrificed significant years of their working lives and their family lives to see a Study Group recognized by the IPA. They are necessarily strong charismatic and passionate personalities, as described by Basseches (2019).

Aisenstein (2019) mentions the book *"Fanaticism in psychoanalysis, upheavals in Psychoanalytic institutions,"* by Manuela Utrilla, that offers a close study of the psychic construction of "leaders."

According to Utrilla (2013), "charismatic leaders" always create their "followers."

Passion for their ideals, conviction, and positive narcissism (as described by André Green) are indispensable traits in becoming a charismatic leader. In order to surround oneself with a group, to carry it onward, to fight to have it recognized, one needs a passion for ideals with which the subject risks ending up identifying himself totally.

So, in such men or women these characteristics probably exist in an embryonic state but are barely discernible. What are the conditions that lead them to their climax? And how could we best manage them?

Aisenstein (2019) mentions that several scenarios may exist. There are "leaders" whom the exercise of power tranquilizes and improves.

Others, on the other hand, seem incapable of living without what they consider their *mission*: that is, for those to whom she is referring, to educate, to convince, to transform others *in their own image*. But when they feel they are losing their power, it often happens that they become destructive both for the group and for themselves.

This is where she thinks we could see ING playing a role. Those kind of initial fights between 2 or 3 historic leaders will be transmitted to their analysands and supervisees and create tensions and hate within the group.

Aisenstein (2019) thinks that often we believe in continuity, but continuity is sometimes a trap. According to her experience, Sponsoring and Liaison Committees are themselves vulnerable and may remain too close to leaders. Or, on the other hand, they may unwittingly push groups into conflict with their "founders."

Now I will get back to the fictional example of a split into a society and the formation of a new study group in that city. While reading and summarizing the ideas put forward by Aisenstein and Basseches, another possible way of understanding that split came to my mind. The first idea is that it was an example that a split may be a positive outcome for a conflict, as it happened in that situation. The other idea is connected with the charismatic leader, so well described by them and by Manuela Utrilla. It is possible that the so-called preferred brother was a charismatic leader, both on the positive and negative versions of this kind of character. In any case, we must take into account the huge effort of the founding officers and be more careful and compassionate when they reach the final steps of their productive careers. We had had situations in which the ING was able to help some of these colleagues and their groups, but this is where confidentiality draws a line.

Concerning the issue of leadership, my own experience includes the opportunity of working with several different leaders, as well as observing different leaders of new groups and sponsoring committees, and, last but not least, occupying the role of leader on many different circumstances. I agree with the important points raised by Basseches and Aisenstein, and I would like to add some others.

There is something in a leader that stimulates his or her colleagues to search into themselves for the best way of taking part in the joint enterprise they are all included in. This something is the capacity to lead, to not be afraid of taking risks and to convey to the group the feeling of complete devotion and commitment to his or her mission. It is impossible to be a leader without some amount of narcissism, but what I am stressing here is the fact that a leader needs to be identified with his/her mission and to have a view on what is to be achieved. This ability to inspire and to stimulate can be connected to what Freud (2021) described as the group members projecting their ego ideal into the leader.

Another important trait of the leader is that his/her choices should not be motivated by his/her own interests and that he/she does not appoint or invite people to occupy group functions only among his/her friends. The true leader chooses people according to their expertise and competence. The true leader is able to endure challenges and even heavy criticism or attacks without being destroyed or having the need to retaliate. Another important aspect of the true or charismatic leader is the ability to listen to the colleagues or followers, to try to understand their needs, complaints or criticisms and to change the course of action when new facts and evidences so require. A certain amount of compassion is also required the empathy that allows someone to put himself/herself in the other's shoes and to feel what they are feeling.

I was able to witness and to work with groups that were suffering the situation described by Basseches and Aisenstein of leaders who were unable to withdraw from their position, because they felt this loss would mean their own death. Guilt, hatred, feelings of betrayal and of lack of gratitude were identified in group members, producing a dark atmosphere and the risk of splits, or even their reality. That's why I consider so important for the work of sponsors and liaisons to help all leaders to work through their motivations and the need to stimulate and prepare younger colleagues to take over when the time comes. The democratic structure of all groups, new or old, is of paramount importance, and it needs to be clearly stated on the procedures and into the mind of all members.

I was also able to witness and to work with groups whose leaders had a clear notion of their importance and the centrality of their work, but at the same time were able to accept that new leaders emerged and to help them in the first stages of their work. More than once, I witnessed new leaders expressing their gratitude to old ones, and promising they would remain as eternal consultants and even a kind of guru.

Some of these old leaders felt deeply disappointed when this did not happen; others were able to understand that new leaders need to have their own plans and ways of leading. In short, to be a charismatic leader includes some degree of vulnerability, due to narcissistic needs, as if the power would be for life, thus helping to cope with primitive fears and anxieties. What I mostly witnessed is this kind of leader in our new study groups, colleagues who fully devoted their energy and skills to their task and who, afterwards, were admired and even loved by their colleagues. After some point in their careers, they did not need any formal position, because their colleagues, old and new, knew they were there to help, to give advice, to support, to hold and to contain for the rest of their lives.

ETHICAL ISSUES AND THE DEVELOPMENT OF A CULTURE OF CONFIDENTIALITY

The ethical dimension encompasses the field of our relations with others, mediated, explicitly or implicitly, by codes of prescriptions, for the legitimization of behavioral patterns. However, this ethical dimension involves human beings in reflexive relations, relations to us and to others. The metaphorical figure of the ethical dimension is the home, the place where we live. Etymologically, ethos is the root of habit, practice and home. Home is a place of shelter, hosting the conditions for the possibility of protection, food and pleasure. To take ownership of our work is to gain some kind of serenity to experience life outside the shelter, to experience challenges and possibilities of the double condition of existence, being thrown into a world that is not chosen, and to recognize the need to build an inside and an outside world to be in. Relations with others are built in this mediation, where there is reliability and risk, differentiation and protection, responsibility and challenges. (Figueiredo, 1995)

Ethical issues play a central role in the development of new groups, despite the fact that many times a group of analysts who begin to develop a new group feel so committed to the task and so united around a joint purpose that they cannot even imagine that ethical breaches may happen at some point of their future development. That´s why Sponsoring Committees always include the working on an ethical code, and the discussion on ethical principles and problems among their joint meetings with all group members. Along with this paper, I am stressing the importance of the position of sponsors as collaborators, inspiring objects and providers of guidance and the need to follow and behave according to the IPA procedures and ethical requirements. Seminars, case discussion and open discussion on ethical issues may contribute to a better understanding and even the prevention of future problems.

When ethical breaches really happen, sponsors will direct the study group to seek the help of the IPA Ethics Committee.

Among so many dimensions of ethics and ethical problems, I will focus mainly on the challenge of fostering a culture of confidentiality, and describe some issues and concerns that were discussed within the ING community. In order to do so I will review some relevant points of the Report of the IPA Confidentiality Committee and then I will describe and discuss the current state of our work concerning confidentiality in reports and communications among us.

ABOUT CONFIDENTIALITY

The Report from the IPA Confidentiality Committee from November 2018, is an extremely important resource to help us when facing problems and dilemmas concerning confidentiality. I will highlight some of the main points they express and their main recommendations, since this is a relatively new document. I suppose not many colleagues have had the opportunity of getting in touch with their relevant contributions as is the case with the ING Committee.

In their general conclusions, the Committee mentions that the principle of confidentiality is one of the foundations of psychoanalysis, which is stated by the IPA in its Ethics Code, and this has consequences both for the IPA as a professional organization and for its individual members. Confidentiality is a matter both of ethics and of technique. It is essential for the well-being and future development of psychoanalysis, as well as for the well-being and benefit of patients. Ensuring the maintenance of confidentiality can be a complex, difficult and challenging task. The Committee considers that in our current professional culture there are gaps between the theory and practice of confidentiality, as we know, even if only anecdotally, that in actual psychoanalytic practice the thoroughness with which confidentiality is maintained is highly variable.

In this report they have identified major risks to confidentiality across three broad areas: 1. sharing of clinical material with colleagues, which is for the benefit of individual patients and of patients generally, but which can come into unavoidable and ultimately unsolvable conflict with the need to preserve confidentiality; 2. telecommunications and use of technology, especially but not exclusively in 'remote analysis', which is creating new risks for which only partial protection is possible; 3. requests from patients and from third parties for access to process notes, where ethical and technical considerations are at risk of being subordinated to legal or political ones.

Furthermore, across all three of these areas, problems arise concerning the possibility of obtaining 'informed consent,' given the complications due to the transference in any psychoanalytic situation and the inherent unpredictability of unconscious psychic content at all stages of an analysis. Despite the fact that the IPA has a responsibility to provide guidelines for its members concerning all of these risks, psychoanalysts cannot escape the obligation of making difficult ethical and technical decisions on a case-by-case basis, often with insufficient information. For this they may need not only guidelines but also institutional support. Psychoanalysts generally need to become better informed about the risks to confidentiality. This implies a need for continuing professional development by individual analysts and a corresponding need for the IPA, its committees and its component organizations to develop ways of meeting this need.

The overall recommendation of the Confidentiality Committee is that the IPA should foster and strengthen a culture of confidentiality in every aspect of its operations.

This is something that the ING has already begun trying to do, as I will describe now.

THE ISSUE OF CONFIDENTIALITY IN RELATION TO REPORTS FROM THE ING COMMITTEES

The ING Committee has discussed the issue of confidentiality at its regional meetings with Sponsoring and Liaison Committees, including how reports of visits should be written, reports from Supervisors, the circulation and storage of such reports (including the deletion of them when they are no longer needed). It was stressed that a report should be written with the view that those mentioned in the report will read it. It is important to manage the content of Supervisor reports and recommendations for Direct Membership, ensuring that only the competency of the analyst is addressed —there is no need for information about the case or the patient, biographic data or any information that potentially identifies the patient. The ING is striving to ensure that all of our new groups are mindful of the importance of protecting their patients, candidates and themselves and that groups hold regular Ethical seminars.

The ING has received supervisor reports from key people in Component Societies that contain details concerning the case and the patient. This information is unnecessary and puts the candidate, supervisor and anyone who circulates the information at risk—not to mention the potential emotional damage to the patient should they discover that information about their case has been circulated by email. The ING highlights the problem when it presents itself, by redacting sensitive information and requesting original copies are deleted from computers. However, the issue also needs addressing from the source i.e. the Institutes themselves.

The written case reports from candidates are the most problematic as it is sometimes necessary to include detail in these papers. These papers should be handled with extreme caution, stored on a secure server, protected by a password, not circulated by email and deleted when no longer needed. All Institutes must have a clear procedure for handling these papers. During one of our meetings with our Sponsors and Liaisons it was suggested that one way of handling this problem could be meeting personally with candidates to carry out most of the assessment in order to negate the need for detailed clinical information to be written down and circulated.

Another issue is ensuring that supervision carried out over any form of telecommunications, including fixed and mobile telephones, VoIP applications, email, and any other application which uses the internet is secure. The problem with any such security issues is that they vary from country to country and therefore it is important that those concerned research what is possible in their own country.

SEVERAL IMPORTANT POINTS WERE RAISED DURING OUR DISCUSSIONS.

Some sponsors feel that there is a danger that Committees will submit reports that don't give any information rather than include something that may be problematic, in the sense that we will lose what is essential from a psychoanalytic perspective, and some even considered that the reports may become void of the very soul of analytic essence. It was considered by other colleagues that it is a difficult balance, even if most of them understand the current need to develop a culture of confidentiality.

It was stressed that there is a chain of confidence which negates the need for detailed information. The ING Committee was appointed by the Board and it is not therefore necessary to include detailed information to back up recommendations. We appoint Sponsors because we trust their judgement and the same should be said for supervisors—they make a recommendation based on their knowledge and experience—it is not necessary for them to include details of the case or the candidate to back up their views.

It was suggested that a candidate could give his or her consent to have information about the supervised case shared. It was pointed out that it would not be appropriate to do this when there was information about the patient included in a report as the patient's confidentiality must also be protected.

There were general concerns about how to keep files safe and it was pointed out that some countries have secure email servers for medical information—but as each country was different it would be up to the individual to look into what was available in their own area.

It was suggested that it is easy to give minimal information when the outcome of an assessment or supervision is positive, but when it is negative it is necessary to prove due process. The importance of discussing difficult situations and problematic cases in person during our meetings, or during the sponsors' visits, was extremely valued.

There was also concern about the detailed reports that candidates submit to institutes when being assessed in their training. Although this is not an ING issue it was up to each institute to ensure that there was a secure process for doing this—perhaps meeting personally with the candidates to carry out most of the assessment so there is no need for detailed clinical information to be circulated.

All the issues described about the culture of confidentiality illustrate the work to continue to develop and protect our mutual home, psychoanalysis and the IPA, in a changing world, with its continuous challenges and transformations. The current situation shows the process of transformation from the usual way of communicating and sharing information concerning colleagues and patients into a new way of conceptualizing and protecting the intimacy of analytic work and the delicate process of creating, and developing new analytic groups and societies.

CONCLUDING REMARKS

In my view, psychoanalysis is a work in progress (Eizirik, 2006), and the ING illustrates very well this conviction. Each one of its previous chairs and co-chairs contributed to developing procedures, rules, ways of relating to new groups, sponsors and liaisons, as well as ways of understanding better hopes, expectations, anxieties, frustrations, resistances, devotion, hard work, and an overall commitment with the future of psychoanalysis. From the huge number of activities, experiences, historical and cultural factors involved, conflicts and achievements, I hope I was able to put together some of the main aspects that constitute the vitality and the creativity of this so relevant activity. I hope, also, that I was able to demonstrate the main reasons that make it possible for the ING and to all colleagues involved in the work to developing, holding and containing new psychoanalytic groups into the IPA.

What did I learn from the experience of chairing and working with the ING?

In my view, the work of initiating and developing new groups into the IPA is possibly one of the most challenging tasks of the association. The selection and monitoring of sponsoring committees involves many times what kind of future society will be constituted. The proper and continuous work involving sponsors and the leaders and members of new groups, at each stage of their development, jointly with the ING, can enhance or undermine the construction of a society both solid scientifically and able to have a stimulating training program. The same holds true concerning ethical issues and ethical problems. That´s why I need to emphasize how important it is to pay continuous attention to procedural aspects as well as to the emotional aspects involved throughout the development of a new component society.

My experience with the ING taught me the importance of meetings in person (or at least online, these days) both with sponsors and liaisons and group leaders and members. These meetings should be continued, because they allow us to listen to other colleagues about their feelings, anxieties and concerns, thus being able to help them to face them and to move forward. Maybe another important point would be a more structured training for new sponsors, to better prepare them for the work they are just to begin. Another project could be to include more systematically publications and research on the several issues that I presented in this paper. I understand and described current concerns about confidentiality, but even considering them, it would be possible a further development in the ING activity.

Reflecting on holding and containing, Ogden (2005, p.108) stresses that "Winnicott´s holding and Bion`s container-contained represent different analytic vertices from which to view the same analytic experience. Holding is concerned primarily with being and its relationship to time; the container-contained is centrality concerned with the processing (dreaming) of thoughts derived from lived emotional experience. Together they afford "stereoscopic" depth to the understanding of the emotional experiences that occur in the analytic setting."

In my view, after this immersion into the ING community, it became clear to me that both processes—holding and containing—are at the very core of the activity involved in developing new analytic groups.

As I described in this paper, several procedural requirements need to be acquired along the duration of the whole process of becoming a psychoanalytic society, but what is essential is the acquisition of a psychoanalytic identity, a feeling of intimacy with psychoanalytic theories and technique and the ability to live this experience and becoming able to live it again and again with each patient as well as with the institution that was formed and needs to be protected, hold and contained from now on.

Last but not least, the experience with the ING was an extremely lively one, that produced in me a great admiration, respect and affection for almost all the colleagues involved in this task, and for their love for psychoanalysis and the IPA. In such a challenging period of our culture, with so much fear, hatred, corrupt leadership, uncertainty about the future and lack of trust in so many national and international institutions, I witnessed and I feel proud to be part of a group of psychoanalysts who keep our work in progress full of vitality and creativity.

ACKNOWLEDGEMENTS

I am grateful to Drs. Marilia Aisenstein, Harriet Basseches and Silvia Flechner, ING co-chairs for North America, Europe and Latin America, for our joint work and for their continuous support, friendship and creative ideas, and to Drs. Gabor Szönyi and Maria Teresa Calabrese, liaisons with EPI and FEPAL. This paper could not be written, as well as my work as ING chair could not have been done, without the continuous, friendly, efficient, dedicated and affectionate presence of Joanne Beavis, Head of International New Groups. She is the person who makes all our huge work possible. I am also grateful to Sebastian Montes, for his continuous and effective work. I am indebted to Dr. Gabriele Junkers for her careful reading and relevant comments and suggestions.

REFERENCES

Aisenstein, M. (2019) Splitting in psychoanalysis, splits in psychoanalytic societies. ING European Study Day Meeting, Madrid.

Aisenstein, M. (2019). Challenges and difficulties in establishing and following new groups. ING Panel, IPA Congress, London.

Basseches, H. (2019). The challenge of developing new IPA psychoanalytic groups. ING Panel, IPA Congress, London.

Bion, DW (1961). *Experiences in groups.* London: Tavistock.

Eizirik, C.L. (2011). The IPA administration from 2005 to 2009. In Loewenberg, P & Thompson, N. *100 Years of the IPA,* London, Karnac.

——— (2006). Psychoanalysis as a work in progress. *Int J Psychoanal*:87, 3:645–50.

——— ((2018). Contemporary developments and challenges of analytic training and practice. In Tylim, I & Harris, A. *Reconsidering the Moveable Frame in Psychoanalysis.* London and New York, Routledge.

——— (2019). Splits in psychoanalytic institutions. ING European Study Day Meeting, Madrid.

——— (2019). Fostering a culture of confidentiality in IPA Study groups and Provisional Societies, London, IPA International Congress.

——— & Foresti, G. (2019). *Psychoanalysis and Psychiatry—Partners and Competitors in the Mental Health Field,* London and New York, Routledge.

Erikson, E. (1963). *Childhood and society.* New York: W.W. Norton.

Figueiredo, LC (1995). Foucault e Heidegger. A ética e as formas históricas do habitar (e do não habitar). *Tempo soc.* (online). Vol 7, n.1-2, pp, 136–149.

Flechner, S.(2019). The challenges of developing new psychoanalytic groups. ING Panel, IPA Congress, London.

Freud, S. (1913). Totem and Taboo. *S.E.* 13:69–102.

——— (1921). Group psychology and the analysis of the ego *S.E.,* 18:65–143.

Jaques, E. (1976). *A general theory of bureaucracy.* New York: Halsted.

Kernberg, O. (1998). *Ideology, Conflict and Leadership in Groups and Organizations,* New Haven and London, Yale University Press.

Ogden, T. (2005). On holding and containing, being and dreaming. In *This Art of Psychoanalysis,* London and New York, Routledge.

Report from the IPA Confidentiality Committee, November 2018.

Utrilla, M.(2013). *Fanaticism in Psychoanalysis Upheavals in the Institutions,* London, Karnac.

Table 1

Assignment of Hue in the Chromatic Series

Class I stimulus forms		Class II stimulus forms		
Object	**Series** Incongruent hue (red seal)	**Object**	**Series** Congruent hue (tan lion)	**Series** Incongruent hue (purple lion)
fork	purple	evergreen tree	green	orange (tan)
pliers	green	giraffe	orange (tan)	red
frying pan	purple	lips	red	yellow
seal	red	banana	yellow	red
snake	red	violin	orange (tan)	green
sword	yellow	grapes	purple	orange (flesh)
elephant	orange (flesh)	hand	orange (flesh)	green
squirrel	green	cactus	green	red
gun	orange (flesh)	fire hydrant	red	purple
tree trunk	red	lion	orange (tan)	purple

Note: Two of the series (black seal and black lion) do not appear in this table since all items in these series were achromatic

Table 2

The Experimental Design

Groups	Stimulus forms presented	
	Class I **Achromatic objects**	**Class II** **Chromatic objects**
Group A ($N = 45$) Achromatic stimuli	10 congruent items black seal series (Class I norm series)	10 incongruent items black lion series
Group C-1 ($N = 45$) Chromatic stimuli	10 incongruent items red seal series	10 congruent items tan lion series (Class II norm series)
Group C-2 ($N = 45$) Chromatic stimuli		10 incongruent items purple lion series

Note: This design provides for two different types of statistical comparison between congruent and incongruent series (a) Comparison of related samples presented one class of stimulus forms in congruent and the other class in incongruent color (horizontal comparisons for Group A and for group C-1) (b) Comparison of independent groups presented the same class of stimulus forms in either congruent or incongruent colors (vertical comparisons of two groups for Class I forms and three groups for Class II forms). For all groups the congruent and incongruent items were intersperse in a single continuous series, for group C-2 special congruent chromatic items had to be added to fill out the series.

Table 3

Group Results for the Various Series, Reaction Times in Seconds

Group	Class I forms			Class II forms		
	Series	Media	Mean	Series	Media	Mean
A (*N* = 45)	black seal	1 015	1 158	black lion	1 025	1 225
C-1 (*N* = 45)	red seal	1 078	1 261	tan lion	1 018	1 212
C-2 (*N* = 45)				purple lion	1 155	1 438

Note: Group medians are based on each S a median reaction time for 10 items, group means are based on individual means.

Table 4

U Tests between Series with the Same Stimulus Forms in Congruent and Incongruent Colors

Series compared	Individual median time scores			Individual mean time scores		
	U	z	*p*	*U*	z	*p*
black lion tan lion	1076 5	52	60	1074 5	50	62
red seal black seal	1335 0	2 60	0094	1374 0	2 92	0036
purple lion tan lion (*8 stems*)	1451 5 1421 5	3 54 3 30	0004 001	1469 5 1370 5	3 69 2 89	0002 0038
(*Norm series*) tan lion black seal	1126 0	92	36	1232 0	1 77	08

Table 5

Wilcoxon Signed-Ranks Tests between Series with the Same *Ss* for Congruent and Incongruent Items

Group	Series compared	T	z	p
C-1 (N = 43)	red seal tan lion	245 4	1 75	006
A (N = 43_	black lion black seal	393 0	97	33

Note: Two *S*s in each group were not included since they showed a zero difference in reaction time for the series compared

Table 6

Frequencies of Various Types of Responses

Class I stimulus forms			
		Frequency in each series	
Form	**Responses scored correct**	**Congruent (black seal)**	**Incongruent (red seal)**
1	fork (pitchfork)	45	45
2	pliers (tongs, pincers)	36	42
3	frying pan (pan, skillet)	40	39
4	seal (walrus)	40	41
5	snake (cobra, serpent)	41	39
6	sword (dagger, knife, sabre)	45	42
7	elephant (— head, trunk)	39	38
8	squirrel	44	41
9	gun (pistol, revolver)	44	45
10	tree	44	45
	Total Frequencies		
	Correct responses	418 (93%)	418 (93%)
	Other responses	29	24
	Detail responses	3	7
	Rejections	0	1

Class II stimulus forms				
		Frequency in each series		
		Congruent (tan lion)	**Incongruent**	
Form	**Responses scored correct**		**black lion**	**purple lion**
11	tree (fir, pine, Xmas)	45	44	42
12	giraffe	39	40	42
13	lips (mouth, — imprint)	43	44	43
14	banana	44	42	42
15	violin (fiddle, guitar, bass,	44	43	42
16	viol, cello)	40	26	13
17	grapes	44	45	44
18	hand	41	44	43
19	cactus	45	44	39
20	fire hydrant (fireplug)	34	33	21
	lion			
	Total Frequencies			
	Correct responses	419 (93%)	405 (90%)	371 (82%)
	Other responses	31	35	65
	Detail responses	0	6	6
	Rejections	0	4	8

Note: Only responses listed here were scored correct.

Table 7

U Tests between Median Reaction Times of Adjusted and Maladjusted *Ss*

Series	U	z	p	Direction
Achromatic congruent (black seal)				negative[b]
Adjusted (N = 23) *vs* maladjusted (N = 22)	310 5	1 31	19	
Achromatic incongruent (black lion)				
Adjusted (N = 23) *vs* maladjusted (N = 22)	339 0	1 95	05	
Chromatic congruent (tan lion)				
Adjusted (N = 19) *vs* maladjusted (N = 25)	272 5	83	41	positive
Chromatic incongruent (red seal)				
Adjusted (N = 19) *vs* maladjusted (N = 25)	315 5	1 85	03[a]	positive
Chromatic incongruent (purple lion)[c]				
Adjusted (N = 25) *vs* maladjusted (N = 19)	313 5	1 80	036[a]	

[a] One-tailed test.

[b] A negative direction means that shorter reaction times are associated with maladjustment. For mean reaction times, z = 2 42, *p* = 016

[c] Abbreviated series of eight items

Table 8

Order of Difficulty of the Types of Stimulus Forms for Adjusted and for Maladjusted *Ss*

Adjusted *Ss*		Maladjusted *Ss*	
Order	Median R T	Order	Median R t
Chromatic Congruent (tan lion)	1 015	Achromatic Incongruent (black lion)	935
Achromatic Congruent (black seal)	1 03	Achromatic Congruent (black seal)	995
Achromatic Incongruent (black lion)	1 035	Chromatic Congruent (tan lion)	1 055
Chromatic Incongruent (red seal) (purple lion)[a]	1 045 1 073	Chromatic Incongruent (red seal) (purple lion)[a]	1 10 1 15

[a] Abbreviated series of eight items

www.ingramcontent.com/pod-product-compliance
Lightning Source LLC
Chambersburg PA
CBHW051542030726
47592CB00001B/93